Diversity in Organizations

The Claremont Symposium on Applied Social Psychology

This series of volumes highlights important new developments on the leading edge of applied social psychology. Each volume concentrates on one area in which social psychological knowledge is being applied to the resolution of social problems. Within that area, a distinguished group of authorities present chapters summarizing recent theoretical views and empirical findings, including the results of their own research and applied activities. An introductory chapter integrates this material, pointing out common themes and varied areas of practical applications. Thus each volume brings together trenchant new social psychological ideas, research results, and fruitful applications bearing on an area of current social interest. The volumes will be of value not only to practitioners and researchers but also to students and lay people interested in this vital and expanding area of psychology.

Books in the Series

Interpersonal Processes, *Stuart Oskamp and Shirlynn Spacapan, Editors*

The Social Psychology of Health, *Shirlynn Spacapan and Stuart Oskamp, Editors*

The Social Psychology of Aging, *Shirlynn Spacapan and Stuart Oskamp, Editors*

People's Reactions to Technology, *Stuart Oskamp and Shirlynn Spacapan, Editors*

Helping and Being Helped, *Shirlynn Spacapan and Stuart Oskamp, Editors*

Gender Issues in Contemporary Society, *Stuart Oskamp and Mark Costanzo, Editors*

Violence and the Law, *Mark Costanzo and Stuart Oskamp, Editors*

Diversity in Organizations, *Martin M. Chemers, Stuart Oskamp, and Mark Constanzo, Editors*

Diversity in Organizations

New Perspectives for a Changing Workplace

Martin M. Chemers
Stuart Oskamp
Mark A. Costanzo

Editors

The Claremont Symposium on
Applied Social Psychology
The Kravis-deRoulet Leadership Conference

SAGE Publications
International Educational and Professional Publisher
Thousand Oaks   London   New Delhi

For information address:

SAGE Publications, Inc.
2455 Teller Road
Thousand Oaks, California 91320
E-mail: order@sagepub.com

SAGE Publications Ltd.
6 Bonhill Street
London EC2A 4PU
United Kingdom

SAGE Publications India Pvt. Ltd.
M-32 Market
Greater Kailash I
New Delhi 110 048 India

Printed in the United States of America

Library of Congress Cataloging-in-Publication Data

Chemers, Martin M.
    Diversity in organizations: New perspectives for a changing workplace / Martin M. Chemers, Stuart Oskamp, Mark A. Costanzo.
        p.   cm.   — (The Claremont symposium on applied social psychology)
    Includes bibliographical references and indexes.
    ISBN 0-8039-5548-0. — ISBN 0-8039-5549-9 (pbk.)
    1. Diversity in the workplace.   I. Oskamp, Stuart.   II. Costanzo, Mark.   III. Title.   IV. Series.
HF5549.5.M5C48 1995
331.11'43—dc20   95-8231

This book is printed on acid-free paper.

96 97 98 99 10 9 8 7 6 5 4 3 2

Sage Production Editor: Astrid Virding

FTW
AJA2222

Contents

An Introduction to Diversity in Organizations

MARTIN M. CHEMERS
MARK A. COSTANZO
STUART OSKAMP

S cientists and practitioners have become increasingly aware of the changing demographic characteristics of the American workforce. In the latter part of this century and into the next, the largest percentage of new entries into the workforce will be individuals who are sometimes labeled "nontraditional" employees. The term *nontraditional* refers to the fact that until very recently the U.S. working population, especially at the managerial and professional levels, primarily comprised white males of European descent. In the coming decades, most new entries will be women, ethnic minorities, and immigrants. Although changes at the managerial level are slower, those ranks are also becoming more diverse and more representative of the U.S. population.

The changing demographic characteristics of the workforce present both challenges and opportunities to individuals and to the organizations of which they are a part. On the positive side, people who had heretofore been denied the opportunity for full development of their talents will be afforded a greater chance to realize their potential. At the same time, organizations will stand to benefit from diversity on a number of fronts. In terms of selection and placement, a broader talent pool means more high-quality employees from which to choose. In terms of creativity, innovation, and performance, demographic diversity can also mean diversity of perspectives and ideas.

Diversity also holds the potential for negative effects. As Sessa and Jackson point out in Chapter 5 of this volume, "different" has often meant wrong, bad, or alien. Traditional organizational policies and practices may not fit the new nontraditional employees. The new employees may feel misunderstood and unappreciated, while both new and traditional organizational members may approach their interactions with anxiety and apprehension. Tension, misunderstanding, and sometimes outright hostility between the old and new groups can create problems of coordination and cohesion for newly diverse organizations.

Our ability, as individuals, organizations, and a society, to garner the benefits of organizational diversity while reducing the disadvantages will depend on our understanding of the dynamics of organizational diversity. It is to that end that this volume was conceived and written. In it we have brought together many of the top theorists in diversity management, intergroup relations, and organizational effectiveness. Diversity is not only present in the title of this book. The chapters offered here are extremely diverse in terms of perspective, intellectual roots, foci, levels of analysis, and recommendations for dealing with organizational diversity.

Many scientific disciplines have useful perspectives on questions of diversity and intergroup relations, and the chapters collected here reflect multidisciplinary influences. Across chapters, and often within a single offering, we can discern theoretical influences from anthropology, sociology, management, social, organizational, and cross-cultural psychology as well as from feminist/ deconstructionist studies. Issues of perception, social cognition, status, power, group cohesiveness, communication, decision making, organizational structure, and cultural evolution inform the viewpoints and arguments included here.

The study of diversity has expanded from an exclusive emphasis on demographic diversity, such as race, gender, and ethnicity, to include more task-related dimensions such as functional specialization and organizational level. Likewise, the measures of outcomes of diversity have expanded to include not only the emotional responses and satisfaction of individuals but also individual performance and organizational productivity.

The chapters in this volume address multiple levels of analysis. As might be expected in a psychological analysis, attention is paid to the reaction of individuals (e.g., the perception of personal identity). In addition, however, various chapters analyze the effects of diversity on dyadic interactions (e.g., mentoring and superior-subordinate managerial relationships); small group dynamics (e.g., cohesion, communication, and leadership); and organizational outcomes (e.g., organizationwide demographic patterns and interdepartmental integration).

The varied perspectives and approaches and the comprehensive scholarly coverage provided by these chapters should make this book a very useful resource for students interested in understanding diversity issues and for scholars seeking integrative perspectives. The chapters also offer forward-looking suggestions for future research and for practical changes in organizations. A common feature across the many perspectives and approaches is a sense of hopefulness. The authors recognize the complexity of diversity issues and are well aware of the extent to which barriers to the full acceptance of all people remain firmly entrenched and resistant to change. Yet the analyses point the way toward redressing the problems and realizing the enormous potential of diverse organizations in a pluralistic society.

Overview of the Volume

The nine contributions in this volume are organized into three sections based on which level of analysis is the dominant focus of the chapter—the individual, the group, or the organizational level.

In Part I, the treatments by Triandis, Ferdman, and Cox and Finley are most concerned with individual reactions to diversity (primarily affective reactions such as comfort or satisfaction). Implicit in each analysis is the assumption that differences between social categories (i.e., racial, gender, ethnic, or functional groups) are real and affect the values, needs, expectations, and reactions of group members. The concern in each chapter is understanding how these group differences and their effects are experienced and understood by members of divergent groups.

In the opening chapter, Harry Triandis provides a theoretical framework that can serve as the basis for research as well as interventions to improve interpersonal relationships among diverse organizational members. The framework, which draws on both the cross-cultural and the intergroup relations literatures, integrates a broad set of variables that impinge on the quality of interpersonal relationships. The centerpiece of the integrative framework is the construct of perceived similarity—a major determinant of the quality of interpersonal relationships. Variables such as cultural distance (i.e., differences in lifestyles, traceable to economic, political, religious, historical, ecological, linguistic, and social structural variables), acculturation, history of intergroup relations, opportunities for contact, social approval of contact, stereotypes, sociotypes (valid stereotypes), isomorphic attributions, perceived control, culture shock, and interpersonal attitudes are organized in terms of how they determine or are determined by perceived similarity.

In Chapter 2, Bernardo Ferdman argues for the importance of considering both group differences and individual uniqueness. Ferdman maintains that, although group differences are significant, researchers need to pay more attention to within-group variation and multiple group memberships. Cultural identity—defined as the individual's image of the cultural features that characterize his or her group(s) and of the reflection (or lack of reflection) of these features in his or her self-representation—provides a conceptual vehicle for connecting the individual and the group. In contrast to the focus of self-categorization theory and social identity theory, whose emphasis on group identities and group boundaries results in the depersonalization of self-perception, Ferdman's chapter focuses on the individual personalization of group perception. This analysis emphasizes the fact that each individual member of any social category has a personal interpretation of what features characterize the category, in general, and how those features relate to him- or herself, specifically.

In Chapter 3, Taylor Cox and Joycelyn Finley emphasize that work specialization and organizational level should be considered as dimensions of diversity because these dimensions, in ways that are similar to differences in group identities, have a strong impact on career outcomes. Cox's (1993) Interactional Model of Cultural Diversity is described, and two studies that investigate the key predictions of the model are presented. These studies tested for possible influences of work specialization and organizational level on affective outcomes of work (employment satisfaction, organizational identification, and job involvement) and achievement outcomes (job performance, compensation satisfaction, and promotion opportunity). Cox and Finley predicted that, in some respects, work specialization and organizational level would produce effects on career experiences similar to those that have been observed for gender and race. Although results were mixed, the findings offer some support for their hypotheses with important implications for future research and for the practice of management.

The chapters included in Part II shift focus not only in terms of the level of analysis from individual-level phenomena to dyadic and group-level processes, but also from an emphasis on differences in values, beliefs, and expectations across groups (what Sessa and Jackson refer to as "horizontal differentiation") toward the implications of social categories for "vertical differentiation" (i.e., differences in power and authority). A shift also occurs in the assumptions about the importance of value and attitude differences between groups. In the analyses by Ragins (Chapter 4) and by Sessa and Jackson (Chapter 5), differences between groups are acknowledged, but more emphasis is placed on how categorical affiliations affect power and authority than on how those differences affect communication and understanding. The shift is more explicit in the analysis offered by Chemers and Murphy (Chapter 6). They cite an extensive literature on leadership style and behavior, including some of the same work addressed by Ragins, and argue that gender and ethnic differences in leadership are not well supported. Rather than true differences in leadership behavior, they argue that it is stereotypical beliefs and expectations about women and ethnic minority individuals as leaders that hamper their access to and deployment of power. Chemers and Murphy raise the question of whether it may not be more useful to address these stereotypical beliefs than to train people to be sensitive and responsive to group differences.

In Chapter 4, Belle Ragins continues the integrative orientation of Triandis, Ferdman, and Cox and Finley, and offers another useful theoretical framework. She develops a multilevel model of organizational change and diversity and then uses the model to establish theoretical linkages among the literatures on diversity, power, and mentorship. Her analysis incorporates cultural, structural, and behavioral influences that are thought to combine synergistically to determine the development of power among women and minorities in organizations. Mentoring is shown to be related to the development of power. Ragins illustrates how cultural, structural, and behavioral factors can reduce opportunities for effective mentoring and thus promote exclusionary power relationships between groups, but also how mentoring can influence and change those relationships. She proposes that diversified mentoring relationships may provide a medium for achieving egalitarian power relationships and effective organizational change. She also suggests provocative research propositions and agendas.

In Chapter 5, Valerie Sessa and Susan Jackson provide an insightful analysis and integration of the effects of diversity on decision making in groups and teams. They show that diversity may be categorized along two dimensions: horizontal (e.g., functional background, gender, ethnicity) and vertical or hierarchical (e.g., organizational level). Much of the past research in psychology, using a cognitive and rational approach, has concentrated on the impact of horizontal diversity within teams. Sociological research, based on the understanding that team processes and outcomes may be shaped by irrelevant and unintentional dynamics among team members, has more often looked at the impact of vertical diversity or status within teams. Although the two dimensions would predict different behaviors and outcomes, rarely have the two types of diversity been considered within the same framework. This chapter discusses the differential impact of the two dimensions of diversity on team processes and team outcomes and shows where more theory and research are needed. Additionally, the chapter discusses how organizations may benefit from diversity and limit their liabilities by hierarchical status reduction, diversity training, and the use of mediation technology in team interaction.

In Chapter 6, Martin Chemers and Susan Murphy examine leadership issues related to diversity in organizations. They approach the topic from two directions. First, do leaders from different social categories (e.g., men and women; European, African, Asian American, Latino leaders) differ in their leadership motivation, behavior, or performance? Second, how can leaders most effectively influence and coordinate the efforts of followers who are diverse, whatever the origins of that diversity? Chemers and Murphy make a strong case that gender and ethnic differences between leaders are exaggerated, and that it is the mistaken stereotypes about women and minority leaders that influence expectations and reactions to such leaders. They present a functional model of effective leadership and raise the point that good leadership always involves attentiveness to the unique needs and desires of each follower and to the successful coordination of the efforts and ideas of diverse followers, regardless of the origins (i.e., racioethnic, functional, or personal) of follower uniqueness or differences in perspective.

In Part III, chapters by Tsui, Egan, and Xin, by Smith, and by Thomas adopt an organization-level perspective. These offerings tend to stand farther back and observe how diversity affects the organization as a whole.

In Chapter 7, Anne Tsui, Terri Egan, and Katherine Xin review the demographic research about organizational diversity and conclude that diversity is both a dynamic and a contextual phenomenon. They emphasize that demographic research using the field research paradigm provides useful knowledge that complements and enriches the discussions by diversity theorists. Their chapter concludes with an analysis of the organization both as a social category itself and as a context that may modify the meaning of other demographic variables.

In Chapter 8, Daryl Smith makes a cogent argument that the increasing diversity of college students, faculty, and staff requires the rethinking of many of the fundamental issues of higher education. The chapter describes the evolving concept of diversity and its implications for higher education, and also addresses how the social sciences, particularly psychology, will need to reframe and reconstitute their approaches to research to respond to change of this magnitude. She maintains that it is time to move from considering diversity as a challenge or a problem to a recognition that it is essential to engage diversity in all its dimensions, for only by doing so will education be adequately positioned for the future.

In Chapter 9, Roosevelt Thomas emphasizes that the emotionally charged issues of race and gender as aspects of "workforce diversity" often prevent managers from grasping the true meanings of diversity and adopting mechanisms for actually managing diversity. He offers a framework for managerial and organizational practice that provides prescriptions for determining where the manager should focus attention as well as descriptions of the available action options. Further, he illustrates how the framework might be used by applying it to the topics of functional diversity, acquisitions and mergers, and work/family issues. He contends that issues less emotionally charged than race and gender might provide more productive arenas for learning about diversity, and that when such lessons have been gleaned they can be transferred to the more traditional and familiar workforce challenges.

Acknowledgments

The joint meeting of the Claremont Symposium on Applied Social Psychology and the Kravis-deRoulet Leadership Conference provided an ideal opportunity to bring together issues of organizational research and practice on the topic of diversity. The conference received financial support from a variety of sources including the Claremont Graduate School (CGS), the Kravis Leadership Institute at Claremont McKenna College (CMC), and the Society for the Psychological Study of Social Issues (SPSSI).

We are indebted to the many people who helped to make the conference a success. We thank the authors of this volume as well as Claude Steele of Stanford University, who participated in the conference but was not able to contribute a chapter. We cannot overstate the importance of the help we received from Administrative Assistants Jane Gray and Pamela Hawkes, whose devotion to duty was matched by their insight and foresight. Finally, we thank the CGS and CMC students who gave freely of their time and energy to help with various logistic needs. We hope that the readers will benefit as much as we have from the combined efforts of all these contributors.

PART I

INDIVIDUAL REACTIONS TO DIVERSITY

1

A Theoretical Framework
for the Study of Diversity

HARRY C. TRIANDIS

The future workplace, worldwide, will become increasingly more diverse, and this will be especially true in the economically most developed countries. The reasons are many.

Demographically, the populations of the developed countries are reaching a plateau (Ingelhart, 1990), while those of the developing countries are increasing. Thus migration from the developing to the developed areas of the world is likely to accelerate. This hydraulic model of population change suggests that the developed will accept those from the less developed so as to have services that only those from the poor parts of the world are willing to perform, and those from dense regions will move to the less dense to improve their standards of living. The pressure to do so can be seen in numbers; in the 18th century, the ratio of the gross national products per capita of the rich and poor nations was 2 to 1; in 1950, 40 to 1; in 1990, 70 to 1 (George, 1993). Productivity is accelerating geometrically in certain activities. For example, the introduction of word processors has increased my writing speed, I estimate, by 100%. However, the poor countries are still struggling, largely without such devices.

In addition, globalization means that professionals from the developed parts of the world will live among the workers from the less developed countries. At the same time, environmental degradation will create environmental refugees. The United Nations expects 20% of the population of the world to become environmental refugees by the year 2020 (George, 1993) because of the deterioration of their physical environments, lack of water, and the like. To give you a sense of the enormity of this problem, I will mention one point: The number of environmental refugees in the year 2020 is expected to be the same as the total population of the world was in 1926, when I was born.

The design-production-distribution processes of the 21st century will involve extreme diversity. For example, the design of a product may occur in Germany, financing might be obtained from Japan, execution of the plans might be directed from the United States, the clerical work might be done in Bulgaria, the manufacturing work in China, and the distribution may include a universalist sales force. The interfaces among those activities will require highly diverse workplaces.

In the developed countries, the shift from manufacturing to service and information economies will require that the sales force be as diverse as the populations of customers (Jackson & Alvarez, 1992).

This chapter examines the issues that will be faced by the managers of tomorrow in these diverse workplaces. It begins with definitions of the meaning of culture, race, ethnicity, and nationality. It examines the changes in the workplace that diversity requires. Then it explores basic issues such as whether the melting pot or multiculturalism are desirable or possible directions of social change, and the ways in which multiculturalism can be accommodated. Next it presents a theoretical model that should prove helpful in keeping in mind, at one time, the major relationships among the key variables that define diversity and its consequences.

Definitions

Culture is to society what memory is to individuals (Kluckhohn, 1954). In short, it consists of ways of perceiving, thinking, and deciding that have worked in the past and have become institutionalized in standard operating procedures, customs, scripts, and unstated assumptions that guide behavior.

Culture consists of both objective elements (tools, roads) and subjective elements (concepts, beliefs, attitudes, norms, roles, and values) (Triandis, 1972). A culture must have been adaptive and functional at some point in the history of a group of people who spoke the same language so they could develop shared beliefs, attitudes, norms, roles, and values, and it got transmitted from one generation to the next. Members of a culture must have had a common language so as to communicate the ideas that were later shared, and must have lived during the same time period in areas that were geographically close enough to make communication possible. Thus language, time, and place are three criteria that can be used to identify a culture.

According to this analysis, there are about 10,000 cultures in the world (it is estimated that there are about 6,170 distinct languages; Moynihan, 1993, p. 72). Because there are fewer than 200 members of the United Nations, it means that most nations are multicultural.

There are many factors, in addition to language, that help communication. Living in the same neighborhood, being members of the same physical type (colloquially called a race), having same occupation, same descent from particular ancestors (ethnicity), same gender, age, and so on provide opportunities to develop similar subjective cultures, reflected in similar attitudes and the like. A major dimension of cultural variation is between collectivist and individualist cultures. This dimension has received prominent treatment in studies of culture and work (Erez & Earley, 1993; Triandis, Dunnette, & Hough, 1994).

Ideologies About Diversity

Cultures emerge in different ecologies and are shaped in such a way that people can solve successfully the problems of existence (Berry, 1967, 1976). The schedules of reinforcement that people experience in each ecology result in unique ways of perceiving the social environment (Triandis, 1972). These perceptions occur along dimensions that have a neutral point, called the level of adaptation (Helson, 1964). This point shifts according to the experiences that people have in a particular environment. For example, in wealthy countries, the neutral point for financial compensation is much higher than in poor countries. A salary of $16,000 per year seems "low" in the United States, but its equivalent, 500,000 rupees per year, seems "high" in India. In short, the same stimulus has different meanings, depending on whether it falls above or below the level of adaptation, which shifts according to the experience that people have in a particular environment.

Two polar points of view have been proposed to deal with diversity. On the one hand, there is the *melting pot* conception (Zangwill, 1914), which argues that the best country has a single homogeneous culture. Japan has refused to receive migrants, on the ground that this will reduce the quality of life in that society. On the other hand, there is the *multiculturalism* conception, which assumes that each cultural group should preserve as much of its original culture as is feasible, without interfering with the smooth functioning of the society. Canada has an official multicultural policy.

The multiculturalism viewpoint requires, ideally, that each individual does develop a good deal of understanding of the point of view of members of the other relevant cultures. One aspect of this understanding is that each person should give approximately the same meaning to observed social behavior that the actor of this behavior gives. For example, in cultures where people are trained to give respect to powerful others by not looking at them in the eye, it is common for people to look down when spoken to by others. Yet in cultures that are more egalitarian, looking away can be attributed to being distracted, disinterested, hostile, or noncooperative. Thus people do not make the same attributions concerning the causes of this behavior. A multicultural person learns to make approximately the same attributions that the actors make in explaining their own social behavior (Triandis, 1975). Thus using multiple cues, such as ethnicity, social class, gender, and so on, the observer may say "perhaps this person is showing respect by looking away."

Ethnocentrism

Most humans are *ethnocentric* (i.e., they judge events as good if they are similar to the events that occur in their own culture). That is inevitable, because we all grow up in specific cultures and view those cultures as providing the only "correct" answers to the problems of existence (Triandis, 1994). As we encounter other cultures, we may become less ethnocentric, but it is only if we reject our own culture that we can become nonethnocentric, and that is relatively rare.

Because all humans are ethnocentric, they make "ethnocentric attributions." For example, when I went to India the first time in 1965, I wrote to a Western hotel and asked for a reservation and got back a card that had two lines: "We have," and "we do not have a room for the dates you requested." There was an X next to "we do not have a room." I made the ethnocentric attribution that an X meant that they did not have a room. The correct attribution, however, as I found out later, was that "they cancel the category that does not apply." In short, I misunderstood the message, because I assumed that they use X-marks the same way I do.

Myriad examples of this kind can be given. Let me add just two. Many people from collective cultures (Triandis, 1988, 1990) find receiving "personal credit" quite embarrassing, because they believe that the *group* should receive credit for a job well done. The expression of public appreciation can embarrass many Asians and Native Americans. Of course, from a Western point of view, credit and public appreciation are perceived as very positive events, but that is often an ethnocentric attribution.

Another example concerns treating everyone equally or in a personalized way. Western bureaucratic theory emphasizes treating everyone the same. In short, if you are going to praise Mr. Jones, you must praise Mr. Tanaka, if both did an equally good job. But what if Mr. Tanaka does not want public exposure?

When people from different cultures work together, their ethnocentrism will result in misunderstandings and lower levels of attraction. The greater the distance between two cultures, the lower the rewards experienced from work together. If the behavior of the other people in the workplace does not make sense, because individuals do not make sufficiently similar attributions, one experiences a loss of control. Such loss of control results in depression (Langer, 1983) and culture shock (Oberg, 1954, 1960) and dislike of the other culture's members.

The more the interactions with these members are *intergroup* (emphasizing their membership in groups), the more the cultural differences will be emphasized. If they become *interpersonal* (paying attention only to the personal attributes of the other and ignoring the cultural aspects of the other's behavior) and the perceiver has had positive experiences with the other person, it is possible to like the member of the other culture *in spite* of the cultural distance (Tajfel, 1982). However, there are some necessary conditions. Contact has to lead to the perception of similarity. This can be achieved if there is no history of conflict between the two cultures, if the person knows enough about the other culture to anticipate the culturally determined behaviors of the other person, if the person knows the other's language, and if they have common friends and common goals (Triandis, Kurowski, & Gelfand, 1994).

The Need for a
Theoretical Framework

Social psychologists have long examined intergroup relations (e.g., Stephan, 1985). There are numerous studies and theoretical frameworks, but the relationships appear to be operating the way a balloon reacts: If you push in one place, you get a change in many other places. To understand how the variables operate together as a *system*, we need a theoretical framework that places the main variables in relation to each other. This chapter will describe such a framework, which I hope can be the basis for more systematic research in the future. The framework is conceived as appropriate for the study of intergroup relations in situations where there is considerable "cultural distance" (differences in social class, language, religion, family structure, or political systems).

One problem with such a framework is that to make it comprehensive the number of variables that must be included is very large. Of course, the more complex the framework, the more difficult it is to test it. Furthermore, if we include the most important variables, we cannot include the less important even when they are relatively important, to avoid complicating the framework beyond the possibility of testing. Thus I have chosen *not* to include some variables in the framework itself but to mention them in the discussion of the framework. Similarly, Figure 1.1 does not include all the arrows that are important, but some of the relationships not shown in this figure are discussed in the text.

Tests of this framework are not yet available, but there is a vast literature that is consistent with it. Furthermore, the framework suggests numerous intervention strategies. If such interventions prove successful, the framework will be supported.

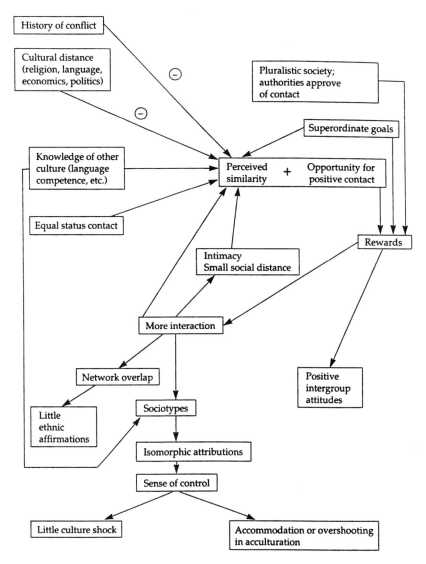

Figure 1.1. A Theoretical Model for the Study of Diversity
SOURCE: From Triandis, Kurowski, and Gelfand (1994).

The rest of this chapter first defines and suggests methods for the measurement of the key concepts of the framework. It then presents the framework and suggests how it can be used to test interventions.

Definitions and Measurements

Task Structure

Tasks differ in structure. That is, they vary in the extent that one and only one solution, method of doing them, or approach is optimal (high structure) as opposed to tasks that can be done with many methods, that is, are susceptible to many satisfactory solutions and approaches (low structure). For example, teaching that 2 + 2 = 4 is, by this definition, a high-structure task; exploring the meaning of "virtue," the way Socrates did in ancient Athens, is a low-structure task.

History of Relationship

Each relationship—such as African Americans versus European Americans, men versus women, bisexuals versus heterosexuals—has its own history. This history structures the meanings that people give to interpersonal contact. When the history has been one of negative interactions (e.g., exploitation), people tend to see the out-group as the "enemy" and to be predisposed toward negative stereotyping, attitudes, and behaviors. Authoritarian personalities are especially likely to see the in-group as "totally in the right" and the out-group as "totally in the wrong," in such confrontations.

Cultural Distance

Cultures are similar or different (distant) to the extent that they include many similar or different elements. Such elements can be objective or subjective. Objective distance depends on the linguistic distance of the two cultures, and the differences in the social structures, religions, and political and economic systems in use. Subjective distance depends on the dissimilarity of the subjective cultures of the two groups.

Linguists have identified language families, revealing why it is very easy to learn French if one already knows Italian, but more difficult to learn English, and even more difficult to learn Hindi. But all those languages belong to the

Indo-European language family, and all the speakers of these languages will have great difficulties with a tonal language, such as Chinese, or one of the African languages that depends on click-sounds. It is possible to measure objectively the distance among languages by noting their location in the clusters formed by language families.

Social structures are also objective. The kind of family structure, such as patrilineal, matrilineal, monogamous, polygynous, polyandrous, and the like, provides objective data about cultural similarities or distances. Todd (1983) has identified seven types of family structure; if two individuals come from families with different structures, that adds to their cultural distance. Anthropologists have used both language families and family structures to identify "cultural regions" (Burton, Moore, Whiting, & Romney, 1992). Thus Africa south of the Sahara is a different region than "the Old World," which includes Europe and the Middle East, and that region is different than South Asia, East Asia, Polynesia, North America, and South America (of course, I refer here to the native peoples).

Many modern cultures are complex mixtures of the "basic cultures" that constituted them historically. For example, in the United States, the influences from the European cultures are very strong, but African and Asian elements can also be identified. There are also pockets of more or less "pure" cultures from all over the world, that have been transplanted in particular neighborhoods. Or, to take another example, in Mexico we see elements of the native American cultures mixed with the European cultural elements, in different degrees, according to region and social class. The seven basic regions discussed by Burton et al. are more distant from each other than are the cultures within any one of these regions.

Other objective distances can be derived from *religion* (e.g., the different varieties of Christianity or Buddhism are closer to each other than Christianity is to Buddhism), *political* systems (e.g., those political systems where there is extensive participation of the population in policy formation are more similar to each other than they are to political systems where only a few people or one person makes all the policies), and *economics* (those with similar incomes, such as the "jet set," are more similar to each other than to those with different incomes).

Subjective cultural distance can be measured by studying the attitudes, beliefs, norms, roles, values, and other elements of subjective culture (Triandis, 1972) that characterize a group of people who speak the same language and live in the same time period and geographic region. For example, one can administer a questionnaire, sampling such elements, and correlate the responses of every person with the responses of every other person. A cluster analysis generated from these data would provide the distances among these people. If we do this analysis on the data of people from two cultures, we can test the distance of the two groups by examining if the between-groups variance of the responses to the questionnaire is larger than the within-groups variance. One can repeat this for each of the elements of subjective culture.

Ronen (1994) has done numerous cluster and smallest space analyses of work-related attitudes and needs and has identified countries that emphasize the satisfaction of different needs through work. Two dimensions distinguish various samples: (a) individualism (emphasis on advancement, recognition, autonomy) versus collectivism (good relations with coworkers, manager) and (b) nonmaterial (challenge, good relations with coworkers) versus material (benefits, earnings) rewards from working. Presumably, the most cultural distance would occur if two ethnic groups differ on both dimensions (e.g., individualist, material versus collectivist, nonmaterial).

In addition, one can obtain "subjective ratings" of the cultural distance (e.g., "How different do you think your language is from the language of X?" "How different do you think your income is from X's income?"). Ward and Kennedy (1992) used the items provided by Babiker, Cox, and Miller (1980), who asked people to rate on five-point scales the extent of the differences between their own background and the background of the people in another group.

Other criteria can include sociological data, such as the frequency of intergroup marriages, as a measure of small cultural distance, or data about the frequencies and levels of success of business partnerships, on the assumption that the greater the cultural distance, the less likely a partnership is to occur or succeed.

There are empirical findings suggesting that cultural distance is an important variable. For example, there is a considerable literature concerning the adjustment of foreign students to the United States that indicates that those from Europe have less difficulty adjusting to the United States than those from Africa. Suicide rates among immigrants seem to reflect cultural distance (Furnham & Bochner, 1986). Dunbar (1992) found that U.S. personnel in managerial positions abroad had less trouble adjusting to Europe than to non-Western or Third World settings.

Cultural distance increases intergroup anxiety (Stephan & Stephan, 1992). Intergroup anxiety results in negative attitudes toward the out-group (Islam

& Hewstone, 1993). The latter authors found that intergroup (as opposed to interpersonal) contact leads to anxiety, while high frequencies of contact and good quality contacts (equal, voluntary, intimate, cooperative), decrease anxiety. In addition, Stephan and Stephan (1992) found that high ethnocentrism increases anxiety.

Perceived Similarity

There is considerable research indicating that we are attracted to those we see as similar (for a review, see Triandis, 1977). Perceived similarity can be obtained on simple rating scales or can be manipulated (e.g., Byrne, 1971). It is obvious that cultural distance is inversely related to the probability that others will be perceived as similar.

A critical question is whether perceived similarity will lead to the judgment that one is dealing with "one of us" (in-group) or "one of them" (out-group). This is especially important in the case of collectivist cultures (Triandis, 1990) where the distinction between behavior toward in-groups and out-groups is much more pronounced than is the case in individualistic cultures.

People differ in their experience with others who are different from themselves. The impact of "difference" on social perception can be examined with the help of Helson's (1964) concept of the "level of adaptation." As mentioned earlier, the level of adaptation is the neutral point for the judgments made on any dimension. Psychophysical research has shown that, for instance, people who handle heavy weights judge most objects as "light" and those whose job makes them deal with light weights judge the very same objects as "heavy." Every time a human meets another human, there is an implicit judgment concerning similarity/difference. The neutral point of the small-large difference dimension shifts according to whether most of the people that the individual has met were perceived as similar or different.

In a cosmopolitan environment, people who differ in language, clothing, and even religion occur very frequently, and the level of adaptation moves in the direction of larger differences. Thus people who are different on many attributes may still be seen as "one of us." By contrast, in a homogeneous social environment, the level of adaptation is very close to the small difference point on the small-large difference dimension. Thus the same person who in a cosmopolitan environment is seen as "one of us" is likely to be seen in a noncosmopolitan environment as "one of them."

Kinds of Contact

Islam and Hewstone (1993) tested a path model that included intergroup attitudes as the dependent variable, and (a) the frequency of contact, (b) the quality of contact, and (c) whether contact was intergroup or interpersonal as the independent variables.

Frequency of Contact Is Related to the Opportunity for Interaction. In different settings, there are variations in the opportunities for interaction. For example, neighbors are more likely to interact than are people who live far apart. In a particular job, there may be more or less opportunity for interaction. This variable can be obtained by asking people in the particular context to judge how frequently they could interact with others, if they had the inclination to do so. The *quality of contact* reflects the extent to which the contact is equal status, voluntary, intimate, cooperative, and so on (Amir, 1969). Contact, as Amir has shown, is not effective by itself in improving intergroup relations. It is only effective if it results in rewarding experiences. The current framework will suggest that contact is rewarding *only* in the context of perceived similarity.

It is also useful to distinguish between threatening and nonthreatening contact (Stephan & Stephan, 1992). The threat may be symbolic or realistic. Threatening contact (e.g., in restaurants, cafes, nightclubs, bars, streets, parks, open markets) has been found (Stephan & Stephan, 1992) to increase anxiety about the intercultural contact, while nonthreatening contact (e.g., in cultural events, sporting events, movies, parties, schools, hospitals) has been found to decrease anxiety. Threat is linked to rejection of the other cultural group (Stephan, 1994).

When contact is rewarding, we have a situation in which the number of positive interactions is greater than the number of negative interactions. Working with marital couples, Gottman and Levenson (1992) found that those couples who discussed problem areas in ways that led to improved relationships had a ratio of positive over negative interactions five times as large as the couples who entered a spiral of deteriorating relationships. That high a ratio may not be necessary in the case of less ego-involving interactions.

Nevertheless, it seems safe to say that only when positive interactions are more frequent than negative ones is the relationship likely to move into a more intimate, satisfying phase, and is there likely to be accommodation of one group in the direction of the position of the other group. *The intergroup versus interpersonal* aspect is also important. Members of collectivist cultures have a tendency to see contact in intergroup terms. This is also the case when there is a history of conflict between two groups, when there is conflict over resources and there are incompatible goals, when members are strongly attached to their in-group, and when there is anonymity and deindividuation (Zimbardo, 1969).

Also, when people can move from one group to another with ease, such as happens when people move from the United States to Canada or vice versa, they are more likely to see others in interpersonal rather than in intergroup terms. Interpersonal perceptions have the advantage that they do not reflect stereotypes, ancient histories of conflict, and "us" versus "them" cognitions. Thus interpersonal perceptions are likely to lead to perceptions of similarity, and hence to interpersonal attraction.

Societal Approval
of Intercultural Contact

Societies differ in the extent to which they prohibit or encourage contact. For example, Nazi policy in Germany prohibited contact with Jews, and Germans who contacted Jews in nonauthorized settings were often punished. On the other hand, Canada has a policy of multiculturalism, where authorities encourage contact and clearly state that they hope the contact will be rewarding, while at the same time they encourage each group to maintain its culture. This variable can be measured by examining the official policies, legal documents, and other products of the culture and by rating the extent that authorities approve of the contact.

Acculturation

Berry (1980) has described four ways for two cultures to relate to each other. One can try to maintain or not maintain one's own culture, and one can try to have or not to have contact with the other culture.

Integration is defined as the type of acculturation where each group maintains its culture, and also maintains contact with the other culture. It is the same as additive multiculturalism (Triandis, 1976), in which a person adds skills for interaction with the other culture, as opposed to negative multiculturalism, in which the person loses skills, perspectives, or aspects of identity.

Assimilation occurs when a group does not maintain its culture but maintains contact with the other culture. It is a consequence of the "melting pot" ideology. *Separation* occurs when the group maintains its culture but does not maintain contact with the other culture. Finally, *marginalization* occurs when neither maintenance of own culture nor contact with the other culture is attempted.

Berry has argued that integration is far better than the other processes from the point of view of mental health (see Berry, Poortinga, Segall, & Dasen, 1992, for a review).

If there is contact with the other culture (i.e., in the case of integration or assimilation), a culture can move toward adopting some of the subjective culture of the out-group. Such movement is called *accommodation*.

However, in some cases such movement is quite extreme, so that there is *overshooting*. For example, Greeks who migrate to the United States sometimes unnecessarily change their name to an Anglicized version (Leondaridis to Lyons). Finally, when a group attempts contact and is punished for such attempts, or is rejected due to discrimination, there is *ethnic affirmation*, in which the group becomes even more extreme in manifesting its original culture than groups who have not attempted to relate to the other culture. For example, some African Americans dress and behave in ways that are more African than the Africans, and more African than those African Americans who have little interest in contact with European Americans. It is possible to identify the patterns of acculturation by examining the subjective cultures of people from each cultural group and seeing whether over time one group is moving toward or away from the other group (Triandis et al., 1986).

Stereotypes

Stereotypes are the assumed characteristics of a group of people. They can be measured through a checklist (e.g., Check 10 out of the following 100 traits as being most typical of Germans), through an estimate of the percentage of a group having the attribute (e.g., What percentage of Germans are warm?), through a rating of the extent that the group has an attribute (e.g., Do Germans tend to be warm? Not at all, somewhat, frequently, always), or through multidimensional scaling of traits and group terms (e.g., How similar are the words *German* and *warm*?). These methods often converge when they are used in the same study (Stephan et al., in press).

Stephan (1994) recommends that the perceived percentage of members of the group who have an attribute be multiplied by the degree of affect toward that attribute, and the products be summed to obtain a measure of the total affect attached to the stereotype. The typical correlation between this sum and the evaluation of the ethnic group is of the order of .40. In one of Stephan's studies, hierarchical multiple regression, predicting the evaluation of an ethnic group from this sum, as well as from various types of threat, resulted in the prediction of 83% of the variance in evaluation.

The more competitive the relationship between in-group and out-group, the more negative are the stereotypes that each group has about the other (Avigdor, 1953).

Sociotypes

While stereotypes are generally invalid, there are some elements of the stereotypes that are valid, in the sense that they agree with the relevant social science research findings. Valid stereotypes are called *sociotypes*. The more a person has contact with another group, the more likely it is that the stereotype will change into a sociotype (Triandis, 1972; Triandis & Vassiliou, 1967). One way to find sociotypes is to identify the common elements between the autostereotype (e.g., how Israelis see Israelis) and the heterostereotypes of a group (e.g., how Americans see Israelis, how Germans see Israelis).

More elaborate procedures include self-ratings. In short, one could ask a representative sample of Israelis if they think they are personally "kind," and also obtain the autostereotype (Are Israelis kind?) and the heterostereotypes (say, Germans indicating whether they think Israelis are kind) from several national samples, and identify the items on which there is convergence. Those items on which all samples agree are the sociotype. One might think that there are no such items, but research shows considerable convergence between auto- and heterostereotypes (e.g., Triandis et al., 1982). For example, in that study, 71% of the Anglos and 72% of the Hispanics thought that Chicanos are "family oriented."

Isomorphic Attributions

When a behavior is perceived, it is usually attributed to some cause. If P perceives O doing Y, P is likely to see X as the cause of Y. If O also sees X, or a cause similar to X, as the cause of his or her own behavior, then P and O are making isomorphic attributions (Triandis, 1975). That is, they give the same meaning to the behavior. To avoid misunderstandings in intercultural relations, it is desirable for those who interact to make isomorphic attributions. Measures of the extent to which people make isomorphic attributions can be obtained by presenting scenarios of social interaction to members of the two groups, and providing four or five attributions under each scenario. Pretest data from the target group can indicate which attribution is most probable ("correct") in that culture. If a person selects that "correct" attribution to explain the behavior of members of the other culture, that person is making an isomorphic attribution. If several heterogeneous scenarios are used, the percentage of the attributions that are correctly identified is a measure of the extent to which the person is making isomorphic attributions.

Sense of Control

People in some situations feel that they have no control over the course of actions in that situation, and that is an extremely uncomfortable feeling. In fact, old people who do not feel that they are in control are more likely to die than old people who feel in control of their lives (Langer, 1983). One way to measure this variable is to ask people to examine scenarios and to indicate what they would do in each of these situations and later ask what is the probability that if they did that they would obtain a desired outcome. Those who see low probabilities of successful outcomes would have a low sense of control. Bandura's (1989) concept of self-efficacy is also related to this construct. It reflects the extent to which the person feels able to obtain successful outcomes.

Culture Shock

When people move from one culture to another, they experience a loss of control, and this results in both physical symptoms (e.g., asthma, headaches) and psychological ones (feeling depressed) (Oberg, 1960). This condition has been called "culture shock" and is explained by the lack of control over the rewards and punishments that one can obtain from the environment. Measures of well-being (e.g., Diener, Emmons, Larsen, & Griffin, 1985) may be used to estimate this variable.

Network Overlap

The more people one knows in common with another person, the more the two individuals are in the same social network, so that there is network overlap. One can use sociometric measurements to obtain an estimate of such overlap. Obviously, if two people are asked to name their friends and they name the same persons, there is much network overlap.

Superordinate Goals

These are goals that each person or group cannot reach without the help of the other person or group (Sherif, 1958). In many cooperative situations, there are goals of this type. In fact, cooperative work environments have been found to result in constructive conflict resolution, when conflict occurs (Deutsch, 1993). Measures of superordinate goals can be obtained by asking people to indicate how important are specific goals and the extent that they are committed to reaching these goals. As a second step, they can respond with estimates of whether they can reach their goals without the help of the other group.

The Framework

Figure 1.1 presents the theoretical framework. Most of the terms have been defined, but a few have not been defined because they are obvious.

Let us begin with *Perceived Similarity*. The framework states that the greater the *History of Conflict* (both length and intensity of conflict, wars, memories of one group killing members of the other group, and so on), the lower is the *Perceived Similarity*.

Also, the greater the *Cultural Distance,* the lower the *Perceived Similarity.* This is simply a generalization of the Byrne (1971) research.

The relationship between *Knowledge of the Other Culture* and *Perceived Similarity* is complex. When cultural distance is small, the more we know about another culture, the more we discover that the other is similar. For example, Stephan and Stephan (1984) found that Anglo high school students who knew much about Chicano culture were attracted to Hispanics in their school (actually, it could also be that those who were attracted learned more about that culture; correlation does not imply causation). Furthermore, in situations of small cultural distance, the more cross-cultural training (Landis & Brislin, 1983) given to a group, the more likely is that group to perceive the other group as similar. But when cultural distance is large, the more *Knowledge,* the less the *Perceived Similarity.*

Learning about other cultures changes the learner. The learner acquires skills and perspectives that actually make him or her more similar to the members of the other group. For example, the culture assimilator (Albert, 1983; Fiedler, Mitchell, & Triandis, 1971) presents 100 or so episodes of interaction that include members of two cultures and, after each episode, four attributions concerning the behavior of a member of the "other culture." The trainee guesses which attribution is the correct one from the point of view of the members of the other culture, receiving feedback concerning this choice, and thus learns to make "isomorphic attributions," that is, to attribute the behavior of members of the other culture to the same causes that members of that culture attribute to their own behavior. That means that objectively the trainees become more similar to the members of the other culture than they were before the training. Objective similarity leads to perceived similarity. But when the cultural distance is large, *Knowledge of the Other Culture* can result in perceived dissimilarity.

The greater the actor's *Language Competence* in the other person's language, the greater the *Perceived Similarity.* Obviously, those who speak our language appear to us to be more similar than those who do not speak our language. The greater the *Network Overlap* with the other person, the greater the *Perceived Similarity.* The more social objects two people have in common, including friends and acquaintances, the more they will see each other as similar.

The more *Equal Status Contact* between the two, the more they will see each other as similar, and hence the greater the *Perceived Similarity* (Amir, 1969). Of course, unequal status is an impediment to good relations, but here the "level of adaptation" (see above for definition) must also be considered. *Equal Status Contact* can be subsumed under two other points; equality of *Power* and equality of the *Number* of in-group and out-group members both increase perceived similarity. Obviously, equality by definition implies similarity. But over and above that, inequality of power sharpens the distance. Unequal numbers also have the effect of making one group feel like a minority, and thus different.

The more *Superordinate Goals* there are, the more the *Perceived Similarity.* Of course, any element (age, gender) that people have in common will increase their perceived similarity, but goals are especially important.

Now let us consider what happens when two people who perceive themselves as similar have much opportunity for contact. Similarity leads to feeling good (Byrne, 1971) and to interpersonal attraction. In short, the greater the *Perceived Similarity* and the *Opportunity for Contact,* the more *Rewards* are experienced, which results in *More Interaction* as well as in more positive *Intergroup Attitudes.* However, positive *Intergroup Attitudes* can be eliminated or seriously reduced if there is much *Intergroup Anxiety.* Cultural distance increases intergroup anxiety. Any factor that increases uncertainty about how to behave in social situations, or the individual's sense of control over the outcomes of the social interaction, increases anxiety. Thus, to obtain positive intergroup attitudes, it is necessary to overcome those factors that lead to intergroup anxiety. *Rewards* are also experienced when the in-group and out-group are high in *Competence,* because people feel more positive about situations in which they are successful than unsuccessful.

The *Rewards* will be especially satisfying when *Authorities Approve of the Contact.* Such approval tends to amplify the rewards.

We know that organisms emit more behaviors that have been rewarded than behaviors that have not been rewarded. In fact, behavior is shaped by its consequences (Skinner, 1981). Thus *Rewards* lead to *More Interactions.*

High rates of interaction result in knowing more about the other person, and that makes *Intimacy* possible. They also may result in higher levels of *Perceived Similarity,* if the participants are basically similar (which the model has made probable because real and perceived similarity are related; see Newcomb, 1956).

More Interaction results in more *Network Overlap.* The *More Network Overlap,* the lower the probability that there will be *Ethnic Affirmation.*

People who feel included in a friendship network are more likely to exhibit accommodation than ethnic affirmation.

The *More Interaction,* the more likely it is that *Stereotypes* will change into *Sociotypes* (Triandis & Vassiliou, 1967).

The presence of *Sociotypes* implies accurate perception of the other group; hence that increases the probability of *Isomorphic Attributions.*

Making *Isomorphic Attributions* means that one can predict what the other person will do much better, and that increases the *Sense of Control.*

Sense of Control results in *Accommodation* and there is *Little Culture Shock.* Positive *Attitudes* and *Accommodation* will make the contact more *Rewarding,* thus amplifying the effects of *Contact.*

We can reverse the signs of all the variables to see how they operate. When there is a history of conflict, much cultural distance, little knowledge of the other culture, no knowledge of the other language, no network overlap, differences in status, and no superordinate goals, there is a maximum of perceived dissimilarity. If there is an opportunity for interaction, this results in a punishing experience, which will lead to avoidance or aggression. Such hostile interactions will lead to no network overlap and to high probabilities of ethnic affirmation (i.e., my group is the best), to invalid stereotypes, and nonisomorphic attributions. Under these circumstances, the most effective way to establish control is to kill the other. If the other is dead, one has total control over the situation.

The final point is that there are (a) individual and (b) task structure differences in the extent to which this framework is applicable. It is more applicable (a) for persons who are open to new experiences and are nonethnocentric (Stephan & Stephan, 1992) than for those who are ethnocentric and (b) for low task structure than for high task structure.

Ethnocentrics may not be able to make isomorphic attributions, and thus obtain control over the situation; thus they may not show accommodation but may show ethnic affirmation in most cases.

In the case of high task structure, it is possible to get results through coercion. The slave owners of the seventeenth and eighteenth centuries enriched themselves by exploiting their slaves, and they did not have to perceive their slaves as similar to themselves or experience rewarding interactions with them. In fact, in situations of large power distance between two sets of people, those with power want to maximize their *dissimilarity* from those without power. In the slave owners' plantations, the task was very simple, so this framework would not be applicable.

However, the lower the task structure, the more the framework is likely to be supported by the data. Low task structure often means that cooperation is necessary to achieve goals. If there are many different ways to achieve a task, coordination is essential.

This implies that to test the framework adequately we must make sure we work with ordinary people and that the task is low in structure. Extreme (pathological) ethnocentrics probably can only be modified with clinical interventions.

Summary and Conclusions

This framework suggests that the key variables that must be considered in thinking about diversity are cultural distance, perceived similarity, and a sense of control as well as culture shock. If there is too large a cultural distance, it may be better to keep the ethnic groups separate and select those among each group who are objectively similar to work together and coordinate the actions of the separate groups, rather than to mix the individuals directly. The United Nations provides a model along these lines. The representatives of each nation have a lot in common, belong to similar socioeconomic groups, and thus can work together.

On the other hand, if the cultural distance is small, one can introduce a variety of factors, such as cross-cultural training, superordinate goals, and equal status contact, that are likely to lead to positive intergroup attitudes, a sense of control, and little culture shock.

We need research that will specify quantitatively how much cultural distance is "too much." We just do not know that.

If the groups are to be separate, that does *not* mean that they will have unequal power. That should be avoided. In fact, their representatives should have equal power in the committees that coordinate the actions of the separate groups.

There is research (Jackson & Alvarez, 1992) showing that diversity is good for creativity but is undesirable from the perspective of job satisfaction or commitment to stay in the organization. Thus it is not a panacea or a plague. It depends on the kind of job and the kind of criterion that we want to maximize. We should take an experimental perspective, identifying the jobs, people, groups, and organizations that are likely to benefit from diversity and the jobs, people, groups, and organizations where we want to keep people who are diverse in different social environments and select individuals who are objectively similar to coordinate their activities. We should also keep in mind that it may not be possible to maximize one criterion without getting very bad results on other criteria, so that in the final analysis the judgment about how to assemble groups will be political rather than scientific.

Interventions

The framework suggests numerous interventions.

1. One can search for superordinate goals and create such goals. Along this line, I am a strong believer in employee ownership, meaningful profit sharing, and especially the Lincoln Electric Co. of Cleveland incentive management plan. This small company has been effective for more than half a century by using a compensation plan that essentially divides the annual profits about equally between innovations (equipment improvements), compensation of shareholders, and bonuses for the employees. At Christmastime, the employees often receive bonuses as large as their yearly income. With such incentives, the employees work at twice the speed and efficiency found in comparable companies; thus Lincoln is able to sell its product slightly below market price, and its employees always have plenty of work.

2. One can increase similarity by making sure that those who interact are similar in as many attributes as possible—dress, behavior, and subjective culture. For example, Japanese companies use uniforms that are worn by both managers and workers. That seems like a good idea. One can also search for historical incidents of cooperation and emphasize those, at the same time deemphasizing past conflicts.

3. The more that lifestyles are similar, the more people will see each other as similar. This suggests that income dissimilarities must be examined from the point of view of motivation. I do not believe that the American wage structure is optimal. Far too often top managers write their own checks, no matter what the success is of their companies. The enormous income gap between the top and the bottom is demotivating to those at the bottom and increases the disparity of lifestyles. At the same time, some income disparity,

say, of the order of up to 10 to 1, is necessary to make sufficiently attractive the top jobs that require more years of preparation, and more tension, requiring that people be workaholics.

4. One can decrease the significance of dissimilarity. Dissimilarity can be seen as desirable (e.g., it increases creativity) or undesirable (e.g., it increases infighting). One can emphasize one over the other.

5. One can learn about the other culture through culture assimilator (Albert, 1983; Fiedler et al., 1971) and other forms of cross-cultural training (Triandis, 1994, chap. 10). This must include learning the other's language, songs, food, and use of symbols.

6. One can find common friends. A good strategy is to develop more social contexts (e.g., sporting events) where people feel similarity and feel good together (parties, picnics, and so on).

7. Make sure that contact is equal status by eliminating symbols of status and large discrepancies in the numbers of people from each group who work in the same setting (e.g., one or two token Black women cannot feel good about the job).

8. Emphasize cooperative learning (e.g., Johnson & Johnson, 1983) in the company's training programs. This is the situation where people get rewarded for teaching each other, and rewards are given to the group rather than to individuals. In individualistic cultures, such as the United States, far too much training is provided in competitive settings, when success in the modern world requires cooperation. A car has 5,000+ components. No one individual can produce it, let alone design it and market it. The success of the collectivist cultures of the Far East is in part due to their cooperative tendencies that are fostered by cooperative training.

9. People in individualistic countries have the tendency to emphasize *ability* more than is necessary, and to underemphasize *effort*. In collectivist cultures, the reverse is true. Yet, there is good evidence (Schneider, 1993) that people can learn to do very complex tasks even if they have modest abilities, provided they persist and work hard. For example, ordinary people have been trained to learn how to remember 80-digit numbers! It just takes 200 trials, and a lot of hard work, but it can be done. This approach will create more equal competencies in the workforce. Effort is something that people can do something about. It is such changeable qualities that we must emphasize.

10. Make sure that the interaction situation is rewarding. This can be achieved by ensuring that people are more successful (which depends on

good training), and it is more likely when the corporation supports diversity efforts.

All of the above, in some combination that is as yet unknown, can be attempted in different settings, and the results can be evaluated to determine the relative effectiveness of each combination of interventions.

The framework discussed here provides a blueprint for research concerning interventions. If structural equations (path analysis) were used, such research would provide excellent guidance about the way to assign resources to each kind of intervention.

References

Albert, R. D. (1983). The intercultural sensitizer or culture assimilator: A cognitive approach. In D. Landis & R. W. Brislin (Eds.), *Handbook of intercultural training* (Vol. 2, pp. 186-217). New York: Pergamon.

Amir, Y. (1969). Contact hypothesis in intergroup relations. *Psychological Bulletin, 71*, 319-342.

Avigdor, R. (1953). Etudes experimentales de la geneses des stereotypes. *Cahiers Internationale de Sociologie, 5*, 154-168.

Babiker, I. E., Cox, J. L., & Miller, P. M. (1980). The measurement of cultural distance and its relationship to medical consultation, symptomatology, and examination performance of overseas students at Edinburgh University. *Social Psychiatry, 15*, 109-116.

Bandura, A. (1989). Perceived self-efficacy in the exercise of personal agency. *The Psychologist: Bulletin of the British Psychological Society, 10*, 411-424.

Berry, J. W. (1967). Independence and conformity in subsistence level societies. *Journal of Personality and Social Psychology, 7*, 415-418.

Berry, J. W. (1976). *Human ecology and cognitive style*. Beverly Hills, CA: Sage.

Berry, J. W. (1980). Acculturation as varieties of adaptation. In A. Padilla (Ed.), *Acculturation: Theory, models, and some new findings* (pp. 9-25). Boulder, CO: Westview.

Berry, J. W., Poortinga, Y., Segall, M., & Dasen, P. (1992). *Cross-cultural psychology*. New York: Cambridge University Press.

Burton, M. L., Moore, C. C., Whiting, J. W., & Romney, A. K. (1992, February). *World cultural regions*. Paper presented to the meetings of the Society for Cross-Cultural Research, Santa Fe, NM.

Byrne, D. (1971). *The attraction paradigm*. New York: Academic Press.

Deutsch, M. (1993). Educating for a peaceful world. *American Psychologist, 48*, 510-517.

Diener, E., Emmons, R. A., Larsen, R. J., & Griffin, S. (1985). The satisfaction with life scale: A measure of life satisfaction. *Journal of Personality Assessment, 49*, 71-76.

Dunbar, E. (1992). Adjustment and satisfaction of expatriate U.S. personnel. *International Journal of Intercultural Relations, 16*, 1-16.

Erez, M., & Earley, C. (1993). *Culture, self-identity, and work*. New York: Oxford University Press.

Fiedler, F. E., Mitchell, T., & Triandis, H. C. (1971). The culture assimilator: An approach to cross-cultural training. *Journal of Applied Psychology, 55,* 95-102.

Furnham, A., & Bochner, S. (1986). *Culture shock: Psychological reactions to unfamiliar environments.* London: Methuen.

George, S. (1993). One-third in, two-thirds out. *New Perspectives Quarterly, 10,* 53-55.

Gottman, J. M., & Levenson, R. W. (1992). Marital processes predictive of later dissolution: Behavior, physiology and health. *Journal of Personality and Social Psychology, 53,* 221-233.

Helson, H. (1964). *Adaptation level theory.* New York: Harper & Row.

Ingelhart, R. (1990). *Culture shift in advanced industrial societies.* Princeton, NJ: Princeton University Press.

Islam, M. R., & Hewstone, M. (1993). Dimensions of contact as predictors of intergroup anxiety, perceived out-group variability, and outgroup attitude: An integrative model. *Personality and Social Psychology Bulletin, 19,* 700-710.

Jackson, S. E., & Alvarez, E. B. (1992). Working through diversity as a strategic imperative. In S. E. Jackson et al. (Eds.), *Diversity in the workplace: Human resources initiatives* (pp. 13-36). New York: Guilford.

Johnson, D. W., & Johnson, R. T. (1983). The socialization and achievement crises: Are cooperative learning experiences the solution? In L. Bickman (Ed.), *Applied social psychology annual* (pp. 119-164). Beverly Hills, CA: Sage.

Kluckhohn, C. (1954). Culture and behavior. In G. Lindzey (Ed.), *Handbook of social psychology* (Vol. 2, pp. 921-976). Cambridge, MA: Addison-Wesley.

Landis, D., & Brislin, R. (1983). *Handbook of intercultural training* (3 vols.). New York: Pergamon.

Langer, E. J. (1983). *The psychology of control.* Beverly Hills, CA: Sage.

Moynihan, D. P. (1993). *Pandaemonium.* Oxford: Oxford University Press.

Newcomb, T. (1956). The prediction of interpersonal attraction. *American Psychologist, 11,* 575-586.

Oberg, K. (1954). *Culture shock* (Reprint series, No. A-329). New York: Bobbs-Merrill.

Oberg, K. (1960). Culture shock: Adjustment to new cultural environments. *Practical Anthropology, 7,* 177-182.

Ronen, S. (1994). An underlying structure of motivational need taxonomies: A cross-cultural confirmation. In H. C. Triandis, M. Dunnette, & L. Hough (Eds.), *Handbook of industrial and organizational psychology* (Vol. 4, pp. 241-270). Palo Alto, CA: Consulting Psychologists Press.

Schneider, W. (1993). *Getting smart quicker: Training more skills in less time.* Washington, DC: Federation of Behavioral, Psychological, and Cognitive Sciences.

Sherif, M. (1958). Superordinate goals in the reduction of intergroup conflict: An experimental evaluation. *American Journal of Sociology, 63,* 349-356.

Skinner, B. F. (1981). Selection by consequences. *Science, 213,* 501-504.

Stephan, C. W., & Stephan, W. G. (1992). Reducing intercultural anxiety through intercultural contact. *International Journal of Intercultural Relations, 16,* 89-106.

Stephan, W. G. (1985). Intergroup relations. In G. Lindzey & E. Aronson (Eds.), *Handbook of social psychology* (2nd ed., pp. 599-658). New York: Random House.

Stephan, W. G. (1994, January 15). *Stereotypes and prejudice: From Russia to Mexico.* Lecture given to the Texas Social Psychology Association, El Paso.

Stephan, W. G., Ageyev, V., Stephan, C. W., Abalakina, M., Stefanenko, T., & Coates-Shrider, L. (in press). Measuring stereotypes: A comparison of methods using Russian and American samples. *Journal of Intercultural Relations.*

Stephan, W. G., & Stephan, C. W. (1984). The role of ignorance in intergroup relations. In N. Miller & M. B. Brewer (Eds.), *Desegregation: Groups in contact* (pp. 229-265). New York: Academic Press.

Tajfel, H. (1982). *Social identity and intergroup relations.* New York: Cambridge University Press.

Todd, E. (1983). *La troisième planète.* Paris: Editions du Seuil.

Triandis, H. C. (1972). *The analysis of subjective culture.* New York: Wiley.

Triandis, H. C. (1975). Cultural training, cognitive complexity, and interpersonal attitudes. In R. W. Brislin, S. Bochner, & W. J. Lonner (Eds.), *Cross-cultural perspectives on learning* (pp. 39-77). Beverly Hills, CA: Sage.

Triandis, H. C. (1976). The future of pluralism. *Journal of Social Issues, 32,* 179-208.

Triandis, H. C. (1977). *Interpersonal behavior.* Monterey, CA: Brooks/Cole.

Triandis, H. C. (1988). Collectivism and individualism: A reconceptualization of a basic concept in cross-cultural psychology. In G. K. Verma & C. Bargley (Eds.), *Personality, attitudes, and cognitions* (pp. 60-95). London: Macmillan.

Triandis, H. C. (1990). Cross-cultural studies of individualism and collectivism. In *Nebraska Symposium on Motivation* (pp. 41-133). Lincoln: University of Nebraska Press.

Triandis, H. C. (1994). *Culture and social behavior.* New York: McGraw-Hill.

Triandis, H. C., Bontempo, R., Betancourt, H., Bond, M., Leung, K., Brenes, A., Georgas, J., Hui, C. H., Marin, G., Setiado, B., Sinha, J. B., Verma, J., Spangenberg, J., Touzard, H., & de Montmollin, G. (1986). The measurement of etic aspects of individualism and collectivism across cultures. *Australian Journal of Psychology, 38,* 257-267.

Triandis, H. C., Dunnette, M., & Hough, L. (Eds.). (1994). *Handbook of industrial and organizational psychology* (Vol. 4). Palo Alto, CA: Consulting Psychologists Press.

Triandis, H. C., Kurowski, L. L., & Gelfand, M. J. (1994). Workplace diversity. In N. C. Triandis, M. Dunnette, & L. Hough (Eds.), *Handbook of industrial and organizational psychology* (Vol. 4, pp. 769-827). Palo Alto, CA: Consulting Psychologists Press.

Triandis, H. C., Lisansky, J., Setiadi, B., Chang, B., Marin, G., & Betancourt, H. (1982). Stereotyping among Hispanics and Anglos: The uniformity, intensity, direction, and quality of auto- and heterostereotypes. *Journal of Cross-Cultural Psychology, 13,* 409-426.

Triandis, H. C., & Vassiliou, V. (1967). Frequency of contact and stereotyping. *Journal of Personality and Social Psychology, 7,* 316-328.

Ward, C., & Kennedy, A. (1992). Locus of control, mood disturbance, and social difficulty during cross-cultural transitions. *International Journal of Intercultural Relations, 16,* 175-194.

Zangwill, I. (1914). *The melting pot: Drama in four acts.* New York: Macmillan.

Zimbardo, P.G. (1969). The human choice: Individuation, reason, and order versus deindividuation, impulse, and chaos. *The Nebraska Symposium on Motivation, 17,* 237-307.

2

Cultural Identity and Diversity in Organizations

Bridging the Gap Between Group
Differences and Individual Uniqueness

BERNARDO M. FERDMAN

The concept of *diversity* as it has been employed by organizational researchers, theorists, and practitioners can encompass a broad range of differences. Most agree, however, on the group-based nature of human heterogeneity. At an individual level, no two persons are alike in every respect, and thus they can be regarded as diverse relative to each other. But it is those features that make us like some specified group of people and different than other groups that constitute the principal thrust of much current work on diversity in organizations. Thus diversity in organizations is typically seen to be composed of variations in race, gender, ethnicity, nationality, sexual orientation, physical abilities, social class, age, and other such socially meaningful categorizations, together with the additional differences caused by or signified by these markers.

AUTHOR'S NOTE: I would like to thank Carolyn Bendik, Maria Frailey, Dixie Galapon, and the other members of my research seminar at CSPP for insightful comments on earlier drafts of this chapter and useful discussions about the concepts discussed here. I am also grateful to Belle Rose Ragins, the editors of this volume, and the participants in the Claremont Symposium for their many helpful suggestions.

Yet at the same time, particularly in an individualist society such as the United States, many people view their individuality and uniqueness as a significant part of themselves that they would not like to be overlooked. When they are described primarily in group terms, many Americans experience this as a threat to their individuality. Given a societal and a social scientific preference to view the self as an "independent, bounded, autonomous entit[y]" (Markus & Kitayama, 1994, p. 568) that "(a) comprises a unique, bounded configuration of internal attributes . . . and (b) behaves primarily as a consequence of these internal attributes" (p. 569), many people choose to see themselves and others as distinct from particular collectives. As Markus and Kitayama (1994) describe it, this "individualist ideal . . . occasions a desire not to be defined by others and a deep-seated wariness, in some instances even a fear, of the influence of the generalized other, of the social, and of the collective" (p. 568). In this construction, individual uniqueness is typically construed as the ways in which a person is separate from and different than other individuals and independent of the collective. While not all societies view the self in this individualist manner (Markus & Kitayama, 1991, 1994; Triandis, 1989), this is a tendency that must be addressed in working with diversity in the United States.

Whether or not persons are constructed essentially as members of collectives, there is a great deal of within-group variation that must be considered if we are to have a complete picture of the dynamics of diversity in organizations (Ferdman, 1992; Ferdman & Cortes, 1992). Part of this variation is due to the processes accompanying the intergroup contact inherent in a diverse society. It must be remembered, for example, that individuals are at once members of many cross-cutting categories. Thus, from a social psychological perspective, group-level accounts of diversity are insufficient if they do not provide a means to consider the linkages between collectives and their individual members.

In this chapter, I seek to bridge the gap between a focus on group differences and a focus on individual uniqueness by elaborating the concept of *cultural identity*, which may be defined as the person's individual image of the cultural features that characterize his or her group(s) (Ferdman, 1990) and of the reflection (or lack of reflection) of these features in his or her self-representation. This construct provides a vehicle by which researchers, theorists, and practitioners can pay attention to within-group variations while also taking seriously the very real ways in which groups differ. It also permits exploring systematic variations in how people see themselves as connected to their group(s), including those differences based on multiple group memberships. Thus the concept of cultural identity can serve as a psychological lens to examine the experience and impact of diversity at the level of the individual while maintaining in focus the reality of group-level differences.

Two Current Approaches to Understanding the Dynamics of Diversity

Many explorations of the dynamics of diversity typically seem to follow one of two approaches (Ferdman, 1992). A categorization or labeling approach —a predominant one in social psychology—focuses on the impact of the boundaries between groups. The intercultural approach—a more interdisciplinary perspective—highlights the implications of actual between-group differences in culture.

The traditional approach within social psychology to understanding intergroup relations has focused on the negative dynamics associated with the highlighting of group memberships. These correlates include prejudice, stereotyping, and discrimination (for reviews, see Alderfer, 1986; Brewer & Kramer, 1985; Cox, 1993; Ferdman, 1992; S. Fiske, 1993; Hogg & Abrams, 1988; Messick & Mackie, 1989; Tajfel, 1981; Taylor & Moghaddam, 1987; Worchel & Austin, 1986). A great deal of work in the social psychology of intergroup relations shows that the dynamics of interaction between the members of different groups often can be understood in terms of the significance to individuals of the intergroup boundaries themselves, rather than in terms of any specific differences between the groups.

Indeed, much work on ameliorating negative intergroup relations in organizations has focused on helping people work better across group boundaries. From this perspective, this is accomplished most effectively by emphasizing the common ground individuals may have as members of the same social system (e.g., Brewer, 1994; Gaertner, Dovidio, Anastasio, Bachman, & Rust, 1993; Gaertner, Mann, Murrell, & Dovidio, 1989). In many cases, these approaches are based on moving people "beyond" perceiving and treating each other as members of different groups and toward working together as individuals (e.g., Brewer & Miller, 1984, 1988; Miller & Brewer, 1986).

This strategy is largely premised on a notion of the person as "self-contained" (Sampson, 1988), one whose essence is distinguishable and separate from his or her ascribed characteristics (see also Appiah, 1990). In this construction, the core of "who I am" is based on characteristics that are strictly unique to me and that distinguish me from those around me, rather than on those features that make me similar and connect me to others. Because this notion views the boundary between self and other as quite firm and control of action and outcome as located in the person, those subscribing to this idea do not consider it problematic to suggest that individuals can in some way "let go" of their group memberships. Even when it is not presumed that it is possible (or desirable) for the person to be symbolically detached from the group, a strict categorization or labeling viewpoint emphasizes the goal of living with intergroup demarcations such that their negative consequences are avoided.

In line with the focus on diversity as group-based difference, however, a central theme in much of the current work on diversity in organizations is the cultural nature of heterogeneity. In the intercultural approach, the emphasis is on the *content* of the differences that are denoted by, but not the same as, the group boundaries. For example, Cox (1993) defines cultural diversity as "the representation, in one social system, of people with distinctly different group affiliations of cultural significance" (p. 6). The major tenet in this approach is that because social groups vary in their preferred patterns of values, beliefs, norms, styles, and behaviors—in short, in their cultural features— our memberships in these social groups distinguish us not only in name but also in our views of the world, in our construction of meaning, and in our behavioral and attitudinal preferences. The intercultural view emphasizes that all of us are in an essential sense cultural beings, shaped by and oriented in the world by the cultures of the groups to which we belong. Thus a significant component of the diversity in an organization is constituted by cultural differences among its members.

This focus on the cultural aspects of diversity has led to increasing attention paid by organizational scholars and practitioners to the many cultural differences among various types of groups. This newer line of work looks at the implications of cultural differences for interpersonal and organizational processes and outcomes when members of these various groups work together or otherwise come in contact. As evidenced by trends in teaching (Ferdman, 1994; Ferdman & Thompson, 1994), in research and theory (see, e.g., Adler, 1991; Arvey, Bhagat, & Salas, 1991; Boyacigiller & Adler, 1991; Cox, 1993; Ferdman, 1992; Hofstede, 1991; Triandis, Dunnette, & Hough, 1994), and in organizational practice (see, e.g., Cross, Katz, Miller, & Seashore, 1994; Jackson et al., 1992), today many authors view a complete understanding of organizational behavior as necessarily incorporating consideration of the role of cultural differences. At the same time, psychology in general is grappling with the implications of a cultural view of human behavior (e.g., Berry, Poortinga, Segall, & Dasen, 1992; Betancourt & Lopez, 1993; Jones, 1991; Markus & Kitayama, 1991; Schweder & Sullivan, 1993; Smith & Bond, 1993; Sue, 1991).

From this work, we have learned that ignoring or attempting to suppress cultural differences can result in many negative outcomes for organizations, groups, and individuals. These perspectives have led to an increasing emphasis on organizational interventions aimed at helping people to understand, accept, and value the cultural differences between groups, with the ultimate goal of reaping the benefits of cultural diversity. Such views and approaches have also typically meant looking at individuals in the context of their particular groups, and thus being cognizant of and sensitive to their (and our) cultural group memberships.

Separating (and Reconnecting)
the Group and the Individual

While the use of culture as a focal concept has been very important in framing the positive aspects of diversity, considerations and descriptions of culture have tended to focus primarily on the group level. Culture is by definition a concept used to describe a social collective. For example, Betancourt and Lopez (1993) cite Rohner's (1984) view of culture:

> [He] proposed a conceptualization of culture in terms of "highly variable systems of meanings," which are "learned" and "shared by a people or an identifiable segment of a population." . . . Perhaps the most distinctive characteristic of Rohner's formulation is the explicit statement of aspects such as the learned, socially shared, and variable nature of culture. (Betancourt & Lopez, 1993, p. 630)

Betancourt and Lopez go on to advocate the utility of focusing on subjective culture "defined in terms of psychologically relevant elements, such as roles and values" (p. 630).

Specific accounts of cultural elements (e.g., Berry et al., 1992; A. Fiske, 1992; Hofstede, 1980; Triandis, Kurowski, & Gelfand, 1994) usually describe a particular group or set of groups, without providing much guidance regarding the degree to which such accounts might apply to given individuals (Ferdman & Cortes, 1992). In using these cultural descriptions to focus on diversity in organizations, we need to avoid the ecological fallacy (e.g., Hofstede, 1980; Smith & Bond, 1993) of assuming that something that is true at the group level is true for every individual member of that group. For example, "this fallacy would be the mistaken belief that, because two cultures differ, then any two members of those cultures must necessarily also differ in the same manner" (Smith & Bond, 1993, p. 41).

Where Is the Group's Culture?

Nevertheless, while descriptions of cultures are focused on the group level, they typically include values, norms, and behaviors expressed by individuals. Although culture is meaningful only with reference to the group, it is enacted by individuals. To understand the individual manifestations of culture while avoiding the ecological fallacy, we are faced with the problem of locating culture: Is the group's culture in the mind of each member, or is it an abstract notion at the collective level (Ridgeway, 1983)? Keesing (1974), in considering cultures in a broad sense, and Ridgeway (1983), in her analysis of small group culture, resolved this by saying that the group culture exists in the mind of each individual member as that person's theory of the code that the other members are following. Each member's theory may be unconscious, but it is used to interpret events and also affects decisions about how to behave (Ridgeway, 1983). So the culture of the group as a whole is located in the interaction of the members with each other:

> When members meet, each with their own theory of the group culture, they enact together their shared symbols, meanings, ideas of themselves and their situation. Even though the members' conceptions of their culture are not identical, these shared meanings emerge from their mutual adjustments to one another and the substantial overlap among their views. (Ridgeway, 1983, p. 247)

In any specific interaction, one finds only part of the group culture, and any individual carries basically a personal theory of the group culture, not necessarily a complete or a static picture.

This perspective—that individuals within a group vary in their image of the group's culture—constitutes the root for the concept of cultural identity developed in this chapter. Before going on to describe cultural identity in more detail, I discuss additional arguments for the need to link group-level notions of culture with individual variation, and then review some current models of identity that focus on the role of culture and group membership in the self-concept.

Individuals often resist overgeneralizations about them, making it difficult to frame cultural differences positively, but the differences are no less real. In my work with Hispanic managers in a largely Anglo organization (Ferdman, 1988; Ferdman & Cortes, 1992), I found a good deal of resistance to being typecast. Many of the managers I interviewed were very clear that they did not want to be seen simply as Hispanics. They very much resisted categorical statements. For example, one Puerto Rican man whom I'll call Eddie told me:

> Even though you consider yourself one of the guys, American, and a professional, a manager, you have a lot of different statuses outside your Hispanicity, people have subtle ways of letting you know that when they look at you they see a Señor first or a Hispanic first. Maybe not first, but at least, . . . one of the first things, they look at you, and they say, "Well he's a manager, but he's also a Hispanic." . . . I've been called Jose, and I've been called San Juan.

Another manager, a woman, said to me:

> I've been told very nicely, "Gee, you're Puerto Rican? You don't look Puerto Rican." And my answer to that is, "What do Puerto Ricans look like?"

For these two managers and their colleagues, one consequence of feeling that they had to fight stereotypes was that they had difficulty in articulating positive and differentiated visions of what it meant to be Hispanic. In their construction, being seen primarily as a Hispanic diminished their sense of being respected as individuals.

But Eddie also told me in an interview: "Sometimes [it's] a different you when at the job and away from the job." Eddie and many of his Hispanic coworkers were quite clear about their sense of being different than the other managers. They believed that, in various ways, they were not the same, even though they did not appreciate being typecast as "the Hispanic." For example, in the same organization, another manager said that her "family wouldn't recognize me here." A third interviewee, explaining why he found little in common with the usual networks in the company, said that "the things which other people [at the company] think are important are not the same things I think are important."

Clearly, in each of these cases, they were not simply describing individual uniqueness. They were not just talking about the ways in which they were different than others along some individual dimensions. They were referring in large part to some of the implications of group differences and some of the ways that they experienced those. However, the experience of difference was not restricted to or focused solely on their identity as Hispanics. As Eddie pointed out, he saw himself as being constituted by a variety of group memberships.

Diversity goes beyond group differences to include within-group differences. The differences within groups are an important part of the multifaceted and complex nature of diversity. In a diverse society with a multitude of cultural groups in constant contact with each other, there will naturally be a great deal of within-group variation (see, e.g., Boekestijn, 1988; Ferdman & Cortes, 1992; Ferdman & Hakuta, 1985; Gurin, Hurtado, & Peng, 1994). Individuals can relate in a variety of ways not only to other groups but also to their own. For example, in some cases the extent to which an individual manifests the group's typical cultural features may reflect processes of acculturation (Berry, 1993). Also, related to this, individuals may change over time in the degree to which they exhibit cultural patterns characteristic of the group.

Every individual belongs to multiple groups. Individuals are part of many types of groups at once. This means that even when we take seriously the cultural perspective on diversity, the meaning that each of us gives to any particular group membership may very well be related to the constellation of our other identifications. Gurin et al. (1994), for example, showed how Chicanos (persons of Mexican descent born in the United States) and Mexicanos (immigrants to the United States born in Mexico) constructed their social identities quite differently, such that each had different associations among family, class, gender, nationality, and ethnic identities. Among Chicanos, but not among Mexicanos, these identities were correlated with the reported amount of contact with a variety of other groups. As Hurtado, Rodríguez, Gurin, and Beals (1993)—building on Tajfel and Turner's (1986; Tajfel, 1981) social identity theory—pointed out:

Different social experiences, even among people who share an objective categorical membership, can encourage the perception and establishment of subtle and detailed group distinctions. Mexican descendants recognize that some members of this category are farmworkers, others working-class; some are Catholic, others Protestant; some are recent immigrants, others third-generation. They go on to use these distinctions to construct different social identities. (p. 133)

In discussing the "multidimensional nature of social identity," these authors also cited research by Rodriguez-Scheel (1980), who presented Chicanos in Detroit with a set of labels and asked each respondent to select one label to define him- or herself. Nonethnic categories, for example, occupational, family-related, racial, religious, and/or linguistic, were picked at least as often as ethnic labels. Hurtado and her colleagues (1993) concluded: "To isolate one criterion as capturing the essence of ethnicity is to artificially limit and simplify its nature and to represent the Mexican-descent population as a homogeneous aggregate" (p. 133).

The issue for the present discussion is that, while group-level descriptions may be accurate, much more information is necessary before they can be used to understand a specific individual. This point was made in my conclusion to a study of Hispanic managers:

The findings . . . highlight some of the ways in which the individual expression of group-level cultural features is modified by and interacts with other variables. Some of these include organizational demands, minority roles, specific situations, and both organizational and individual perceptions of ethnicity. For both the Hispanic managers at XYZ, as well as for organizational researchers, it is difficult to "see" culture at the individual level. Nevertheless, as the patterns we found indicate, group-level patterns are present in individual behavior. That we can abstract such group-level features, however, does not mean that we can then directly apply them back to individuals. The Hispanic managers at XYZ varied widely in their specific behavior and outlook, as well as in how they thought about culture. (Ferdman & Cortes, 1992, p. 273)

Individual Uniqueness as
the Constellation of Social Identities

When we focus at the individual level and take seriously the multiplicity of group memberships of any particular person, it then becomes unnecessary to separate the person from the group to view others (and ourselves) as unique.

While I may share a particular identity with others, for example, Latino, the specific expression of that group membership is defined by its coexistence with the variety of my other identities, for example: Jewish, parent, professor, and diversity consultant.

In this view, even when I think about myself in terms of my social identities (i.e., my group memberships), I can experience these as contributing to and forming an essential part of my individual uniqueness. This contrasts with the position taken in self-categorization theory (Turner, Hogg, Oakes, Reicher, & Wetherell, 1987; Turner, Oakes, Haslam, & McGarty, 1994), which distinguishes personal and social identity such that

> as shared social identity becomes salient, individual self-perception tends to become *depersonalized*. That is, individuals tend to define and see themselves less as differing individual persons and more as the interchangeable representatives of some shared social category membership. (Turner et al., 1994, p. 455, italics in original)

Instead of the depersonalization of self-perception, the focus here in considering the links between group differences and individual uniqueness is on the *personalization of group perception*. Rather than distinguishing personal and social identity as "two different levels of self-categorization" (Turner et al., 1994, p. 454), the view posited here is that my social identities can be an important part of my personal identity, that is, who I am as an individual. It is quite possible that, given a distinctive set of group memberships, I can experience these as making me quite unique.

New Directions

These considerations lead us to pose questions of a sort not typically addressed in connection with current psychological approaches to diversity in organizations. Such questions include the following:

- How can we understand the individual experience and impact of diversity?
- How can we honor individual uniqueness and at the same time better accept, explore, and value group differences?
- How do individuals develop and maintain differentiated and positive images of the group(s) to which they belong?

People identify with or accentuate different aspects of themselves and their relationships to groups. We often experience certain aspects of ourselves as quite personal, but they may not be. I might believe that certain characteristics of myself are simply something about me as an individual, and yet according to the way others perceive me, there may well be some kind of cultural connection. Or I may grow, over time, to see a cultural connection.

In context, it can be difficult to see things or to experience one's behaviors, values, and beliefs as culturally rooted, in part because the whole group culture does not exist in any one individual and in part because each of us belongs to a variety of groups at once. Another reason this association is difficult is that in the United States, in particular, it is often seen as negative to connect an individual's features to the group. As alluded to earlier, the United States has been described as a society that subscribes to an individualist notion that strongly rejects the interdependence of the self and the collective and displays a "fear of the collective" (Markus & Kitayama, 1994).

Because of the history of oppression of some cultural groups (see, e.g., Cross et al., 1994) and the way group differences have been used to devalue some people as less worthy than others, a frequent response is attempts to discount group memberships. This is captured by the oft-heard phrase, "Treat me for who I am, not what I am." Indiscriminate interpretation of individual characteristics as expressions of group-level features is what we call *stereotyping*, and this must be avoided if we are to manage diversity positively. In particular, people from marginalized groups have often felt that they had to separate themselves from the group to be seen positively (Crocker, Luhtanen, Blaine, & Broadnax, 1994; Tajfel, 1981; Tajfel & Turner, 1986; Taylor & McKirnan, 1984).

When we try to shift from this perspective so that we view ourselves through a cultural lens, it can become very difficult, because we cannot readily separate the personal from the collective. Who is to say definitively which aspects of my individual uniqueness are cultural and which are idiosyncratic? And can they ever be truly disentangled?

My position is that, from the individual level, we have to ask the question differently. The issue is not so much what is "true," that is, what are the actual cultural differences (though as discussed earlier that can be a very important question from the group level). From the individual level, the question should become, not what is happening "objectively" but, instead: How does the person construct her- or himself as a cultural being? How do I see myself as a cultural being? What do I believe is the reflection of the collective in me?

Models of Cultural
Diversity at the Individual Level

Various theorists and researchers have addressed the links between the group and individual levels in the context of diversity. Their work describes the individual construction of the self as a cultural being in terms of the person's relationship to the groups in the environment. Two such approaches are briefly discussed here: models of biculturalism and acculturation, and Cox's (1993) model of "culture identity structure."

Biculturalism and
Acculturation Models

Approaches that deal with acculturation (e.g., Berry, 1980, 1993; Marín, 1993) focus on the ways in which individuals incorporate the influence of two or more "autonomous cultural systems" (Social Science Research Council, 1954, p. 974, cited in Marín, 1993)—one belonging to their culture of origin and the other(s) to cultures with which they come in contact. Similarly, work on biculturalism seeks to describe the implications for individuals of having more than one culture as a reference group. For example, in a review of theory and research on the psychological impact of biculturalism, LaFromboise, Coleman, and Gerton (1993) list five types of models that have been used "to describe the psychological processes, social experiences and individual challenges and obstacles of being bicultural" (p. 395). These include (a) assimilation models, which describe how individuals give up one culture to be absorbed into another, more dominant one; (b) acculturation models, which describe the development of competence in a dominant culture by members of minorities; (c) alternation models, which address the two-way nature of intercultural contact and describe how individuals can move between two cultures without giving up either; (d) multicultural models, which describe how individuals can maintain their cultures of origin while interacting with members of other cultural groups; and (e) fusion models, which describe the melting pot notion in which two or more cultures are blended on an equal basis into a new combination.

The concepts of acculturation and of biculturalism are quite rich and very useful for understanding aspects of the dynamics of diversity. In terms of the issues that are the focus of this chapter, however, these models can be problematic when they are based on an either/or view of cultures at the group level. The cultures are viewed as being separate from their members and as somewhat static. Individuals then decide, or are influenced by a variety of factors, to move back and forth between cultures, to move permanently from one to the other, or to develop a blend (e.g., Rotheram-Borus, 1993). Such models presume the primacy of the group-level cultures as the stimuli driving individuals' adaptation strategies.

Most problematic, however, is that these approaches tend not to specify the nature of the group-level cultures, usually either implicitly or explicitly viewing these in a unitary and relatively objective fashion. Thus, for example, Berry (1993) writes about cultural transmission in the context of "two cultures in contact (A and B)." From the perspective of the present analysis, it is possible that each of these cultures may appear quite different to different individuals, whether or not they are original members of the groups. If there is a great deal of individual variation not only in the way that cultural contact is handled but also in the way in which individuals subjectively construct the cultures (i.e., what the cultures are understood to be), then acculturation and biculturalism models could benefit by incorporating concepts to represent this dynamic.

Cox's Model of
Culture Identity Structure

Taylor Cox, Jr. (1993) uses the concept of *culture identity structure* to refer to an individual's particular configuration of membership in cultural groups. In this view, individuals may view themselves in terms of their membership in many different groups at once, and also may vary in the weight that they perceive each group as having in their self-concept. Figure 2.1 shows examples of culture identity structures generated by four of Cox's students. In these pie charts, the presence of a slice indicates that the group affiliation is important in that person's self-concept, and the size of the slice represents the relative importance of that affiliation in the overall identity. Comparing Examples 2 and 4, *Male* or *Man* is given a similar weight, suggesting that each student sees his gender as constituting the same proportion of the self-concept. In contrast, in Example 2, Black constitutes approximately one quarter of the self-concept based on group affiliations, while in Example 4, *White* is

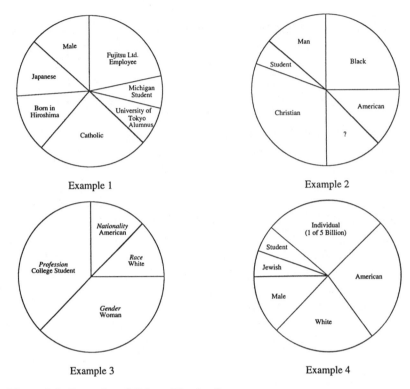

Figure 2.1. Examples of Culture Identity Structure

smaller than one quarter, implying that this student perceives race as less important to his self-concept.

This approach represents an advance in that it allows for multiple group identities that vary from person to person in their configuration. From the individual perspective that I am proposing, however, this is insufficient, because it continues to treat each group as unitary or separate. In the individual's culture identity structure, each piece has its own little box; the objective is to figure out how much of each one there is. Within this model, it is not clear what impact, if any, the various identities have on each other.

Related to this, there is an implicit equivalence of the same group across individuals. The students in Examples 2 and 4 both emphasized being male, and there is an assumption that this might mean the same thing for both of them. The preferable perspective is one that permits considering the ways in which various group memberships interrelate and influence each other.

Toward Connected Identities

A useful way to conceptualize identities from the individual perspective would be to incorporate the connections and interrelations among the various components. For example, we can expect that the meaning of a given ethnicity for the individual will in part be shaped by other identities, such as gender, class, religion, and immigration status. Wealthy members of the English nobility will not have the same conception of what it means to be English as will poor laborers in Liverpool, in spite of a shared ethnic identification. A recent immigrant from Mexico living in a poor neighborhood of Los Angeles will probably have a different conception of Hispanic culture than a sixth-generation landowner in New Mexico, and both of these will differ from a Jewish woman recently arrived from Buenos Aires, although all may well identify as Latinas. The construct of cultural identity is intended as a way of capturing such individual-level variations.

Cultural Identity

Cultural identity is proposed as a concept that represents the individual-level reflection of culture as it is constructed by each of us. Cultural identity addresses our sense of ourselves as cultural beings. It can be seen as the individual's road map of how the group guides her or his behavior, together with her or his reactions to that. Before formally defining it, I want to put it in the context of social identity.

Social identity (Tajfel & Turner, 1986) is an individual-level construct that deals primarily with the boundary around the group, and the individual's image of that boundary. *Social identity* typically refers to the symbolic aspects of social categories—the demarcation between in-group and out-group, between "we" and "they"—and the associated affect. In contrast, cultural identity focuses on what's "inside" the boundary, on what the person perceives to be the behavioral and attitudinal bases or consequences of the categories.

Cultural identity can be defined as one's individual image of the behaviors, beliefs, values, and norms—that is, the cultural features—that characterize one's group(s), together with one's feelings about those features and one's understanding of how they are (or are not) reflected in oneself. Thus cultural identity includes three types of perceptions on the part of the individual:

- What constitutes the group-level culture?
- How (what) do I feel about it?
- Where is it in me? (Where/how/to what degree are the group's cultural features reflected in me and my values/beliefs/style?)

Thus cultural identity is my picture of the relationship between my group's culture and myself. Like social identity, it includes both descriptive and evaluative components.

Via her or his cultural identity, an individual answers the question: What is the culturally appropriate way for someone such as me, for someone having my group memberships, to behave in and to interpret the world? Individual members of a particular group will vary in the extent to which they perceive specific attributes as central to their cultural identity and in the value they give to these attributes. In addition, they will vary in the degree to which they see themselves as having these attributes.

The first aspect of cultural identity is the individual's construction of the group, which can vary across persons. Two individuals may define membership in a group in basically the same way. However, each describes the group's cultural features quite differently. For example, Person 1 may be just as strongly Jewish as Person 2, but their constructions of Judaism and what it means for them, and even their picture of the Jews as a group, can be very different. Similarly, two people who perceive their identification as Hispanics as central to their social identity may define its meaning very differently. For example, a Puerto Rican living in New York and one living in Puerto Rico may share an ethnic identification but have dissimilar experiences and ways of looking at the world, with resulting differences in their cultural identities. For one, minority status and ethnic distinctiveness in an urban environment play a relatively focal role; for the other, the Spanish language and living on the island will be relatively more important (e.g., Flores, 1985; Ginorio, 1987; Safa, 1988). Similarly, some Hispanics more than others may perceive certain values or behaviors, such as balancing work and family life or maintaining close relations with extended family, to be culturally linked.

The second aspect of cultural identity is the individual's feelings about the cultural features ascribed to the group. Two individuals may agree in their depiction of a reference group that they share, but these images may carry quite divergent valences. For example, two Americans may view the U.S. culture as characterized by conservative values about sexuality. One may feel positively about this, however, while the other would prefer that the group were different.

The third aspect of cultural identity is the individual's view of where, how, and to what degree the group culture is reflected in the self. Thus, in the previous example, the individual who has positive feelings about U.S. culture sees himself as having conservative values and believes that this reflects his enculturation as an American. The person with negative feelings about these values may not see these reflected in her own preferences. A third person may perceive similar features in U.S. culture and have somewhat negative feelings about them, but still see these characteristics reflected in himself.

Figure 2.2 depicts schematically the conjunction of these various elements in three different individuals. Each person addresses the questions: What is the group like? How do I feel about it? And where am I in relation to that—what relationship is there between me and the group? In these examples, Persons 1 and 2 describe their reference group's cultural features in relatively similar ways (perhaps they are two siblings in the same family), and they have the same boundaries around those, in terms of who's in and who's out. But Person 1 puts herself close to the group, seeing herself as reflecting the group's culture to a large degree, whereas Person 2 sees very little of the group's culture reflected in herself. So there is some overlap, but not very much. Note that for Person 1, however, it is hard to distinguish in herself between the cultural features attributable to one group versus those features based on membership in another group. Indeed, it is the conjunction of these two groups that she sees reflected in her own styles and values. Person 2 in contrast sees no overlap between the cultural features of her various reference groups. Finally, Person 3 interprets the reference group culture quite differently than Persons 1 and 2, and also sees himself as somewhat but not completely detached from that culture.

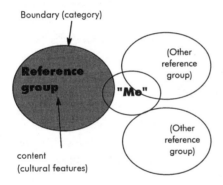

Figure 2.2. Cultural Identity in Three Individuals

Implications for Diversity in Organizations

The concept of cultural identity as discussed here has a number of implications for research and practice regarding diversity in organizations. Some of these can be introduced by considering an experience related to me during a focus group interview with a Hispanic manager whom I'll call Maria:

> I went to Puerto Rico with a peer of mine. . . . She didn't want to read, so she would sit there for hours watching television and not knowing what they're saying. And at one point she looks at me and she goes, "Maria, I finally figured out why you are so outgoing and you talk with the hands and all. All of you are like that." I said "I beg your pardon." She goes, "Yeah, you know, I always thought you were kind of friendly and everything . . . you and [another Puerto Rican coworker], when you talk you're always with the hands and everything, you're very expressive and emotional." I started laughing, but I said, "Wow, that's interesting." She goes, "All of you are like that," from watching TV. It wasn't a negative statement to her. She was just saying that she realized that it was all of us. . . . I started watching Puerto Rican television, and sure enough, the hands are going crazy.

There are at least two dynamics occurring here relevant to the current discussion. First is the traditional notion of intercultural training. Maria's coworker is beginning to see behavior that she previously interpreted as idiosyncratic or individual as connected to the group. Second, Maria is also changing in terms of seeing aspects of herself as connected to the group. So she is beginning to develop an idea about how some of her own style that she previously experienced as individual may actually be related to her membership in a group.

A graduate student, in a recent discussion on this topic, reported a similar experience. She said to me:

> I was reading some of your work about cultural identity, and I was thinking, wow, this is amazing. People have always said to me in graduate school, "You don't seem so professional," or "there is a certain thing about you that we really need to understand," or "there's just something that doesn't match."

She had initially tended to think of herself simply as being different at an individual level and having characteristics that she had to change. And as she read my descriptions of cultural features of Hispanic managers and some of their discoveries of that, she said, "Wow, maybe that's culturally related." So she started changing her theory about what was cultural and what was not. I do not presume here to decide what is "true" and what is not. The point is that each of us has a different construction of how our individuality reflects our group culture(s), and we need to pay more attention to that in our work on diversity.

Organization Socialization

Cultural identity has implications for how people are socialized and incorporated into organizations. The concept of cultural identity suggests that simply having some representatives of a particular group may not adequately reflect the full range of diversity. The process of "joining up" may vary depending on individuals' cultural identities. In developing and instituting mechanisms to help people become more socialized—people whose groups have previously not been represented in an organization, for example—it may be hard to justify having programs of the "one size fits all" type. We need to pay more attention to the process of how socialization works in relation to where the individuals are, and not just our collective constructions of their groups as a whole.

Intergroup Understanding

Cultural identity adds another layer of complexity to descriptions of what we might mean by developing intergroup understanding. Triandis (e.g., Triandis, Kurowski, & Gelfand, 1994) proposes the importance of moving toward making isomorphic attributions, such that members of Group A observing the behavior of a member of Group B learn to explain that behavior in the same way other members of Group B would explain it. The cultural identity concept suggests that intergroup understanding may go far beyond having people make isomorphic attributions. Given individual variations in the construction of the group, it becomes more difficult to know what is an isomorphic attribution. It becomes important to specify the level that we are talking about—group or individual. At the individual level, it would seem quite difficult ever to achieve fully isomorphic attributions, because they are usually based primarily on generalized knowledge of the group, not the individual.

I believe that we have to develop more dynamic and fine-tuned notions of intergroup understanding that include the relationship of the interpersonal to the intergroup aspect. We also need to incorporate means of guiding individuals in accepting their own identities and in understanding where they are now, before they can start working with other groups. This is consistent with approaches to intercultural training that focus on starting with understanding one's own culture and its influence before moving to consider others (see Gudykunst & Hammer, 1983).

Cultural identity suggests that in intergroup understanding there is also a dimension of within-group as well as between-group processes. To the extent that there are variations within a group, an out-group may develop understanding with some of its subgroups and not with others. Related to this, assessment of when intergroup understanding has been reached may vary depending on who is asked. Some group members may be quite satisfied with their interactions with the members of another group, while others perceive these to be problematic.

Diversity Training

Another implication of cultural identity relates to the practical aspects of diversity training. How can we most effectively do what some people call diversity training, which is to help people get the skills they need to work better in more inclusive organizations? Consideration of cultural identity suggests adding another objective to this type of training: learning that individual uniqueness is not compromised by group memberships. In fact, individual uniqueness may be enhanced by group memberships.

In terms of methods for diversity training, the notion of cultural identity suggests that the self—the individual self-constructions—may be a very valuable vehicle in doing this kind of training, and that we certainly need to go beyond presenting lists of cultural features of other groups.

Research Questions and Methods

Thinking about cultural diversity in the manner suggested by this chapter has implications for the type of research questions we might ask and the methods we might use to investigate them. In the acculturation and biculturalism approaches discussed earlier, ethnic and social identities, and perhaps even some aspects of what I call cultural identity, are typically seen as the independent variable. Identities are considered as the precursor or antecedent, and then research examines what effects they may have on other variables. If one looks at cultural identity in the way described here, one needs to think about it as a dependent variable or at least a moderator. What dynamics, what processes, what kinds of contextual factors or experiences will result in different patterns of cultural identity? Then one can begin to ask questions about systematic variations in cultural identity across different kinds of subgroups.

There is some exciting work in education that can be interpreted in this light. Fordham (1988, 1992), for example, showed how Black high school students who wanted to succeed in school felt pressed to construct identities that were "raceless":

> Achieving academic success in a context where a Eurocentric ethos dominates necessitates divorcing one's commitment to a changing yet familiar African American identity and embracing instead an unpredictable, unfolding meaning of both Self and Other. (Fordham, 1991, p. 471)

The texture of these reconstructed identities, however, varied across individuals and subgroups.

In terms of research methods, a consideration of cultural identity suggests that some of our quantitative, structured approaches should be complemented by more qualitative methods that allow people to tell their own stories. Before we can systematize some of the questionnaires we use and some of the assumptions about the differences between groups, we need to first include approaches that allow us to really hear what people think and believe about their own individual uniqueness as it relates to their group memberships. I hope then we will be able to find a better bridge between group differences and individual uniqueness.

References

Adler, N. J. (1991). *International dimensions of organizational behavior* (2nd ed.). Boston: Kent.

Alderfer, C. P. (1986). An intergroup perspective on group dynamics. In J. Lorsch (Ed.), *Handbook of organizational behavior* (pp. 190-222). Englewood Cliffs, NJ: Prentice-Hall.

Appiah, A. (1990). "But would that still be me?" Notes on gender, "race," ethnicity, as sources of "identity." *Journal of Philosophy, 87,* 493-499.

Arvey, R. D., Bhagat, R. S., & Salas, E. (1991). Cross-cultural and cross-national issues in personnel and human resource management: Where do we go from here? *Research in Personnel and Human Resources Management, 9,* 367-407.

Berry, J. W. (1980). Acculturation as varieties of adaptation. In A. Padilla (Ed.), *Acculturation: Theory, models, and some new findings* (pp. 9-25). Boulder, CO: Westview.

Berry, J. W. (1993). Ethnic identity in plural societies. In M. E. Bernal & G. P. Knight (Eds.), *Ethnic identity: Formation and transmission among Hispanics and other minorities* (pp. 271-296). Albany: State University of New York Press.

Berry, J. W., Poortinga, Y., Segall, M., & Dasen, P. (1992). *Cross-cultural psychology*. New York: Cambridge University Press.

Betancourt, H., & Lopez, S. R. (1993). The study of culture, ethnicity, and race in American psychology. *American Psychologist, 48*, 629-637.

Boekestijn, C. (1988). Intercultural migration and the development of personal identity: The dilemma between identity maintenance and cultural adaptation. *International Journal of Intercultural Relations, 12*, 83-105.

Boyacigiller, N., & Adler, N. J. (1991). The parochial dinosaur: Organizational science in a global context. *Academy of Management Review, 16*, 262-290.

Brewer, M. B. (1994, October). *Managing diversity: Can we reap the benefits without paying the costs?* Paper presented at the Conference on Work Team Dynamics and Productivity in the Context of Diversity, Center for Creative Leadership, Greensboro, NC.

Brewer, M. B., & Kramer, R. M. (1985). The psychology of intergroup attitudes and behavior. *Annual Review of Psychology, 36*, 219-243.

Brewer, M. B., & Miller, N. (1984). Beyond the contact hypothesis: Theoretical perspectives on desegregation. In N. Miller & M. B. Brewer (Eds.), *Groups in contact: The psychology of desegregation* (pp. 281-302). Orlando, FL: Academic Press.

Brewer, M. B., & Miller, N. (1988). Contact and cooperation: When do they work? In P. A. Katz & D. Taylor (Eds.), *Towards the elimination of racism: Profiles in controversy* (pp. 315-328). New York: Plenum.

Cox, T., Jr. (1993). *Cultural diversity in organizations: Theory, research, and practice*. San Francisco: Berrett-Koehler.

Crocker, J., Luhtanen, R., Blaine, B., & Broadnax, S. (1994). Collective self-esteem and psychological well-being among White, Black, and Asian college students. *Personality and Social Psychology Bulletin, 20*, 503-513.

Cross, E. Y., Katz, J. H., Miller, F. A., & Seashore, E. W. (Eds.). (1994). *The promise of diversity: Over 40 voices discuss strategies for eliminating discrimination in organizations*. Burr Ridge, IL: Irwin.

Ferdman, B. M. (1988, August). Values and fairness in the ethnically diverse workplace. In F. Crosby (Chair), *Emancipation, justice and affirmative action*. Symposium conducted at the 2nd International Conference on Social Justice and Societal Problems, University of Leiden, the Netherlands.

Ferdman, B. M. (1990). Literacy and cultural identity. *Harvard Educational Review, 60*, 181-204.

Ferdman, B. M. (1992). The dynamics of ethnic diversity in organizations: Toward integrative models. In K. Kelley (Ed.), *Issues, theory, and research in industrial/organizational psychology* (pp. 339-384). Amsterdam: North Holland.

Ferdman, B. M. (Ed.). (1994). *A resource guide for teaching and research on diversity*. St. Louis, MO: American Assembly of Collegiate Schools of Business.

Ferdman, B. M., & Cortes, A. (1992). Culture and identity among Hispanic managers in an Anglo business. In S. B. Knouse, P. Rosenfeld, & A. Culbertson (Eds.), *Hispanics in the workplace* (pp. 246-277). Newbury Park, CA: Sage.

Ferdman, B. M., & Hakuta, K. (1985, August). Group and individual bilingualism in an ethnic minority. In K. Hakuta & B. M. Ferdman (Chairs), *Bilingualism: Social psychological reflections*. Symposium presented at the American Psychological Association, Los Angeles.

Ferdman, B. M., & Thompson, D. (1994, April). *Teaching about diversity in organizations*. Master tutorial presented at the meetings of the Society for Industrial and Organizational Psychology, Nashville, TN.

Fiske, A. (1992). The four elementary forms of sociality: Framework for a unified theory of social relations. *Psychological Review, 99*, 689-723.

Fiske, S. (1993). Social cognition and social perception. *Annual Review of Psychology, 44*, 155-194.

Flores, J. (1985). "Que assimilated, brother, yo soy asimilao": The structuring of Puerto Rican identity in the U.S. *Journal of Ethnic Studies, 13*(3), 1-16.

Fordham, S. (1988). Racelessness as a factor in Black students' school success: Pragmatic strategy or Pyrrhic victory? *Harvard Educational Review, 58*, 54-84.

Fordham, S. (1991). Racelessness in private schools: Should we deconstruct the racial and cultural identity of African-American adolescents? *Teachers College Record, 92*, 470-484.

Fordham, S. (1992). "Those loud Black girls": (Black) women, silence, and gender "passing" in the academy. *Anthropology and Education Quarterly, 24*, 3-32.

Gaertner, S., Dovidio, J., Anastasio, P., Bachman, B., & Rust, M. (1993). The Common Ingroup Identity Model: Recategorization and the reduction of intergroup bias. In W. Stroebe & M. Hewstone (Eds.), *European review of social psychology* (Vol. 4, pp. 1-26). Chichester, U.K.: Wiley.

Gaertner, S., Mann, J., Murrell, A., & Dovidio, J. (1989). Reducing intergroup bias: The benefits of recategorization. *Journal of Personality and Social Psychology, 57*, 239-249.

Ginorio, A. B. (1987). Puerto Rican ethnicity and conflict. In J. Boucher, D. Landis, & K. A. Clark (Eds.), *Ethnic conflict: International perspectives* (pp. 182-206). Newbury Park, CA: Sage.

Gudykunst, W. B., & Hammer, M. R. (1983). Basic training design: Approaches to intercultural training. In D. Landis & R. Brislin (Eds.), *Handbook of intercultural training: Vol. 1. Issues in theory and design* (pp. 118-154). New York: Pergamon.

Gurin, P., Hurtado, A., & Peng, T. (1994). Group contacts and ethnicity in the social identities of Mexicanos and Chicanos. *Personality and Social Psychology Bulletin, 20*, 521-532.

Hofstede, G. (1980). *Culture's consequences: International differences in work-related values.* Beverly Hills, CA: Sage.

Hofstede, G. (1991). *Cultures and organizations: Software of the mind.* London: McGraw-Hill.

Hogg, M. A., & Abrams, D. (1988). *Social identifications: A social psychology of intergroup relations and group processes.* London: Routledge.

Hurtado, A., Rodríguez, J., Gurin, P., & Beals, J. (1993). The impact of Mexican descendants' social identity on the ethnic socialization of children. In M. E. Bernal & G. P. Knight (Eds.), *Ethnic identity: Formation and transmission among Hispanics and other minorities* (pp. 131-162). Albany: State University of New York Press.

Jackson, S. E., & Associates. (1992). *Diversity in the workplace: Human resource initiatives.* New York: Guilford.

Jones, J. (1991). Psychological models of race: What have they been and what should they be? In J. D. Goodchilds (Ed.), *Psychological perspectives on human diversity in America* (pp. 7-46). Washington, DC: American Psychological Association.

Keesing, R. M. (1974). Theories of culture. *Annual Review of Anthropology, 3*, 73-97.

LaFromboise, T., Coleman, H. L. K., & Gerton, J. (1993). Psychological impact of biculturalism: Evidence and theory. *Psychological Bulletin, 114*, 395-412.

Marín, G. (1993). Influence of acculturation on familialism and self-identification among Hispanics. In M. E. Bernal & G. P. Knight (Eds.), *Ethnic identity: Formation and transmission among Hispanics and other minorities* (pp. 181-196). Albany: State University of New York Press.

Markus, H. R., & Kitayama, S. (1991). Culture and the self: Implications for cognition, emotion, and motivation. *Psychological Review, 98*, 224-253.

Markus, H. R., & Kitayama, S. (1994). A collective fear of the collective: Implications for selves and theories of selves. *Personality and Social Psychology Bulletin, 20,* 568-579.

Messick, D. M., & Mackie, D. M. (1989). Intergroup relations. *Annual Review of Psychology, 40,* 45-81.

Miller, N., & Brewer, M. B. (1986). Categorization effects on ingroup and outgroup perception. In J. F. Dovidio & S. L. Gaertner (Eds.), *Prejudice, discrimination, and racism* (pp. 209-230). Orlando, FL: Academic Press.

Ridgeway, C. L. (1983). *The dynamics of small groups.* New York: St. Martin's Press.

Rodriguez-Scheel, J. (1980). *An investigation of the components of social identity for a Detroit sample.* Unpublished manuscript, Occidental College, Psychology Department, Los Angeles, CA.

Rohner, R. P. (1984). Toward a conception of culture for cross-cultural psychology. *Journal of Cross-Cultural Psychology, 15,* 111-138.

Rotheram-Borus, M. J. (1993). Biculturalism among adolescents. In M. E. Bernal & G. P. Knight (Eds.), *Ethnic identity: Formation and transmission among Hispanics and other minorities* (pp. 81-102). Albany: State University of New York Press.

Safa, H. I. (1988). Migration and identity: A comparison of Puerto Rican and Cuban migrants in the United States. In E. Acosta-Belén & B. Sjostrom (Eds.), *The Hispanic experience in the United States: Contemporary issues and perspectives* (pp. 137-150). New York: Praeger.

Sampson, E. E. (1988). The debate on individualism: Indigenous psychologies of the individual and their role in personal and societal functioning. *American Psychologist, 43,* 15-22.

Schweder, R. A., & Sullivan, M. A. (1993). Cultural psychology: Who needs it? *Annual Review of Psychology, 44,* 497-523.

Smith, P., & Bond, M. (1993). *Social psychology across cultures.* Boston: Allyn & Bacon.

Social Science Research Council. (1954). Acculturation: An exploratory formulation. *American Anthropologist, 56,* 973-1002.

Sue, S. (1991). Ethnicity and culture in psychological research and practice. In J. D. Goodchilds (Ed.), *Psychological perspectives on human diversity in America* (pp. 47-85). Washington, DC: American Psychological Association.

Tajfel, H. (1981). *Human groups and social categories.* Cambridge: Cambridge University Press.

Tajfel, H., & Turner, J. C. (1986). The social identity theory of intergroup relations. In S. Worchel & W. Austin (Eds.), *Psychology of intergroup relations* (pp. 7-24). Chicago: Nelson-Hall.

Taylor, D. M., & McKirnan, D. J. (1984). A five-stage model of intergroup relations. *British Journal of Social Psychology, 23,* 291-300.

Taylor, D. M., & Moghaddam, F. M. (1987). *Theories of intergroup relations: International social psychological perspectives.* New York: Praeger.

Triandis, H. C. (1989). The self and social behavior in differing cultural contexts. *Psychological Review, 96,* 506-520.

Triandis, H. C., Dunnette, M. D., & Hough, L. M. (Eds.). (1994). *Handbook of industrial and organizational psychology* (Vol. 4). Palo Alto, CA: Consulting Psychologists Press.

Triandis, H. C., Kurowski, L. L., & Gelfand, M. J. (1994). Workplace diversity. In H. C. Triandis, M. D. Dunnette, & L. M. Hough (Eds.), *Handbook of industrial and organizational psychology* (Vol. 4, pp. 769-827). Palo Alto, CA: Consulting Psychologists Press.

Turner, J. C., Hogg, M. A., Oakes, P. J., Reicher, S. D., & Wetherell, M. S. (1987). *Rediscovering the social group: A self-categorization theory.* Oxford: Blackwell.

Turner, J. C., Oakes, P. J., Haslam, A., & McGarty, C. (1994). Self and collective: Cognition and social context. *Personality and Social Psychology Bulletin, 20,* 454-463.

Worchel, S., & Austin, W. G. (Eds.). (1986). *Psychology of intergroup relations* (2nd ed.). Chicago: Nelson-Hall.

3

An Analysis of Work Specialization and Organization Level as Dimensions of Workforce Diversity

TAYLOR H. COX, JR.
JOYCELYN A. FINLEY

As a topic in the study of organizations, diversity research addresses the impact of differences in group identities of workers on the behavior and performance of individuals, work groups, and organizations. Previous literature on group-identity effects on organizational behavior has focused primarily on gender, race, nationality, and age. However, writers recently have given attention to a broader set of dimensions such as work specialization (e.g., Jackson, 1991) and physical ability (e.g., Stone, Stone, & Dipboye, 1992) and to eclectic theoretical frameworks that are applicable across dimensions (Cox, 1993; Jackson, Stone, & Alvarez, 1993; Triandis, Kurowski, & Gelfand, 1994). This theoretical direction raises new empirical questions such as these: (a) Which of these additional dimensions of difference provide important explanations of organizational experience? (b) To what extent do phenomena that have been observed for gender, race, nationality, and age identity (such as stereotyping, ethnocentrism, and more negative career outcomes for members of minority groups) also occur for other dimensions of difference? This chapter reports research that addresses these questions.

Following this introduction, we present the theoretical framework of Cox (1993) in which our study is grounded. We then review briefly some of the previous empirical research that is relevant to the framework. Finally, we discuss two empirical studies that address work specialization and organization level as dimensions of workforce diversity.

Theoretical Background

Interactional Model of Cultural Diversity

The Interactional Model of Cultural Diversity (IMCD), developed by Cox (1993), is shown in Figure 3.1. This model brings together learnings from a wide spectrum of previous work in psychology (e.g., Mischel, 1977; Triandis, 1976; Wong-Reider & Quintana, 1987), sociology (e.g., Kanter, 1977; Rice, 1969; Tajfel, 1978), anthropology (e.g., Asante & Asante, 1985; Berry, 1983; Hall, 1976), and organizational behavior (e.g., Alderfer & Smith, 1982; Ashforth & Mael, 1989; Bell, 1990; Chatman, 1989; Cox & Nkomo, 1990, 1992; Jones, 1986; Nkomo, 1992; Pettigrew & Martin, 1987; Tung, 1988). The framework suggests that a variety of phenomena related to differences in the group identities of workers combine to create potent effects on their career experiences.

Specifically, the model in Figure 3.1 posits that four individual-level factors (personal identity structures, prejudice, stereotyping, and personality type), three intergroup factors (cultural differences, ethnocentrism, and intergroup conflict), and four organizational context factors (organizational culture and acculturation processes, structural integration, informal integration, and institutional bias) collectively define the diversity climate of an organization.

The diversity climate may influence individual career experiences and outcomes in organizations in two ways. *Affective outcomes* refer to how people feel about their work and their employer. Thus in many organizations employee morale and satisfaction are related to identity groups such as gender, racioethnicity, and so on. Second, the actual *career achievement* of individuals as measured by such things as job performance ratings may be related to group identities in some organizations. These individual outcomes, in turn, are expected to have an impact on a series of first-order organizational effectiveness measures such as work quality, productivity, absenteeism, and

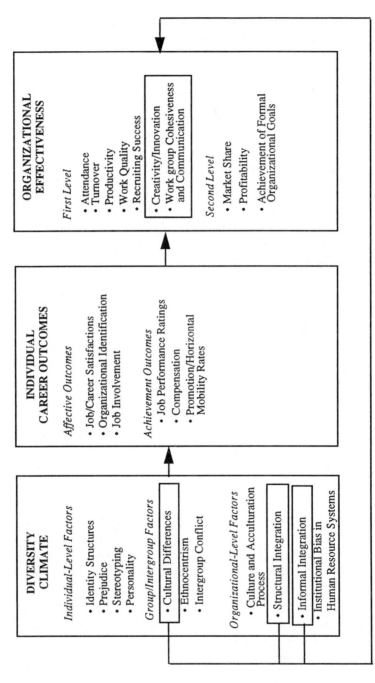

Figure 3.1. Interactional Model of Cultural Diversity

SOURCE: Reprinted with permission from figure 1.1 of *Cultural Diversity in Organizations: Theory, Research, and Practice*, Taylor Cox, Jr., San Francisco: Berrett-Koehler Publishers, Inc., 1993.

turnover. For profit-making organizations, these first-order measures ultimately translate into second-order results such as profitability and market share. In nonprofit organizations, individual contribution is still crucial in determining the extent to which organizational goals will be achieved.

In addition to these indirect effects of group identity, certain aspects of the diversity climate are thought to directly affect organizational performance. Specifically, the amount of diversity in both formal and informal structures of organizations will affect factors such as creativity, problem solving, and intraorganizational communications.

Cox (1993) argues that the basic relationships depicted in the IMCD are relevant across many dimensions of group identification. One example is that when properly leveraged, diversity based on gender, race, and nationality will add value to problem solving, creativity, and innovation in work groups in much the same way that diversity of work function or organizational tenure does. A second example is that factors such as prejudice, stereotyping, miscommunication, and intergroup conflict, which have been observed to lead to differences in career outcomes based on differences of gender, race, or nationality, will sometimes operate in a similar manner based on other differences such as work specialization or organization level. This latter example is the focal point of the empirical research to be presented later in this chapter.

Review of Previous Research

Before reviewing previous research on work specialization and organization level, it may be useful to briefly review some examples of previous work on the more traditional dimensions of workforce diversity. Although empirical support, in various quantities, exists for many of the relationships depicted in Figure 3.1, we will confine ourselves here to examples that bear most directly on the connection between personal identity and individual career outcomes. This is in keeping with the focus of the empirical studies that we report in the next section of the chapter.

Gender, Race, Nationality, and Age. Although some contrary data exist (e.g., Nkomo & Cox, 1989), research on gender effects on career outcomes has generally shown that women have less favorable career outcomes than men on measures of compensation and upward mobility (e.g., Cox & Harquail, 1991; Cox & Nkomo, 1991). Some research also suggests that women have lower job involvement than men (Cox & Nkomo, 1991) and higher rates of absenteeism and turnover, two key indicators of organizational identification and commitment (Cox, 1993). Research has generally not shown gender effects on the career outcomes of satisfaction (e.g., Cox & Nkomo, 1991) and of job performance (e.g., Shore & Thornton, 1986).

The term *racioethnic identity* (Cox, 1990) has been used to label differences of physical and cultural background among members of the same national origin (e.g., African Americans in the United States). It is preferred to *ethnic identity* because the latter is customarily used to distinguish people within a race group (e.g., Euro-Americans of Irish versus German ancestry). Research on the link between racioethnic identity and career outcomes has generally shown that members of racioethnic minority groups have more negative career experiences than those of the majority group. For example, among the career outcomes specified in the IMCD model, research has indicated less favorable experience for non-Anglos compared with Anglo-Americans on job performance ratings (e.g., Cox & Nkomo, 1986; Kraiger & Ford, 1985), upward mobility (e.g., Greenhaus, Parasuraman, & Wormley, 1990), career satisfaction (e.g., Cox & Nkomo, 1991), and job involvement (Cox & Nkomo, 1991). The vast majority of studies to date have included only Anglo-Americans and African Americans; however, a limited amount of research suggests that similar results occur when comparing Anglo-Americans with other racioethnic minority groups (e.g., Fernandez, 1991; Khoo, 1988; Rivera-Ramos, 1992).

The limited research that has compared workers of different nationalities using the career measures of the IMCD is difficult to summarize. In Slocum and Topichak's (1972) study of a matched sample of production workers from the United States and Mexico, for example, the Mexican respondents reported higher job satisfaction than their American counterparts. On the other hand, a study comparing U.S. and Mexican workers for the same U.S.-based employer found that Mexican workers were more likely to experience alienation and more likely to leave the organization (Zurcher, Zurcher, & Meadow, 1965), and a study of American and Chinese managers of U.S. firms operating in Taiwan revealed no differences between the Chinese and the American managers in a measure of overall job satisfaction (Chang, 1985).

There is some evidence that performance appraisal processes are influenced by cultural differences related to nationality but these effects are not as simple as personal prejudice against a minority group. For example, Farh, Dobbins, and Cheng (1991) report that when appraisal processes include the use of self-evaluations, persons of Chinese origin may score lower than most Americans due to a tendency to understate their contributions because of modesty norms in Chinese culture.

Finally, there is some research on age that suggests that older workers are subject to the processes of stereotyping and undervaluation of ability that have often been attributed to women and non-Anglo men in majority Anglo male organizations and that older workers have more negative career outcomes than their younger counterparts. For example, age tends to be negatively correlated with job performance ratings given by supervisors (Waldman & Avolio, 1986), and older workers tend to have lower ratings of promotion potential even when performance and job tenure are held constant (Cox & Nkomo, 1992). Rosen and Jerdee (1976) and Cleveland and Landy (1983) are among those who have explicitly connected the less favorable career outcomes of older workers with identity-group processes such as stereotyping.

Work Specialization. Several streams of past research on work specialization are relevant to contemporary thinking about diversity in organizations. One stream examines the impact of group heterogeneity on team and organizational effectiveness. In general, this research has shown that diversity in terms of functional background increases innovation (Bantel & Jackson, 1989), creativity (Ancona & Caldwell, 1992), problem solving (Wanous & Youtz, 1986), and overall financial performance (Murray, 1989). Some of this research indicates that unmanaged diversity (i.e., where diversity exists in work groups without any conscious effort to educate people about differences or how to leverage them) often leads to no improvement or even to unfavorable outcomes. For example, Ancona and Caldwell (1992) explain that team diversity brings more creativity to problem solving and product development, but impedes implementation because there is less capability for teamwork than there is for homogeneous teams. They further note that teams need to find a way to garner the potential positive effects of diversity and to reduce the potential negative effects.

There is also some evidence that the effect of functional diversity in management teams on group and organization performance is a complex interaction of diversity and contextual factors such as the measure of performance and amount of change and competition that the firm faces (Murray, 1989; Ouchi & Price, 1978; Weick, 1977). These findings suggest that simply changing the structure of teams (i.e., combining representatives of diverse function and tenure) will not necessarily improve performance.

A second stream of research suggests that work specialization is an important dimension of diversity because the various functional areas of firms tend to have their own distinctive cultures. For example, Hambrick and Mason (1984) note that marketing-oriented people have outlooks different than those with production backgrounds, and a recent book on organizational culture devotes an entire chapter to occupational groups as subcultures (Trice & Beyer, 1993).

Finally, research suggests that work specialization/function may form the basis of ethnocentric behavior in organizations. For example, Dearborn and Simon (1958) found that when a group of executives from different functional areas were presented with the same problem and asked to consider it from a companywide perspective, they defined the problem largely in terms of the activities and goals of their own functional areas. When considered in the context of organizational power structures in which a particular work specialization may be dominant, this kind of parochialism may lead to a devaluing of the contributions of persons from other work specializations.

Research on Organization Level. Some researchers have argued that different levels of organizations represent different cultural constellations in much the same way that different work specializations do (Hood & Koberg, 1991; Reynolds, 1986). This is one of the ways in which organizational level may be said to operate as a dimension of diversity. However, a line of research closer to the interest of the present study demonstrates that persons at lower organization levels tend to have different career experiences and to perceive their work setting very differently than people at higher levels in organizations. For example, in a study of 122 employees (89 males and 33 females) from eight large public accounting firms, Hood and Koberg (1991) investigated the relationship between hierarchical level and five dependent measures including job satisfaction, job involvement, and propensity to leave the organization. Results indicated that partners (the highest level) reported significantly higher job satisfaction and involvement and significantly lower propensity to leave the organization than either managers or senior staff members. Although it seems clear that these results, to some degree, simply reflect the greater stake that partners have in the success of the firm and their higher level of control over decision making, research on equity theory suggests that people evaluate their opportunities and rewards in light of their contributions (Bateman & Zeithaml, 1990). Thus it seems to us that persons at lower levels will feel involved, satisfied, and willing to stay as long as their recognition and sense of being valued is viewed as appropriate to their level, not equal to people at higher levels.

Similar results, indicating more favorable work outcomes for persons at higher organization levels, have been found by other researchers. Kline and Boyd (1991) examined possible job satisfaction differences in hierarchical level among managers from 120 different organizations (183 men and 27 female private sector managers) from four major Canadian urban centers. Overall, managers at the highest level reported the most job satisfaction. Presidents reported higher satisfaction with pay than middle managers did. Vice presidents reported greater satisfaction with promotional opportunities than presidents did. The researchers note:

> Consistent with previous findings, these results generally support the notion that the higher one is in the organizational hierarchy, the more satisfied one is with the firm and the salary but the less satisfied one is with promotional opportunities, presumably because there are fewer of them. (Kline & Boyd, 1991, p. 310)

Gannon and Demler (1971) examined the relationship between organizational level and five job attitudes among 237 government workers: interest in work innovation, job motivation, acceptance of job changes, willingness to disagree with supervisors, and identification with the organization. They found that persons at higher organizational levels reported significantly higher scores on three of the attitudes: interest in work innovation, job motivation, and willingness to disagree with supervisors.

Leigh and Futrell (1985) investigated 395 marketing managers enrolled in an executive development program. Subjects at higher managerial levels had more favorable perceptions of their jobs and were more satisfied with them. Relative to marketing managers and district sales managers, presidents and marketing vice presidents had greater job satisfaction and higher satisfaction with pay and promotions.

We identified two studies containing results that contradicted the "higher-is-better" ideology. Both addressed job involvement as the dependent variable. Singh (1987) examined the effect of occupational level on job involvement among 100 supervisors and 100 workers. Results indicated no significant difference between job involvement scores of supervisors and those of workers. Finally, Anantharaman and Begum (1982) investigated the difference in job involvement among bank managers. They interviewed 10 managers, 50 officers (supervisors), and 100 clerks using the Lodahl and Kejner (1965) job involvement scale. These researchers found no difference in job involvement across levels.

It is interesting to note that, although both the study by Anantharaman and Begum and that of Singh were conducted in India, neither addressed the issue of culture. Anantharaman and Begum suggest that their findings may be due to the fact that the working conditions, salaries, and nature of the work for all subjects were similar. However, Singh investigated an industrial plant and also found no significant differences between job involvement scores of supervisors and those of workers. Though the authors, in each case, make no claims that cultural differences had an impact on findings, it is reasonable to question the influence of cultural norms. For instance, Hofstede's (1980, 1984) research on cross-national cultural differences has shown that individuality is a strong cultural norm in most Euro-Western organizations while Asian countries adhere to more collectivist cultural orientations. Such differences may translate into different perspectives from which to assess equity of treatment and other factors related to affective responses to work.

A recurring theme in the previous research relating group identity to career outcomes is that members of the majority sociocultural group (in terms of numbers and/or power) tend to experience more positive outcomes than members of "minority" groups (groups of comparatively smaller numbers and/or substantially less power). While this line of thinking is well established regarding differences of gender and racioethnic identity, the extent to which this is a general phenomenon of workforce identity groups needs further exploration. This is the line of inquiry that our empirical research addresses, as described in the next section.

Research Focus of the Present Study

In the empirical study reported here, we were interested in testing for possible effects of work specialization and organizational level on the individual outcomes specified in Cox's IMCD model of the impact of diversity in organizations (Cox, 1993). As noted previously, the IMCD model posited that due to phenomena related to intergroup differences, such as stereotyping, ethnocentrism, and intergroup conflict, work outcomes at the individual level will be systematically related to the group identities of workers. At the individual level of analysis, the model specified that the work outcomes that are systematically related to group identity include affective outcomes of work (job satisfaction, organizational identification, and job involvement) and achievement outcomes (job performance, compensation, and job mobility). Most of the theory and research on which the model is based dealt with gender, racioethnicity, and nationality. We were interested in examining the extent to which some basic tenets of the model would also apply to work specialization and organization level. The logic underlying the present research is that members at low organization levels and in nondominant work specializations have relatively low power in organizations and have traditionally been undervalued and marginalized. Thus in many respects they are members of "minority" groups and will tend to have less favorable work experiences in terms of both affect and achievement as compared with members at higher levels and in the dominant work specialization of the firm (i.e., in-group members). As indicated in our literature review, there is some support for this logic in the previous research on organization level and in research on functional areas as subcultures of organizations.

A practical implication of this research is that organizations seeking to employ cross-functional work teams and cross-level problem-solving teams will experience sub-optimal results if the dynamics of in-group favoritism and out-group oppression are operating based on hierarchical level and work specialization. Other writers have noted that organizations are redesigning jobs to emphasize teamwork to meet the demands of increased competition and globalization. They explain that the emphasis is on teamwork that is multifunction-multidepartment because this type of team is believed to improve a company's competitiveness by facilitating production quality and the development of new products that will be both acceptable to customers and efficient to produce (Banas, 1988; Dumaine, 1990; Jackson et al., 1993; Kanter, 1988; Walton & Hackman, 1986). Thus, if the dynamics of diversity operate with respect to work specialization and organization level, the Cox model has important implications for the practice of management as well as for future research.

In summary, we expect that work specialization and organization level will function as dimensions of diversity in that they will differentiate work experiences and perceptions of workers. Furthermore, we expect that less favorable career outcomes for members of "minority" groups, which have heretofore been observed for gender and racioethnicity, will also result from work specialization and organization level. Based on the logic and previous research presented, the following hypotheses were tested:

Hypothesis 1: Members of the dominant work specialization in organizations will tend to have more favorable career outcomes than members of other work specializations.

Hypothesis 2: Members at higher organization levels will tend to have more favorable career outcomes than members at lower organizational levels.

Method

Data were taken from two separate studies. The first database was obtained from a survey of managerial and professional employees in a U.S. research and development company (referred to hereafter as Study 1). The second database was taken from a survey of all employees in a medium-sized U.S. financial services company (hereafter referred to as Study 2).

Sample and Data Collection Method

Study 1. A survey designed by one of the authors was sent through internal company mail to 368 managerial and professional personnel who were scheduled to participate in a diversity awareness training program. Those scheduled included all of the management-level employees at the eastern location of the company and a stratified, random sample of professional employees that included engineers, scientists, and administrative personnel. The bases of sample stratification were gender and race. This was done to meet the research objective of comparing work experiences based on gender and race.

The survey was part of an organizational assessment process on managing diversity and asked for respondents' perceptions on a wide range of subjects related to their employment experiences. In addition to the survey, some career information was obtained on respondents from the human resource computer information system of the company. Data obtained in this fashion included performance ratings, promotion potential, starting and current job level, compensation, education, and other demographic data such as departmental affiliation, gender, race, and age. Survey responses were matched with file data by means of a research code that appeared on both the survey and the file data. No names were made available to the researcher so as to protect the anonymity of the respondent. Respondents were assured that their confidentiality would be fully protected in handling the data. A total of 298 usable surveys were returned for an 81% response rate; however, 23 surveys were not used because they could not be matched to file data, leaving a sample for statistical analysis of 275 (75% of the recipients).

The sample was 71% male and 74% Anglo-American; 12% of the sample were Asians, 7% were African American, and 7% Latino. As suggested previously, women and non-Anglo men were somewhat overrepresented in the sample (compared with the total organizational population) due to the objectives of the broader assessment.

Study 2. A survey similar to that used in Study 1 was sent to all permanent employees of a financial services company. A response of 51% yielded a sample of 1,500. Respondents were compared with nonrespondents on age, departmental affiliation, company seniority, gender profile, race profile, geographic region, and organization level. There were no significant differences between the profile of the sample and that of the overall workforce on any of these dimensions. The sample was 46% male and 69% Anglo-American. Of the 31% non-Anglos, 6% were Asian, .3% were Native American, 2.5% were Latino, and the remaining 22% were African American; 71% of the sample were in entry or lower level professional jobs, 13% were in lower level managerial jobs, and 16% were in middle or upper management jobs. Similar to Study 1, demographic data and career experience data such as performance ratings, promotion rates, and compensation were obtained from the human resource computer file of the company and matched to survey data by research codes. Also as in Study 1, explicit assurances of confidentiality were provided to respondents.

Measurement of Variables

The independent variables of focus in the study were work specialization and organization level. The control variables used in the multivariate analyses of the study included gender, race, and company seniority.

Work Specialization. In Study 1, work specialization was operationalized as either engineer ($n = 112$) or other ($n = 159$). This categorization was chosen because engineering was the culturally dominant function in the power coalition of the organization and, in keeping with the intent of the study, there was an interest in contrasting experience of persons affiliated with the dominant specialization with experience of those from other ("minority") backgrounds. Several pieces of evidence indicated that engineering was the dominant specialization; all of the members of the senior management committee of the firm were engineers; 80% of the members of the management committees at the department level in the firm were engineers; and 90% of the 268 respondents to a survey question asking how important various factors were in obtaining promotion to senior management jobs said that having an engineering background was very important.

In Study 2, work specialization was operationalized as marketing ($n = 644$) versus other specializations ($n = 827$) with persons from administration excluded. Administration consisted mainly of human resource management personnel. They were excluded from the analyses because many of these respondents were responsible for creation of the human resource policies and practices that we wanted to assess. We felt that their sense of ownership and responsibility for creation and monitoring of the practices would tend to bias their views on the effects of policies and practices.

Marketing was chosen for comparison because of indications that it was the culturally dominant specialization in the firm. Evidence of this included the fact that 43% of the employees of the company (and in the sample) were from marketing. In addition, on the survey question asking about the importance of various factors in obtaining promotion to senior positions in the company, 78% of the respondents said that having experience in the marketing function of the organization was important or very important.

Organization Level. As suggested previously, the intent was to compare the experience of persons working at higher levels in the organization with that of those working at lower levels. The preferred base of comparison, where distinctions of perception and experience were expected to be greatest, was managers versus nonmanagers. In Study 2, this point of comparison was accomplished with data on managers ($n = 463$) compared with nonmanagers ($n = 1,008$). However, because the sample in Study 1 included only managerial or professional personnel (e.g., persons at a similar level on the technical career ladder), organization level was operationalized as senior managers ($n = 59$) and lower level managers/professionals ($n = 212$).

Control Variables. Gender was treated as a dichotomous variable: men or women. Race was also treated as a dichotomy of Anglo-Americans compared with other racioethnic groups, and company seniority was the total number of years of service in the organization.

The dependent variables in the study were employee satisfaction, organizational identification, job involvement, job performance, compensation satisfaction, and promotion opportunity. As noted previously, these variables were identified as individual career outcomes in the model of diversity suggested by Cox (1993). In that model, the first three variables are labeled as affective outcomes and the last three are labeled achievement outcomes. Study 1 did not include a measure of job involvement, and therefore only five of the dependent variables were analyzed here for Study 1.

Employment Satisfaction. In Study 1, six items, each measured on a four-point Likert-style scale, were used as a measure of overall satisfaction with employment. Scale anchors ranged from "strongly disagree" to "strongly agree." Results of a principal component factor analysis employing varimax rotation indicated that the six items did appear to be measuring the same underlying construct. A sample item: "Overall, I am satisfied with my career at _____ up to this point in time."

This same measure was used in Study 2 except that one item used in the Study 1 version of the survey instrument was deleted in the Study 2 version. The deleted item read, "All things considered, I am satisfied with my employment experience at _____." This item was deleted because it was somewhat redundant with other items in the scale.

Organizational Identification. In both studies, this variable was operationalized as "intent to stay" in the organization. Respondents were asked to indicate their level of agreement-disagreement with the following statement: "If given the opportunity, I expect to continue working for _____ for at least the next 3-5 years (or until retirement)." Higher levels of agreement with this statement were interpreted to indicate higher levels of organizational identification and vice versa.

Job Involvement. The job involvement scale was deleted from the survey in Study 1 by the organization in the interest of questionnaire brevity. Therefore this variable was measured only in Study 2. It was measured by a four-item scale developed by Lodahl and Kejner (1965). Each item was answered in a four-point Likert-style agree-disagree format. The Cronbach coefficient alpha for the scale in this study was .75 indicating internal consistency reliability. A sample item: "I avoid taking on extra duties and responsibilities in my work" reversed scored.

Job Performance. Job performance ratings for respondents were obtained from the official human resource records of the company. No individual performance forms were involved. The researcher received a list of research codes and ratings. Only those persons authorized by the company had access to the names and rating data. In Study 1, ratings were obtained for the two most recent rating years and were averaged to get one score. The scores are reported here as a derivative of the original ratings used to further protect the confidentiality of the company. The derivative is a simple transformation of the original scores (i.e., by multiplying all scores by the same factor). The scale used for scores in the analysis has a theoretical range of 1 to 10 with higher values indicating higher performance.

In the second study, the measurement of performance ratings was more complicated because the organization had changed performance rating plans one year earlier and used different rating scales for exempt (not covered by the Fair Labor Standards Act) versus nonexempt personnel. As a result of these conditions, we used only the rating for the most recent performance year rather than an average rating for two years. We also conducted separate analyses for exempt versus nonexempt employees. For exempt employees, ratings were given on an 11-point scale with higher numbers indicating a higher performance. Nonexempt employees were rated on a 7-point scale with higher numbers indicating better performance.

Compensation Satisfaction. Although salary data were available for both studies, the lack of comparability of jobs across departments and professional fields suggests that no analysis of this measure of compensation would be fruitful. Therefore we compared satisfaction with pay. In Study 1, compensation satisfaction was measured by the following two items: (a) "I am satisfied with information the company gives about pay issues of concern to me" and (b) "I feel I am compensated fairly relative to others at _____ and elsewhere doing similar work." These items were answered on the same four-point, strongly disagree-strongly agree scale as the other survey items. The Cronbach's alpha coefficient for this two-item scale was .69. In Study 2, due to more flexibility to lengthen the survey instrument, compensation satisfaction was measured by a four-item scale developed by Heneman and Schwab (1985). The Cronbach's alpha coefficient for this scale was .86, indicating that the scale had high internal consistency. A sample item was "I am satisfied with my overall level of compensation."

Promotion Opportunity. In Study 1, promotion opportunity was measured by the difference between an individual's current level and the level specified in his or her promotion potential rating. This measure produced a range of values of 0 to 20.5 with a mean of 2.59 and a standard deviation of 2.47. In Study 2, promotion opportunity was measured by the historical rate of promotion defined as number of promotions divided by the years of company seniority. This measure produced scores ranging from 0 to 2.0 with a mean of .275 and a standard deviation of .364. The difference in measurements between studies is partly due to differences in methods used to track promotion potential in the two organizations (e.g., in the second organization, no formal promotion potential ratings were done by managers).

Results

Hypothesis 1 predicted that individuals with backgrounds in the dominant work specialization would experience more favorable career outcomes than persons in other work specializations. Table 3.1 provides a comparison of mean scores for each of the dependent variables.

In Study 1, a comparison of mean scores indicates that engineers (the dominant specialization) did, as predicted, have higher scores than nonengineers on four of the five available measures. The exception was promotion rates, where the difference between current level and the promotion potential rating was 2.34 for engineers versus 2.66 for other work specializations. In Study 2, persons from a marketing background (the dominant specialization) had higher scores than others on four of six measures. The exceptions here were performance ratings and promotion rates.

To determine whether or not there were significant differences in scores based on work specialization, a series of analyses of covariance was conducted using the GLM program of the SAS computer software package. This enabled us to test for significant differences in the means presented in Table

Table 3.1
Means by Group Affiliations

	Study 1				Study 2			
	Work Specialization		Organizational Level		Work Specialization		Organizational Level	
	Engineer	Others	Exec.	Others	Mktg	Others	Mgmt.	Non-Mgmt.
	(n = 112)	(n = 159)	(n = 59)	(n = 212)	(n = 644)	(n = 827)	(n = 463)	(n = 1,008)
Employment satisfaction	2.92	2.72	2.95	2.76	2.80	2.75	2.88	2.74
Organizational identification	3.56	3.39	3.64	3.41	3.42	3.34	3.30	3.41
Job involvement	NA[a]	NA	NA	NA	2.97	2.86	2.91	2.91
Job performance nonexempt					5.06	5.25	NA	NA
exempt	6.55	6.04	5.66	6.42	7.19	7.51	7.92	7.02
Compensation satisfaction	2.75	2.55	2.82	2.58	2.65	2.59	2.75	2.58
Promotion opportunity	2.34	2.66	2.04	2.66	.219	.320	.230	.290

a. NA = not applicable or not available.

78

Table 3.2
Results of Analysis of Covariance: Study 1

Independent Variables	Dependent Variables (F Statistics)				
	Employment Satisfaction	Organizational Identification	Job Performance	Compensation Satisfaction	Promotion Opportunity
Work specialization	3.64[a]	.41	5.27[b]	.47	.97
Organization level	.44	.05	5.17[b]	.54	.71
Gender	1.90	3.88[b]	5.76[b]	8.42[b]	.32
Race	8.29[c]	8.58[c]	11.92[c]	3.05[a]	.51
Seniority	.02	3.87[b]	9.38[c]	.71	.00
Model statistics	$R^2 = .07$	$R^2 = .11$	$R^2 = .10$	$R^2 = .08$	$R^2 = .04$
	$F_{5,263} = 4.13^c$	$F_{5,259} = 6.51^c$	$F_{5,263} = 5.68^c$	$F_{5,257} = 4.22^c$	$F_{5,226} = 1.78$

a. $p < .10$.
b. $p < .05$.
c. $p < .01$.

3.1 while controlling for certain other factors. We were concerned that differences in representation on other diversity factors might account for differences between work specializations. For example, if there were proportionately more women in the nonengineering areas, then observed differences in career outcomes between engineers and nonengineers could be due to gender and not work specialization. To address this concern, we included organization level, gender, race, and company seniority in each of the analyses of covariance on work specialization. Thus the models essentially examined the effect of work specialization for people at the same organization level, of the same gender and race group, and with similar seniority.

Tables 3.2 and 3.3 show the results of the multivariate analysis for work specialization. Due to the relatively small sample size, a probability of error of .1 was specified for significance in Study 1 rather than the .05 used for Study 2.

In Study 1, the data indicated that even with the specified controls, engineers had significantly higher scores than nonengineers on overall employment satisfaction ($F = 3.64$, $p < .10$) and job performance ratings ($F = 5.27$, $p < .05$). No significant differences were found on organizational identification, compensation satisfaction, or promotion. Study 1 also produced significant effects for some of the other dimensions of diversity used as control variables. Gender made a significant difference in organizational identification (men = 3.54,

Table 3.3
Results of Analysis of Covariance: Study 2

	Employment Satisfaction	Organizational Identification	Job Involvement	Job Performance[1]		Compensation Satisfaction	Promotion Opportunity
Independent Variables				*Dependent Variables (F Statistics)*			
				NE	EX		
Work specialization	2.28	2.22	18.23^c	2.82	6.47^a	1.77	21.03^c
Level	10.68^b	3.27	.15	NA	58.87^c	12.95^c	7.71^b
Gender	.59	1.99	10.20^b	1.90	7.02^b	.54	.93
Race	10.93^b	2.64	.41	8.71^b	12.66^c	26.49^c	.57
Seniority	4.60^a	3.45	16.55^c	1.35	7.21^b	.48	91.47^c
Model statistics	$R^2 = .02$	$R^2 = .01$	$R^2 = .03$	$R^2 = .05$	$R^2 = .09$	$R^2 = .03$	$R^2 = .10$
	$F_{5,1410} = 6.18^c$	$F_{5,1379} = 3.64^b$	$F_{5,1410} = 8.19^c$	$F_{3,60} = 4.278^b$	$F_{5,912} = 18.69^c$	$F_{5,1411} = 9.99^c$	$F_{5,1181} = 27.65^c$

NOTE: 1. NE = nonexempt; EX = exempt personnel.

a. $p < .05$.

b. $p < .01$.

c. $p < .001$.

women = 3.29), job performance (men = 6.34, women = 6.04), and compensation satisfaction (men = 2.74, women = 2.38) with women having lower scores than men on all three measures. Race produced significant effects on employment satisfaction (Anglos = 2.86, others = 2.63), organizational identification (Anglos = 3.54, others = 3.24), job performance (Anglos = 6.43, others = 5.70), and compensation satisfaction (Anglos = 2.68, others = 2.52), with non-Whites having significantly lower scores than Whites on all four measures. Finally, more senior people had significantly higher scores on organizational identification ($r = .27$) and lower job performance ratings ($r = -.13$) than less senior people.

In Study 2, persons from marketing backgrounds had significantly different scores than those from other backgrounds on job involvement ($F = 18.23, p < .001$) and on job performance ratings for exempt personnel ($F = 6.47, p < .05$). The significant difference for job performance is contradictory to hypothesis 1 in that we expected job performance to be higher for those from the dominant specialization (as in Study 1) whereas, in Study 2, exempt personnel from marketing backgrounds had lower average performance ratings (7.19) than those from other specializations (7.51). A second finding contradictory to our hypothesis was that promotion rates of persons in the marketing area were significantly lower than those of persons from other areas ($F = 21.03, p < .001$).

The data from Study 2 also produced several significant results on the other dimensions of diversity examined as control variables. Gender had a significant effect on job involvement and job performance with women having lower job involvement scores (2.87 versus 2.96 for men) and higher job performance ratings (7.43 versus 7.34) than men. In connection with the latter result, it is relevant to note that women outnumbered men in this organization and had experienced considerable recent success in promotion to managerial jobs. Race had a significant effect on employment satisfaction (Anglos = 2.83, others = 2.67), job performance ratings (Anglos = 7.51, others = 6.95), and compensation satisfaction (Anglos = 2.70, others = 2.47) with non-Anglos having lower scores than Anglos on all three measures. Finally, job involvement ($r = -.10$), job performance ratings ($r = -.07$), and promotion rates ($r = -.29$) were related to seniority in that more senior workers had lower scores on all three measures.

In summary, the data produced mild support for hypothesis 1. Of the eleven comparisons of mean scores across both studies, eight were in the predicted direction and three of the eight were significant. The data were more supportive of our hypothesis in Study 1, in which both significant results were in the predicted direction, than in Study 2, in which two of the three significant results were contradictory to our hypothesis and the R squares were very small.

Hypothesis 2 predicted that persons at higher organization levels would have more favorable career outcomes than persons at lower levels. Referring again to Table 3.1, the comparison of means shows that, in Study 1, persons in senior management jobs did have higher scores than persons in lower management and professional jobs on employment satisfaction, organizational identification, and compensation, but lower scores on job performance ratings and on promotion. In Study 2, persons in management jobs had higher scores than persons in nonmanagerial jobs on employment satisfaction, job performance, and compensation, but lower scores on organizational identification and promotion. There were no differences in mean scores between managers and nonmanagers on the measure of job involvement.

The statistical test of hypothesis 2 was the same as for hypothesis 1 except that organization level was the predictor variable and work specialization was treated as a control variable along with the other controls of gender, race, and seniority. Referring now to Tables 3.2 and 3.3, we see that in Study 1 the only significant effect of level was for job performance where, contrary to our prediction, senior managers had lower scores than the group of lower managers/professionals ($F = 5.17$, $p < .05$). In Study 2, managers had significantly higher scores than nonmanagers on employment satisfaction, on job performance, and on compensation. These results are supportive of hypothesis 2. However, contrary to hypothesis 2, persons in the nonmanagement group had a higher rate of promotion than persons in the management group ($F = 7.7$, $p < .01$).

In summary, for hypothesis 2, the data again provided mild support for our predictions. Six of the eleven comparisons of means across both studies were in the predicted direction. Five statistically significant results were observed; however, only three of these were supportive of our hypothesis while two were contradictory.

Discussion

Although the mixed nature of the findings makes it difficult to draw firm conclusions about the issues under investigation, several observations seem appropriate. First, the research supports the basic proposition that work specialization and organization level are group affiliations around which work experiences differ among employees. Of the six career outcomes studied, significant results for either work specialization or organization level were observed on five (the only exception being organizational identification). We believe the data suggest that work specialization and organization level operate as important dimensions of diversity in at least two ways.

First, different specializations or levels may represent different work cultures. For example, the differences in rates of promotion and in job performance ratings may be attributable to different opportunity structures and different performance expectations across groups, rather than to the deleterious effects of out-group dynamics on which our hypotheses were based. Other results, such as the lower employment satisfaction for nonengineers in Study 1 and for nonmanagers in Study 2, are very consistent with the viewpoint that diversity climate factors such as stereotyping and ethnocentrism combine with a power structure that features underrepresentation of "minority" group members, to produce less favorable career outcomes for members of the latter. This belief is further supported by a supplemental analysis of data from Study 2 (note that these data were not available for Study 1) dealing directly with the diversity climate. Respondents were asked the extent to which stereotyping, miscommunication, and intergroup conflict occurred in the organization for various group identities. The data indicated the following:

1. A majority of respondents agreed that stereotypes existed related to organization level (60%) and work specialization (62%). To better understand the nature of the stereotyping, respondents were asked to provide some written comments. A sample of their responses is given below.

Low level and clerical staff are discriminated against in many of the same ways as racial/gender groups. They are talked down to, and not viewed as promotion material.

I think some stereotyping goes on between the exempt and nonexempt levels in that exempt staff see their positions as overly important. This affects nonexempt staff as they are sometimes seen as "second-class" citizens.

Although a great deal of verbiage is spent claiming_____to be a team-oriented work-place, more emphasis seems to be placed on maintaining a hierarchical structure, rather than acknowledging the contribution of all parties regardless of job-level or function.

I took the receptionist position due to department downsizing. All of a sudden, people I have worked with for years treated me as though I had put my brains in the desk drawer.

One analyst on my team views programmers as unthinking monkeys who should defer all decisions and innovative thinking to the analysts.

People in "less important" work functions are not as highly regarded by upper management.

Our operations group are the "mules," while sales staff are the "stars."

2. A large percentage of respondents agreed that intergroup conflict existed in their department related to organization level (44%) and work specialization (60%).

3. The percentage of people saying that the quality of communication across group boundaries was good was lower for organization level and work specialization than for any other basis of identity (e.g., 67% said communications were good between people of different levels compared with 83% saying communications were good between men and women). These data strongly suggest that work specialization and organization level were perceived to be influenced by similar intergroup dynamics as those that have been found to apply to core group identities like gender and race.

A second point is that affective outcomes may be more influenced by differences of work specialization and organization level than the achievement outcomes of the model proposed by Cox (1993). For example, if we reanalyze the data in Table 3.1 by type of outcome, we find that 8 of the 10 comparisons of means for the affective outcomes (satisfaction, identification, and involvement) were in the predicted direction compared with 6 of 13 for the achievement outcomes. Further, the statistically significant results that were contrary to hypotheses occurred among the achievement outcomes.

A third point of interpretation is that the data suggest that the effects of group identity are organization specific and cannot necessarily be generalized across organizations. For example, while persons in the dominant work specialization did have significantly higher job performance ratings in Study 1, we found the opposite result in Study 2. This result highlights the importance of the work context in determining whether or not group identities will be systematically related to work outcomes, a point emphasized in the model of diversity offered by Cox (1993). Thus future research should address contextual effects such as the extent to which the organization has invested in organization change to break down group-identity-related barriers. Our research has implications for management practice. It suggests the importance of doing organization-specific diagnostic work to determine which dimensions of diversity are of greatest significance in a particular setting.

The finding from Study 2 that nonmanagers had a higher number of promotions per year of service may be due to the fact that persons at higher levels of the organization are more likely to be plateaued. This finding is also consistent with those of previous research, which shows that persons at higher levels are less satisfied with promotional opportunities than those at lower levels (Kline & Boyd, 1991). The finding that persons from the marketing specialization in Study 2 had significantly lower promotion rates than persons in other functions runs counter to the logic that members of the dominant function would be favored for promotion. This result may be due to different vacancy rates across departments. Although we did not collect data on vacancy rates, we did observe during the data collection process that the information systems area (the second largest specialization in terms of head count in the entire firm) had experienced a high rate of growth during recent years.

The fact that job performance ratings were higher for lower level managers/professionals in Study 1 and for nonmarketing people compared with marketing people in Study 2 is difficult to explain. One notion is that expectations are lower for persons at lower levels and in nondominant specializations, making it easier to achieve a high rating. However, this idea certainly would not apply to "minority" groups generally because the control variable analysis revealed that minority gender and race groups had lower ratings than the corresponding dominant groups (with the one exception of gender in Study 2).

In conclusion, we believe that the data offer enough support for our hypotheses to encourage additional research employing the same theoretical premise used here. Our research suggests that, at least to some degree, the group identifications of work specialization and organization level have effects on career outcomes of individuals. To some extent, workers in less dominant work functions and those at lower organizational levels may experience similar "alienation" effects as have been observed for members of gender and race minority groups. These effects at the individual level may, in turn, lead to consequences for group and organizational performance. Thus as organizations continue to make greater use of cross-functional and cross-level teams for performing work, for solving problems, and for making decisions, attention to intergroup dynamics related to work specialization and organization level will be increasingly important for both academics and practitioners.

References

Alderfer, C. P., & Smith, K. K. (1982). Studying intergroup relations embedded in organizations. *Administrative Science Quarterly, 27*, 5-65.

Anantharaman, R. N., & Begum, K. S. (1982). Job involvement among bank employees. *Indian Journal of Applied Psychology, 19*, 11-13.

Ancona, D. G., & Caldwell, D. F. (1992). Demography and design: Predictors of new product team performance. *Organizational Science, 3*, 321-331.

Asante, M. K., & Asante, K. W. (Eds.). (1985). *African culture*. Westport, CT: Greenwood.

Ashforth, B., & Mael, F. (1989). Social identity theory and the organization. *Academy of Management Review, 14*, 20-39.

Banas, B. A. (1988). Employee involvement: A sustained labor/management initiative at the Ford Motor Company. In J. P. Campbell & R. J. Campbell (Eds.), *Productivity in organizations: New perspectives from industrial and organizational psychology* (pp. 388-416). San Francisco: Jossey-Bass.

Bantel, K. A., & Jackson, S. E. (1989). Top management and innovations in banking: Does the composition of the top team make a difference? *Strategic Management Journal, 10*, 107-124.

Bateman, T. S., & Zeithaml, C. (1990). *Management: Function and strategy*. Homewood, IL: Irwin.

Bell, E. L. (1990). The bicultural life experience of career-oriented Black women. *Journal of Organizational Behavior, 11*, 459-477.

Berry, J. W. (1983). Acculturation: A comparative analysis of alternative forms. In J. Samunda & S. L. Woods (Eds.), *Perspectives in immigrant and minority education* (pp. 66-77). Lanham, MD: University Press of America.

Chang, S. K. (1985). American and Chinese managers in U.S. companies in Taiwan: A comparison. *California Management Review, 27*, 144-156.

Chatman, J. (1989). Improving interactional organizational research: A model of person-organization fit. *Academy of Management Review, 14*, 333-349.

Cleveland, J. N., & Landy, F. J. (1983). The effects of person and job stereotypes on two personnel decisions. *Journal of Applied Psychology, 68*, 609-619.

Cox, T. H. (1990). Problems with research by organizational scholars on issues of race and ethnicity. *Journal of Applied Behavioral Science, 26*, 5-24.

Cox, T., H., Jr. (1993). *Cultural diversity in organizations*. San Francisco: Berrett-Koehler.

Cox, T. H., & Harquail, C. V. (1991). Career paths and career success in the early career stages of male and female MBAs. *Journal of Vocational Behavior, 39*, 54-75.

Cox, T. H., & Nkomo, S. M. (1986). Differential appraisal criteria based on race of the ratee. *Group and Organizational Studies, 11*, 101-119.

Cox, T. H., & Nkomo, S. M. (1990). Invisible men and women: A status report on race as a variable in organizational behavior and research. *Journal of Organizational Behavior, 11*, 419-431.

Cox, T. H., & Nkomo, S. M. (1991). A race and gender group analysis of the early career experience of MBAs. *Work and Occupations, 18*, 431-446.

Cox, T. H., & Nkomo, S. M. (1992). Candidate age as a factor in promotability ratings. *Public Personnel Management, 21*, 197-210.

Dearborn, D. C., & Simon, H. A. (1958). Selective perceptions: A note on the departmental identification of executives. *Sociometry, 21*, 140-144.

Dumaine, B. (1990, May 7). Who needs a boss? *Fortune*, pp. 52-60.

Farh, J., Dobbins, G. H., & Cheng, B. (1991). Cultural relativity in action: A comparison of self-ratings made by Chinese and U.S. workers. *Personnel Psychology, 44,* 129-147.

Fernandez, J. P. (1991). *Managing a diverse workforce.* Lexington, MA: Lexington.

Gannon, M. J., & Demler, J. W. (1971). Organizational level and job attitudes. *Psychological Reports, 29,* 399-402.

Greenhaus, J. H., Parasuraman, S., & Wormley, W. (1990). Effects of race on organizational experiences, job performance evaluations and career outcomes. *Academy of Management Journal, 33,* 64-86.

Hall, E. T. (1976). *Beyond culture.* New York: Doubleday.

Hambrick, D. C., & Mason, P. A. (1984). Upper echelons: The organization as a reflection of its top managers. *Academy of Management Review, 9,* 193-206.

Heneman, H. G., III, & Schwab, D. P. (1985). Pay satisfaction: Its multidimensional nature and measurement. *International Journal of Psychology, 20,* 129-141.

Hofstede, G. (1980, Summer). Motivation, leadership and organization: Do American theories apply abroad? *Organizational Dynamics, 9,* 43-62.

Hofstede, G. (1984). The cultural relativity of the quality of life concept. *Academy of Management Review, 9,* 389-398.

Hood, J. N., & Koberg, C. S. (1991). Accounting firm cultures and creativity among accountants. *Accounting Horizons, 5,* 12-19.

Jackson, S. E. (1991). Team composition in organizational settings: Issues in managing an increasingly diverse workforce. In S. Worchel, W. Wood, & J. A. Simpson (Eds.), *Group process and productivity* (pp. 138-173). Newbury Park, CA: Sage.

Jackson, S. E., Stone, V. K., & Alvarez, E. B. (1993). Socialization amidst diversity: Impact of demographics on work team oldtimers and newcomers. In L. L. Cummings & B. M. Staw (Eds.), *Research in organizational behavior* (Vol. 15, pp. 45-109). Greenwich, CT: JAI Press.

Jones, E. (1986). Black managers: The dream deferred. *Harvard Business Review, 64,* 84-93.

Kanter, R. M. (1977). *Men and women of the corporation.* New York: Basic Books.

Kanter, R. M. (1988). When a thousand flowers bloom: Structural, collective, and social conditions for innovation in organization. In B. M. Staw & L. L. Cummings (Eds.), *Research in organizational behavior* (Vol. 10, pp. 160-211). Greenwich, CT: JAI Press.

Khoo, G. P. S. (1988). *Asian Americans with power and authority in the corporate world: An exploratory investigation.* Unpublished master's thesis, University of California, Santa Cruz.

Kline, T. J. B., & Boyd, J. E. (1991). Organizational structure, context, and climate: Their relationships to job satisfaction at three managerial levels. *Journal of General Psychology, 118,* 305-316.

Kraiger, K., & Ford, J. (1985). A meta-analysis of ratee race effects in performance ratings. *Journal of Applied Psychology, 70,* 56-65.

Leigh, J. H., & Futrell, C. M. (1985). From the trenches to the command post: Perceptual and attitudinal differences among levels in the marketing management hierarchy. *Journal of Business Research, 12,* 511-536.

Lodahl, T. M., & Kejner, M. (1965). The definition and measurement of job involvement. *Journal of Applied Psychology, 49,* 24-33.

Mischel, W. (1977). The interaction of person and situation. In D. Magnussen & N. S. Endler (Eds.), *Personality at the crossroads* (pp. 333-352). Hillsdale, NJ: Lawrence Erlbaum.

Murray, A. I. (1989). Top management group heterogeneity and firm performance. *Strategic Management Journal, 10,* 125-141.

Nkomo, S. M. (1992). The emperor has no clothes: Rewriting race in organizations. *Academy of Management Review, 17,* 487-513.

Nkomo, S. M., & Cox, T. H. (1989). Gender differences in the upward mobility of Black managers: Double whammy or double advantage? *Sex Roles, 21*, 825-839.

Ouchi, W. G., & Price, R. L. (1978). Hierarchies, clans and theory Z: A new perspective on organizational development. *Organizational Dynamics, 7*, 25-44.

Pettigrew, T. F., & Martin, J. (1987). Shaping the organizational context for Black American inclusion. *Journal of Social Forces, 43*, 41-78.

Reynolds, P. D. (1986). Organizational culture as related to industry, position and performance: A preliminary report. *Journal of Management Studies, 23*, 333-345.

Rice, A. K. (1969). *Learning in groups*. London: Tavistock.

Rivera-Ramos, A. N. (1992). The psychological experience of Puerto Rican women at work. In S. B. Knouse, P. Rosenfeld, & A. L. Culbertson (Eds.), *Hispanics in the workplace* (pp. 194-210). Newbury Park, CA: Sage.

Rosen, B., & Jerdee, T. H. (1976). The nature of job related age stereotypes. *Journal of Applied Psychology, 61*, 180-183.

Shore, L. M., & Thornton, G. C., III. (1986). Effects of gender on self- and supervisory ratings. *Academy of Management Journal, 29*, 115-129.

Singh, B. K. (1987). A comparative study of job involvement of supervisors and workers in relation to their occupational level. *Perspectives in Psychological Research, 10*, 3-35.

Slocum, J. W., & Topichak, P. M. (1972). Do cultural differences affect job satisfaction? *Journal of Applied Psychology, 56*, 177-178.

Stone, E. F., Stone, D. L., & Dipboye, R. L. (1992). Stigmas in organizations: Race, handicaps, and physical unattractiveness. In K. Kelley (Ed.), *Issues, theory and research in industrial/organizational psychology* (pp. 385-457). Amsterdam: Elsevier Science.

Tajfel, H. (Ed.). (1978). *Differentiation between social groups: Studies in the social psychology of intergroup relations*. San Diego, CA: Academic Press.

Triandis, H. C. (1976). The future of pluralism revisited. *Journal of Social Issues, 32*, 179-208.

Triandis, H. C., Kurowski, L. L., & Gelfand, M. J. (1994). Workplace diversity. In H. Triandis, M. Dunnette, & L. Hough (Eds.), *Handbook of industrial psychology* (pp. 769-827). Palo Alto, CA: Consulting Psychologists Press.

Trice, H. M., & Beyer, J. M. (1993). *The cultures of work organizations*. Englewood Cliffs, NJ: Prentice-Hall.

Tung, R. L. (1988). Toward a conceptual paradigm of international business negotiations. *Advances in International Comparative Management, 3*, 203-219.

Waldman, D. A., & Avolio, B. J. (1986). A meta-analysis of age differences in job performance. *Journal of Applied Psychology, 71*, 33-38.

Walton, R. E., & Hackman, J. R. (1986). Groups under contrasting management strategies. In P. S. Goodman (Ed.), *Designing effective work groups* (pp. 168-201). San Francisco: Jossey-Bass.

Wanous, J. P., & Youtz, M. A. (1986). Solution diversity and the quality of group decisions. *Academy of Management Journal, 29*, 149-158.

Weick, K. E. (1977). Repunctuating the problem. In P. S. Goodman & J. M. Pennings (Eds.), *New perspectives on organizational effectiveness*. San Francisco: Jossey-Bass.

Wong-Reider, D., & Quintana, D. (1987). Comparative acculturation of Southeast Asian and Hispanic immigrants and sojourners. *Journal of Cross-Cultural Psychology, 18*, 345-362.

Zurcher, L. A., Zurcher, S. L., & Meadow, A. (1965). Value orientation, role conflict, and alienation from work: A cross-cultural study. *American Sociological Review, 30*, 539-548.

PART II

DIVERSITY EFFECTS ON GROUPS AND TEAMS

4

Diversity, Power, and Mentorship in Organizations
A Cultural, Structural, and Behavioral Perspective

BELLE ROSE RAGINS

Theory on diversity in organizations can best be described as being in an early stage of theory construction. There have been few theoretical linkages between diversity and other established fields. There has been some discussion of the relationship between diversity and power (see, e.g., Cox, 1993; Nkomo, 1992), and mentorship has been proposed as a method for attaining diversity (Cox, 1993; Davis & Rodela, 1992; Redmond, 1990; D. Thomas, 1990). Yet, power and mentoring may be viewed as both determinants and outcomes of effective management of diversity in organizations.

The purpose of this chapter therefore is to examine the relationships among diversity, power, and mentorship in organizations. A theoretical framework of organizational change is developed that incorporates cultural, structural, and behavioral changes concerning diversity. This framework is briefly described and then used to establish and develop theoretical linkages among the diversity, power, and mentorship literatures.[1]

A Multilevel
Framework for Analysis

Diversity theorists concur that effective management of diversity requires organizational change (Cox, 1993; Thomas, 1991). This section presents an analytic framework for organizational change involving three levels of analysis: cultural, structural, and behavioral. These levels affect not only organizational change regarding diversity but also the relationship between diversity and the development of power and mentorship in organizations.

Cultural Level of Change

This level of analysis involves change that alters the organization's culture, which is defined as the basic assumptions, values, beliefs, and ideologies that define an organization's view of itself and its environment (Pettigrew, 1979; Schein, 1985). Culture is a vision, often unarticulated but shared by members of an organization. It is a socially constructed reality, a historically determined phenomenon that is manifested in values, rituals, heroes, symbols, and practices (Trompenaars, 1993).

Because values toward diversity are reflected in organizational culture, cultural change is an integral part of an organization's transformation to a pluralistic model that promotes diversity (Cox & Finley-Nickelson, 1991). According to Cox (1993), organizations with pluralistic cultures eschew assimilation and, instead, support the interdependence and preservation of subcultures within the organization. Pluralistic cultures are characterized by a tolerance for ambiguity, an acceptance of a wide range of work styles and behaviors, and the encouragement of diversity in thought, practice, and action.

Although change in organizational culture is critical for effective management of diversity, cultural changes require intensive and long-term efforts aimed at understanding the implicit core assumptions regarding diversity (Trompenaars, 1993). Effective cultural changes regarding diversity often result in changes in vision, traditions, symbols, management practices, and reward structures that value and promote diversity (Thomas, 1991).

Structural Level of Change

The structural level of analysis involves changes in the grouping of positions and departments within the organization. Structural changes in organizations involve changes in positions' formal reporting relationships, hierarchical level, span of control, task functions, and patterns of interaction with other positions (Burns & Stalker, 1961).

Structural changes are necessary for the promotion of diversity in organizations. Women and racioethnic minorities face glass ceilings and walls that prevent them from gaining access to positions of power in organizations (Morrison & Von Glinow, 1990; Morrison, White, & Van Velsor, 1987; Rowe, 1990). These groups are often tracked into powerless departments and positions with limited career paths (Ragins & Sundstrom, 1989). Given these structural barriers, Cox (1991, 1993) observes that structural integration is a necessary component for effective management of diversity. *Structural integration* within a diversity perspective refers to the achievement of proportional heterogeneity in employment positions across rank, department, and specialization. In addition to access to power, structural integration may reduce stereotypes and prejudice by increasing contact among heterogeneous groups (Pettigrew & Martin, 1987).

Behavioral Level of Change

This micro level of analysis refers to changes in behaviors, attitudes, and perceptions among individuals and work groups. Stereotypes, attitudes, and attributions may combine to influence behavior toward women and minorities by individuals and work groups. Stereotypes influence role expectations in work settings, and women and minorities may be rewarded for exhibiting behavior that is congruent with role expectations but ineffective for promotion or career advancement (see, e.g., Powell, 1988; Ragins & Sundstrom, 1989).

Valuing diversity in organizations obviously requires changes in overtly racist, sexist, and homophobic behaviors among members of the organization. However, there are other more insidious and subtle behaviors that may be even more destructive than overt acts (see, e.g., Pettigrew & Martin, 1987). These subtle behaviors may or may not be intentional but have the effect of excluding and marginalizing women and minority groups and ultimately undermining their self-confidence, performance, and development of power. These behaviors, which are sometimes called "micro-inequities" (Rowe, 1990), include exclusion from informal peer support, networking, and mentoring; restricted information and a lack of feedback from supervisors and coworkers; inadequate or inaccurate performance appraisals by supervisors or work groups; and inequitable delegation of tasks.

Behaviors and attitudes regarding diversity are reciprocally influenced by the culture of the organization (Thomas, 1991) and the climate of the work group (Kossek & Zonia, 1993). *Climate* refers to the influence of the work group and organizational environment on employee behaviors and attitudes (Schneider & Reichers, 1983). Kossek and Zonia (1993) define *diversity climate* as the individuals' perceptions and attitudes regarding the importance of diversity in the organization and the perceived qualifications of women and racioethnic minorities. Behaviors and attitudes toward diversity can create a chilly or receptive climate for women and minorities. Climate, in turn, can influence the attitudes and behaviors of organizational members. The nature of these reciprocal relationships is explored in the following section.

Diversity and Change Propositions

A central proposition of this review is that effective management of diversity requires significant and inclusive change in cultural, structural, and behavioral domains, and that change in one domain is insufficient for producing effective organizational change with respect to diversity. For example, an organization may provide training aimed at altering the behaviors and attitudes of employees, but may maintain structures that segregate women and minorities into powerless departments or positions. Another example is the case where an organization achieves structural integration and a culture that values diversity, but still has individual employees operating on the basis of stereotypes and pernicious attributions.

A second proposition is that the scope of diversity efforts must be inclusive toward all groups for diversity efforts to be effective and maintained over time. An example of this is the case where the organization "complies with diversity initiatives" by instituting structural integration for racioethnic groups but maintains a culture that values and promotes homogeneity with respect to religion, sexual orientation, physical abilities, and political thought. The valuing and acceptance of diversity must be directed toward all groups, rather than a limited subset, for effective cultural change to occur.

A third proposition is that the cultural, structural, and behavioral levels are interdependent with respect to their influence, in that change in one domain synergistically affects other levels. By definition, attitudinal and behavioral changes in the individual and work group influence the culture of the organization, and vice versa. Similarly, structural changes that place women and minorities in positions of leadership have a clear impact on the culture of the organization as well as on the attitudes and behaviors of the individual and work group. A theoretical approach that illustrates the interdependence among the levels is Kanter's (1977) structuralist perspective, which proposes that gender differences in access to structural forms of power cause behavioral differences between the sexes.

In sum, a multilevel framework is developed that incorporates cultural, structural, and behavioral factors that influence organizational change regarding diversity. The relationships among diversity, power, and mentoring in organizations are influenced by each of these factors and are discussed in subsequent sections.

Diversity and Power

Definition of Power

Although there are a multitude of definitions of power, most fall into one of four categories (Ragins & Sundstrom, 1989). The first category views power as an individual's ability, or perceived ability, to influence others or change others' behaviors (i.e., Dahl, 1957; Weber, 1947). The second category holds that power is part of the dynamic and reciprocal aspect of interpersonal relationships (i.e., Cartwright, 1959; Dansereau, Graen, & Haga, 1975). The third category of power takes the view that power is a property of the structure of the organization and involves control over persons, information, and resources (i.e., Hinnings, Hickson, Pennings, & Schneck, 1974; Mechanic, 1962; Pfeffer, 1981). Finally, a sociopolitical perspective views power as the cause and outcome of racism, sexism, heterosexism, classism, and other forms of group oppression in society (Clark, 1966; Jones, 1972). This perspective contends that groups with control over resources maintain and develop their power by isolating, dominating, and controlling other groups and their access to power for the purpose of economic gain (Dovidio & Gaertner, 1986; Griscom, 1992; Jones, 1972). While the societal perspective takes a more macro view of power, unequal power relationships in society influence organizational, interpersonal, and individual levels of influence, and ultimately the ability of the individual to develop resources for power (Ragins & Sundstrom, 1989).

In the attempt to integrate the above perspectives, *power* is defined here as the influence of one person over others, stemming from an individual characteristic, an interpersonal relationship, a position in an organization, or membership in a societal group. The cultural, structural, and behavioral influences on the development of power among diverse groups in organizations are discussed in the following sections.

Cultural Influences
on Diversity and Power

The organization's culture has both a direct and an indirect impact on the allocation of power among diverse groups. The values and ideologies inherent in the organization's culture directly determine which behaviors and outcomes will be rewarded (Ferdman, 1992; Schein, 1985). The reward system, in turn, determines which groups are tracked into positions of power and leadership (Ragins & Sundstrom, 1989). Groups with power are invested in maintaining their influence and resources, and may do so by supporting policies, practices, and prescriptions that exclude other groups from power.

Two forces affect cultural prescriptions regarding power and intergroup relations in organizations. First, organizational culture is shaped by the larger societal context in which the organization is embedded (Alderfer & Smith, 1982). Societal values, assumptions, and beliefs regarding power relationships among groups are internalized and reinforced by the organization. Societal culture sanctifies unequal power relationships among groups in organizations. This is most likely to occur in societies where status is salient and accorded on the basis of physical characteristics (Trompenaars, 1993) and in collectivist cultures in which strong distinctions are made between in-groups and out-groups (Triandis, Bontempo, Villareal, Asai, & Lucca, 1988).

Second, organizational culture is shaped and supported by the power-holders of the organization (Schein, 1985). These individuals influence the values, assumptions, and ideologies of the organization's culture. Power-holders use an ethnocentric perspective to define and develop criteria for successful performance. Because most power-holders in America are European American males, their experience is held to be the standard by which performance is evaluated and rewarded. Promotions and resources for power are therefore allocated to individuals who are viewed as being "appropriate" for leadership roles. One result of this is that individuals who share common physical characteristics or values with the power-holders are more likely to gain access to powerful positions than those who are different, thus perpetuating a cycle of exclusionary power relationships among groups in organizations.

One consequence of these processes is that organizations with Euro-Western cultures may define power as a White, able-bodied, heterosexual phenomenon. The very image of power, as reflected in the corporate culture's heroes, often reflects these characteristics and perpetuates the notion of power as a White male attribute. Access to power may therefore be limited to those who are viewed as physically and culturally appropriate for the role.

The proposition that power is defined by those who have it is supported by a postmodernist perspective. This perspective holds that power does not reside in the individual but is a socially constructed phenomenon that is defined by relationships and interpersonal perceptions (Bohan, 1993; Hare-Mustin & Marecek, 1990). Using a constructivist perspective, Miller and Cummins (1992) argue that power is a "gendered concept" and that definitions of power are based on a male perspective. In support of this idea, in their study of 125 women, they found that women were more likely to view power in terms of personal authority or the capacity to change rather than as control over others or resources. Griscom (1992), however, argues that the dichotomy of "power-over" as a masculine perspective and "power-for" as a feminine perspective alienates the experience of women of color, who may experience White women as using "power-over" behaviors. Although there is a lack of agreement on the nature of power, this line of thought suggests that the very concept of power, as it relates to organizational culture, is influenced and defined by those who have power in organizations.

In sum, power relationships among groups in organizations are influenced by the organization's culture, which in turn is shaped by societal factors and the power-holders of the organization. Individuals with power define the organization's culture, determine which groups get power, and may even define the very nature of power in the organization. The process becomes a self-perpetuating cycle that reinforces inequitable and exclusionary power relationships among groups in organizations. As discussed in the next section, these inequitable power relationships become entrenched in the structure of the organization.

Structural Influences
on Diversity and Power

Structural differences in access to power contribute to unequal power relationships. There are three structural indicators of unequal power relationships among diverse groups in organizations: rank, department or career track, and positional power. These indicators reflect both causes and consequences of power differentials among groups in organizations and result in low-power groups being tracked into support substructures of organizations that operate to support and develop the resources of high-power groups.

Rank. Organizational rank is directly related to positional power and control over resources in organizations (Ragins & Sundstrom, 1989) and is the most obvious structural indicator of power in organizations. Women and minorities hold lower ranks and enter organizations at lower levels than their White male counterparts (Brown & Ford, 1977; DeFreitas, 1991; Fierman, 1990; Morrison & Von Glinow, 1990). Because entry level may have a disproportionate influence on mobility and advancement (Beehr & Juntunen, 1990), differences in entry rank may contribute to gender and racioethnic differences in the development of power in organizations (Ragins & Sundstrom, 1989).

One contributing factor to group differences in organizational rank is differences in performance appraisals and promotion rates. Overall, women and minorities receive lower performance appraisals than their White male counterparts, and these effects are amplified when the appraiser is of a different race or gender (see, e.g., reviews by Dipboye, 1987; Kraiger & Ford, 1985; Landy & Farr, 1980). Compared with White managers, Black managers report more restricted opportunities for advancement (Cox & Nkomo, 1991), may be subject to different standards of performance (Cox & Nkomo, 1986), and may receive less favorable assessments of promotability from their supervisors (Greenhaus, Parasuraman, & Wormley, 1990). Similar outcomes have been found with Latino (Bendick, Jackson, Reinoso, & Hodges, 1991; Rodriguez, 1987) and gay and lesbian employees (Lee & Brown, 1993).

However, even if performance appraisals and promotion rates were held constant, there is evidence that women and minorities would not obtain the rank or power associated with promotions. Specifically, female managers have been found to receive promotion rates equivalent to their male counterparts, but do not receive the rank (Stewart & Gudykunst, 1982) or salary (Stroh, Brett, & Reilly, 1992) associated with their promotions. Cox and Nkomo (1991) found that while Blacks were at comparable hierarchical levels to Whites, they reported less involvement with their jobs. Cox and Nkomo conclude that one reason for this is that Blacks may have less authority and responsibility associated with their positions than Whites. Although there has been much discussion and legislation aimed at eliminating discrimination, race and gender wage inequality has increased over the past 10 years (Haberfeld & Shenhav, 1990), suggesting increasing disparities in power among groups.

Career Tracks and Departments. In addition to differences in organizational rank, women and minorities tend to be segregated in staff positions in departments with little power and limited career paths (Ragins & Sundstrom, 1989). The power of a department influences the individual's ability to advance in organizations (Pfeffer, 1981). Department power has a wide scope and may therefore be more important than positional power or rank in the development of an individual's power (Pfeffer, 1981). In short, a low-ranking position in a powerful department may be more influential than a high-ranking position in a powerless department.

Women and minorities tend to be tracked into staff support departments (Jones, 1986; Ragins & Sundstrom, 1989; Rodriguez, 1987), which generally have less power than production or line departments (Davis, 1951). Tracking occurs in recruitment, selection, and training systems, and results in women and minorities being assigned to positions with low power, short career ladders, and restricted opportunities for promotion. As part of the process of differential tracking, women and minorities may be denied access to managerial and technical training reserved for grooming White male counterparts for powerful positions.

One consequence of differential tracking is early career plateaus and career dissatisfaction. Black managers are more likely to plateau in their careers and report more dissatisfaction with their careers and advancement rates than their White counterparts (Cox & Nkomo, 1991; Greenhaus et al., 1990; Morrison, 1992). Premature career plateaus are a primary indicator of the glass ceiling, and those who have broken the ceiling report a reliance on line rather than staff positions in internal career paths (U.S. Department of Labor, 1990).

Positional Power. Positional power involves the discretionary authority involved with planning and implementation of tasks associated with the position, the relevance and importance of the tasks, and the visible control over resources involved with the implementation of job functions (Kanter, 1977). Gender differences in authority and positional power have been well documented (see, e.g., Ragins & Sundstrom, 1989); women are less likely than men to have the power and authority associated with their positions (Wolf & Fligstein, 1979). Similar differences in positional power have been found with other socioethnic groups. Greenhaus et al. (1990), for example, found that Black managers perceived themselves as having less job discretion than White managers. They concluded that the exclusion of Blacks from power structures in organizations may have a detrimental effect on their job performance. Similarly, in a study of hospital employees, Rodriguez (1987) found that Latino and Black employees were at lower ranks and reported less positional power, as measured by self-reported skill level, than White counterparts. Finally, race differences in job satisfaction may reflect differences in positional power. Moch (1980), for example, found that Blacks reported less job satisfaction than Whites, even when controlling for differences in rank, work group composition, and social isolation.

Systemic group differences in positional power have significant implications for diversity and power in organizations. Positional power influences the development of future power in organizations (Lachman, 1989), and differential access to resources and positional power may contribute to group differences in organizational rank and differential career tracking (Ragins & Sundstrom, 1989). While structural integration has received considerable attention with respect to diversity (see, e.g., Cox, 1993), there has been little discussion of group differences in positional power. Although structural integration is an important method for equalizing power across groups, systemic differences in positional power may negate the benefits of structural integration; women and minorities may receive high-ranking positions in powerful departments, but may still lack the authority associated with the positions. The next section provides a perspective for understanding why some of these processes occur.

A Deconstructivist Perspective. A deconstructivist perspective provides insights into the relationships among diversity, power, and organizational structure. This perspective challenges the apparent neutrality of organizational structure and suggests that group differences in power are not just due to differences in rank, department, positional power, or career paths but are due to biases inherent in the structure and processes of the organization. Specifically, Acker (1990) theorizes that assumptions about gender underlie organizational structure and processes. Acker and Van Houten (1974) observe that gender is used to signify power and hierarchical relationships, and that masculine principles are used to develop authority structures, the division of labor, and the development of hierarchical relationships. These theorists go on to connect organizational power with men's sexuality, and contend that male sexual imagery pervades organizational language, metaphors, and even work activities. While these theoretical perspectives have yet to be empirically tested, they do provide insight into the relationship between diversity and power in organizations.

Using a diversity perspective to deconstruct the concept of organizational structure results in a very different view of structure and intergroup power relationships. This perspective suggests that pervasive structural attributes, such as formal reporting relationships, spans of control, and reliance on bureaucratic procedures, all reflect the values and characteristics of the dominant power group of White, able-bodied, heterosexual males. Women and minorities may not only be unfamiliar with such organizational protocol, but may also be viewed, and feel like, "foreigners" in the dominant culture (Kanter, 1977). Perhaps this is one reason they are often advised to learn and play "the White man's game" to advance in organizations (Jones, 1986). However, this advice is inadequate at best, and harmful at worst. This strategy places the burden on the individual and does not recognize the pervasiveness of the biases inherent in organizational structures, processes, and procedures. Moreover, by promoting assimilation (Thomas, 1991), this strategy is detrimental to diversity efforts and may result in increased performance pressures, stress, and a loss of identity (Bell, Denton, & Nkomo, 1993; Cox, 1993; Cox & Finley-Nickelson, 1991). Finally, this strategy assumes that if women and minorities alter their behaviors to conform with White male norms, these behaviors will be perceived accurately and received favorably. As discussed in the following section, existing empirical evidence suggests that there is a sizable gap between minority members' behaviors and the perceptions and reactions to their behaviors in organizations.

In sum, structural differences in rank, department, career path, and positional power create and reinforce unequal power relationships among diverse groups in organizations. These differences are both created and reinforced by organizational structures that reflect power-holders' values and attributes. The lack of structural integration and positional power reinforces the cultural effects discussed previously and the behavioral effects discussed in the next section.

Behavioral Influences
on Diversity and Power

Behaviors, attitudes, and perceptions may all contribute to unequal power relationships among diverse groups in organizations. This section will discuss and review research on group differences in power behaviors, perceptions of power, and reactions to power.

Power Behaviors. One explanation for group differences in organizational power is that groups differ in influence strategies and behaviors. However, this explanation has received relatively little support with respect to gender, and limited support with respect to race and culture.

Research on gender differences in power strategies suggests that observed differences may be due more to differences in rank than gender (see, e.g., review by Ragins & Sundstrom, 1989). Kipnis, Schmidt, and Wilkinson (1980), for example, found no differences between men and women in choice of influence strategies. Influence strategies were, however, related to the relative power of the respondents and their targets of influence; use of more direct forms of influence increased with respondent's rank and power. Other laboratory studies controlled for differences in power and found no gender differences in power-related behaviors (Molm, 1985; Sagrestano, 1992).

Few studies have directly examined the effects of race and culture on influence strategies. In a laboratory study of 160 male and female European and Latino students, Ayers-Nachamkin, Cann, Reed, and Horne (1982) found both gender and race differences: Men and European Americans attempted to influence their subordinates to a greater degree than women and Latinos. Significant differences were also found between Latinas and European American women. Compared with European American women, Latinas displayed influence strategies more similar to men's. In another laboratory study of 137 students in the United States and Mexico, Belk et al. (1988) found gender and race differences in power strategies used in intimate relationships. Counter to their predictions, women were found to use more direct power strategies than men. As predicted, Latinos used more interactive power strategies than European Americans, perhaps reflecting the collectivist culture of Mexico (Triandis et al., 1988). In a study of 129 Chinese law students in Singapore, Nedd (1989) found no differences between men and women in compliance gaining strategies. However, religious beliefs were significantly related to compliance styles for men but not for women, suggesting a potentially complex interaction among culture, religion, and gender.

It is important to recognize that if gender and racioethnic differences in power-related behaviors are found, they may reflect differences in organizational rank, positional power, and other situational factors. While it is necessary to conceptually disentangle these effects, structural segregation may still have a direct impact on power-related behaviors of women and minorities. If low-ranking groups use more indirect and ingratiating influence strategies than high-ranking groups (Kipnis et al., 1980), and women and minorities are found at lower ranks, differences in power-related behaviors should occur. As women and minorities advance in rank, their influence strategies should change to more directive and unilateral influence strategies that are associated with higher ranking positions. However, as discussed in the next section, directive influence strategies may not be accepted or accurately perceived by others in the organization. One consequence of this is that women and minorities may face a "Catch-22" situation whereby they are constrained to use influence strategies that are acceptable to their coworkers but are not appropriate for their position or for developing power and mobility in their organization. The influence of perceptions, attributions, and reactions to power are discussed in the following sections.

Power Perceptions and Attributions. Even if women and minorities display the same power behaviors as their White male counterparts, these behaviors may be perceived differently. Stereotypes may distort and limit perceptions of power and attributions regarding sources of influence (Pettigrew & Martin, 1987; Ragins & Sundstrom, 1989). Perceptual distortions of women and minority members' power may in turn influence their subordinates' compliance with requests, their subordinates' job performance, appraisals of their managerial performance, and ultimately their advancement and structural integration in the organization.

Although there has been a lack of research on racioethnic differences in perceived power, gender differences have been found in a fair number of laboratory studies. Wiley and Eskilson (1982) found that, when holding position and performance constant, male actors were viewed as being more powerful than female actors. The findings of two other laboratory studies suggest that, in the absence of other information, sex role stereotypes may influence perceptions of power. In a simulation study of 161 managers, Gruber and White (1986) found that respondents of both sexes described men as using more stereotypically masculine influence strategies and women as using more feminine influence strategies. Sex role expectations also influenced self-reports of strategies used by the respondents. In a laboratory study of 281 undergraduate students, Johnson (1976) found that coercive, legitimate, expert, and informational power was expected more of men than women, whereas influence attempts based on personal reward and sexuality were expected more of women than men. These findings, however, were not replicated in a field study of subordinates of 110 male and female managers matched on rank, department, and positional power (Ragins & Sundstrom, 1990). Subordinates in this field study perceived female managers as having equivalent reward, coercive, legitimate, and referent power as male managers, and actually perceived the female managers as having more expert power than their male counterparts. This field study suggests that the influence of sex role stereotypes on perceptions of power may be reduced in settings that provide subordinates with direct experience of managerial power over a period of time. One implication of this is that while stereotypes may guide perceptions of power at the beginning of a relationship, the impact of stereotypes may attenuate over the course of the manager-subordinate relationship.

Gender and racioethnic differences may also be found in power attributions. *Power attributions* refer to the reasons given for complying with a manager's requests (Kaplowitz, 1978; Ragins, Sundstrom, & Thomas, 1993). These attributions may influence perceptions of power and the efficacy of power-related behaviors displayed by women and minorities. Ragins et al. (1993) assessed subordinates' power attributions in a field study of matched male and female managers and their subordinates. Although male and female managers gave equivalent reasons for why their subordinates complied with their requests, these perceptions were not shared by subordinates, who gave more reasons for complying with the requests of male managers than female managers.

Although there has been a lack of research on racioethnic differences in power attributions and perceptions of power, race and ethnicity have been found to influence attributional processes (see, e.g., reviews by Ferdman, 1992; Pettigrew, 1979; Pettigrew & Martin, 1987). In a recent study of 322 Black and 426 White managers, for example, Greenhaus and Parasuraman (1993) found that among highly successful managers, the performance of Black managers was less likely to be attributed to ability and effort and was more likely to be attributed to help from others. The researchers found many of the attributional differences attenuated as the respondents gained work experience with the managers, providing support for the view that perceptions and attributions of power may be influenced by the length of the manager-subordinate relationship.

Gender and racioethnic differences in networks may also contribute to differences in perceived power. Network centrality is an important source of power in organizations, and group differences in access to networks may contribute to differences in perceived power (Ibarra, 1993). Ibarra and Andrews (1993), for example, found that network factors shape job-related perceptions, over and above the effects of individual attributes and formal positions. Brass and Burkhardt (1993) found that both the structural position of the individual, as measured through network centrality and rank, and their power behaviors related independently and significantly to perceptions of the individual's power. This research suggests that the perception of minority managers' power may be limited not only by stereotypes and attributions but also by differential access to influential networks in organizations.

Reactions to Power. Even if women and minorities use the same power behaviors as their White male counterparts, and these behaviors are perceived accurately by their subordinates, there is still no guarantee that equivalent behaviors will lead to equivalent outcomes. Women and minorities may get penalized for using "majority" forms of power. For example, Wiley and Eskilson (1982) found that men received more positive evaluations for using expert power, whereas women received higher evaluations when using reward power, and concluded that the adoption of similar power strategies by men and women does not assure equivalent evaluations of their performance.

Negative reactions may be amplified when women and minorities use influence strategies that are inconsistent with group stereotypes. A meta-analysis of studies on gender and leader evaluation concluded that women in leadership positions were devalued relative to their male counterparts when leadership was carried out in stereotypically masculine styles (i.e., autocratic or directive), and that the devaluation was greater when the leaders occupied male-dominated roles and when the evaluators were men (Eagly, Makhijani, & Klonsky, 1992). A related study on gender and group influence found that women in male-dominated groups had less influence on group decisions and were liked less when they used male-typed, internal rationales, such as their expertise, in their attempts to influence group decisions, rather than female-typed, external rationales based on the expertise of others (Taps & Martin, 1990).

Negative reactions to power behaviors are likely to be amplified when individuals are tokens. According to Kanter (1977), token members of minority groups are faced with increased visibility and performance pressures as well as the potential for backlash and retaliation if their performance threatens the majority members. Research on reactions to tokens indicates that individuals are likely to devalue token performance and credibility (Ilgen & Youtz, 1986; Pettigrew & Martin, 1987), particularly when the minority members are viewed as obtaining their position because of affirmative action policies. Heilman, Block, and Lucas (1992), for example, found that individuals depicted as affirmative action hirees were viewed as incompetent and perceived as more passive and less potent than individuals who were not associated with affirmative action policies. This line of research suggests that tokens may face an attenuation of power, in terms of both the perception of power and the reaction to the use of power. Negative reactions to the use of power among tokens may range from simply ignoring the token manager's request to undermining or even sabotaging the manager's attempts to influence. The combined effect of these reactions may serve to reduce the power of women and minorities in organizations.

As an extension of Faludi's (1991) concept, negative reactions to the development of power by women and minorities can be characterized as a form of backlash. This may be called *diversity backlash* when applied to organizations, which occurs when minority members are perceived as attempting to develop power by individual or collective means. Diversity backlash can be characterized as a preemptive strike against the development of power by groups lacking power in organizations. Typically, it occurs before power has actually been obtained by minority groups; it is a reaction to the threat of loss of power by the majority group. Diversity backlash may take a variety of overt and covert forms, and may include attempts to alienate and ostracize groups by stereotyping and accentuating differences, belittling attributes, and excluding individuals from formal and informal networks. Diversity backlash is evident in media reports depicting White males as victims of diversity initiatives, when encountering reverse discrimination as a result of affirmative action policies, and extensive self-censorship in the attempt to avoid sexual harassment suits or charges of being "politically incorrect" (e.g., Galen & Palmer, 1994; Horwitz, 1993). Diversity backlash legitimates unequal power relationships among groups in organizations, supports the cultural status quo in power relations, and provides the majority group with a sense of righteousness regarding their disproportional power in the organization.

In sum, behavioral influences on the development of power include group differences in power behaviors, perceptions, attributions, and reactions to the use of power by women and minorities. Even when holding structural indices such as rank, department, and positional power constant, women and minorities may not be perceived or expected to have power by their subordinates, managers, or coworkers. Moreover, they may encounter negative reactions or diversity backlash if they threaten majority members or are perceived as gaining too much power.

Summary of Power and Diversity. Cultural, structural, and behavioral factors synergistically combine to influence the development of power among women and minorities in organizations. The organization's culture, which is shaped by societal culture and the organization's power-holders, determines the norms and values that define power relationships among groups in organizations. The organization's structure reflects and reinforces the culture by segregating women and minorities into low-power career tracks, departments, and positions. Behavioral factors influence the perceptions and reactions to power, and serve to keep women and minorities "in their place." These factors combine to perpetuate and support exclusionary power relationships and the cultural status quo.

From this discussion, it is clear that, to equalize power relationships among groups, organizations need to direct their efforts toward all three levels of analysis: organizational, structural, and behavioral. The next section uses these three levels to examine the relationships among diversity, mentorship, and power in organizations. It will be argued that by addressing all three levels of analysis, mentorship may provide a medium for organizational change toward achieving egalitarian power relationships among groups in organizations.

Diversity and Mentorship

Definition of Mentors

Mentors generally are defined as individuals with advanced experience and knowledge who are committed to providing upward mobility and support for their protégés' careers (Hunt & Michael, 1983; Kram, 1985; Ragins, 1989). According to Kram (1985), mentors provide two primary types of functions or roles. First, they provide career development roles, which involve coaching, sponsoring advancement, protecting protégés from adverse forces, providing challenging assignments, and fostering positive visibility. Second, mentors provide psychosocial roles, which include such functions as personal support, friendship, acceptance, counseling, and role modeling. Some research has found support for the two mentorship factors of career development and psychosocial functions (Schockett & Haring-Hidore, 1985), whereas other research found role modeling to represent a distinct factor that is separate from psychosocial support (Scandura, 1992). While mentors may provide some or all of these functions, existing research suggests that the more functions the mentor provides, the greater the benefits accrued by the protégé (Dreher & Ash, 1990; Scandura, 1992).

Diversified Mentoring Relationships. The gender or racial composition of the mentoring relationship may differ for women and minorities in organizations. Given the glass ceiling and the demographic composition of male-dominated organizations, women and minorities are more likely to have a mentor of the opposite sex or a different race than are majority members (Murray, 1982; Ragins, 1989; Ragins & Cotton, 1991; D. Thomas, 1990; Thomas & Alderfer, 1989). To extend this concept to other groups, *diversified mentoring* will be defined here as mentoring relationships in which the mentor and protégé differ in race, gender, ethnicity, or other identity-group attributes. Diversified mentoring relationships may involve the pairing of a White male mentor, hereafter referred to as "majority mentor," with a female or minority protégé, or "minority protégé." While less common, diversified mentoring may also involve a minority mentor teamed with a majority protégé. As discussed in subsequent sections, although diversified mentoring relationships may share some commonalities with homogeneous relationships, there are distinct and important differences in mentoring processes and outcomes associated with diversified relationships.

Mentoring and Power

Mentoring is related to the development of power in organizations in at least three ways. First, a consistent relationship has been found between mentorship and advancement; individuals with mentors receive more promotions, advance at a faster rate, and receive greater compensation than those lacking mentors (Dreher & Ash, 1990; Fagenson, 1989; Scandura, 1992; Whitely, Dougherty, & Dreher, 1991).

Second, there is evidence that mentoring is related to positional power. In a study of 518 women and men in high and low organizational ranks, Fagenson (1988) found that regardless of rank or gender, protégés reported greater positional power, greater access to important people, and more influence over organizational policy than nonprotégés.

Third, mentors may help protégés develop interpersonal forms of influence and power by providing coaching, role modeling, and other mentoring functions. Mentors may help protégés recognize the importance of developing power bases in organizations and may provide insights into the development of political skills and strategies. By providing challenging assignments and placing protégés in visible positions, mentors help protégés develop expert power and obtain organizational visibility and influence. Kanter (1977) observes that mentors provide a form of "reflected power" for their protégés; the relationship signals to others in the organization that the protégé has the mentor's powerful backing and resources. By transmitting power, mentors can increase their protégés' influence and buffer their protégés from adverse forces in the organization. This line of thought suggests the following propositions: (a) Mentors provide a variety of resources for power for their protégés, and (b) the greater the mentor's power, the greater the potential for the protégé's development of power.

The influence of cultural, structural, and behavioral factors on the relationships among mentoring, diversity, and power are explored in the following sections. A central proposition of this review is that the relationships are reciprocal; diversified mentoring relationships are influenced by and have the capacity to influence organizational culture, structure, and behaviors.

Cultural Influences
on Mentoring and Diversity

Influence of Culture
on Diversified Mentoring

The values and norms inherent in an organization's culture can support or deter mentoring relationships. An extension of existing theory on culture suggests that mentoring relationships may be more likely to be supported in collectivist than individualist organizational cultures. As applied to societal culture, Triandis and his colleagues observe that vertical relationships (e.g, parent-child relationships) are maximized in collectivist cultures, which emphasize active intervention by parents in providing guidance and direction to children (Triandis, 1989; Triandis et al., 1988). Individualist cultures, on the other hand, promote horizontal relationships (e.g., equal-status friends or spouses), and value parental detachment and the promotion of independence in children. As applied to organizations, collectivist cultures may place a greater value on mentoring relationships, which are conceived as similar to parental relationships (see, e.g., Levinson, Darrow, Klein, Levinson, & McKee, 1978). Mentoring may be viewed as an important and valued activity in collectivist cultures, and mentors may be rewarded informally by peer recognition or formally in performance appraisals (Ragins & Scandura, 1994a). Individualist organizational cultures, on the other hand, emphasize individual attainments and may discredit and discourage cooperative, helping relationships. Mentors in individualist cultures may be viewed as fostering dependency or showing favoritism to protégés. While collectivist cultures may view the mentoring relationship as developmental in nature, individualist cultures may view the relationship as remedial in nature and necessary to compensate for a protégé's deficiency.

By influencing perceptions regarding the purpose of the mentoring relationship, organizational culture may also influence the power outcomes associated with the relationship. If collectivist cultures view mentoring as a strength, and individualist cultures view it as a weakness, power transmittal in mentoring relationships should be more likely to occur in collectivist than individualist cultures. The support provided by collectivist cultures should therefore increase the quality and quantity of the mentoring functions provided, and mentors should have more freedom, latitude, and support to help their protégés advance. Although there has been no research on this topic, this perspective suggests the following hypotheses: (a) Mentoring relationships will be more likely to occur in collectivist rather than individualistic organizational cultures, and (b) mentoring relationships will provide more resources for power in collectivist than in individualistic organizational cultures.

At first glance, it would appear that women and minorities have a better chance for effective mentoring relationships, and the associated resources for power, in collectivist than individualist organizational cultures. However, as discussed earlier, collectivist cultures support unequal power relationships by emphasizing distinctions between in-groups and out-groups. Women and minorities are therefore placed in a difficult position: If they gain mentors in individualistic cultures, where mentoring relationships are viewed as remedial, they may reinforce stereotypes of incompetence and inadequacy. While mentoring relationships are valued in collectivist cultures, the polarization and isolation among groups in collectivist cultures may decrease opportunities for meeting powerful mentors and developing diversified mentoring relationships. In short, both cultures may present barriers to the development of mentoring relationships for women and minorities.

Influence of Diversified
Mentoring on Culture

Mentors may influence and shape organizational culture by articulating and supporting the values and norms of the organization. Wilson and Elman (1990) observe that mentors strengthen and assure the continuity of an organization's culture by socializing protégés and providing them with information on the organization's values, norms, and beliefs. In support of this idea, Ostroff and Kozlowski (1993) found that mentors assisted protégés with socialization and adaptation to organizations, and that protégés were more likely than nonprotégés to obtain information about organizational issues, policies, and practices.

Diversified mentoring relationships have the potential for both negative and positive effects with respect to organizational culture and diversity. In terms of negative effects, by promoting socialization and adaptation to organizational culture, mentors in diversified relationships may advise their protégés to assimilate to the dominant culture rather than maintain their separate identity. In the most extreme form, it has been suggested that some mentors may attempt to stifle the individuality of the protégé or create a protégé "clone." In a study of 62 academic mentors, Blackburn, Chapman, and Cameron (1981) found that mentors nominated as their most successful protégés those whose careers were essentially identical to their own—that is, their "clones." However, another study found that these behaviors may be relatively uncommon in mentoring relationships. In a study of a matched sample of 275 male and female ex-protégés, Ragins and Scandura (1994b) examined reasons for termination of mentoring relationships and found that attempts to "clone" or stifle growth were infrequently reported and that women and men did not differ in this reason for termination. Future research needs to explore the nature and extent of assimilation processes in diversified mentoring relationships.

Diversified mentoring relationships may also have a positive influence on diversity and organizational culture. As discussed earlier, diversified mentoring usually involves the pairing of a senior, White, male mentor with a minority protégé. In fact, formal mentoring programs often involve matching senior executives with female and minority protégés (Phillips-Jones, 1983). This situation creates a unique opportunity for changing corporate culture, which, as argued earlier, may be shaped by the experiences of the power-holders. Due to structural segregation, power-holders in organizations are often insulated from minority members and may have limited exposure and experience interacting with individuals who differ from them. Diversified mentoring relationships provide a one-on-one experience involving support, friendship, and some degree of intimacy. Through this experience, power-holders in diversified relationships can gain an understanding and appreciation of the obstacles to advancement faced by women and minorities. Moreover, because mentors are involved with promoting the advancement of protégés (Kram, 1985), diversified mentors may gain firsthand experience with the cultural, structural, and behavioral barriers to the development of power among women and minorities. This experience may influence the values, beliefs, perceptions, and ideologies of power-holders. To the extent that power-holders influence the culture of the organization, diversified mentoring relationships may have a profound influence on corporate culture. One proposition that can be drawn from this discussion is that corporate cultures are more likely to reflect pluralistic models when their power-holders are involved in diversified, rather than homogeneous, mentoring relationships.

In sum, organizational culture may influence the development and functioning of diversified mentoring relationships. Both collectivist and individualist cultures may present unique barriers to women and minorities seeking mentors in organizations. However, once in a diversified mentoring relationship, protégés can have the potential to influence corporate culture through the power-holders of the organization. While diversified relationships create an opportunity for corporate cultures to accept diversity, they may also function to assimilate the protégé to the existing culture. Diversified mentoring relationships may therefore function either to facilitate an appreciation of diversity or to undermine diversity issues. There is a clear need for future research to understand the individual and organizational predictors of each of these scenarios.

The next section explores the reciprocal relationship between structure and diversified mentoring relationships.

Structural Influences on Mentoring and Diversity

Research on mentoring clearly indicates that individuals with mentors have a distinct advantage over those lacking mentors. Protégés have been found to receive more promotions (Dreher & Ash, 1990; Scandura, 1992), have higher incomes (Dreher & Ash, 1990; Whitely et al., 1991), and report more career satisfaction (Fagenson, 1989) and mobility (Scandura, 1992) than nonprotégés.

Although mentoring is important for all individuals, it is particularly critical for women and minorities (Noe, 1988; Ragins, 1989; Thomas & Alderfer, 1989). However, structural variables may present barriers to the development of mentoring relationships and may determine the gender and racial composition of the mentoring relationship. Diversified relationships may in turn contribute to structural integration and cultural change toward acceptance of diversity. These reciprocal relationships are examined at length in the following sections.

Influence of Structure on Diversified Mentoring

Structure and Access. Organizational structures that promote segregation by rank, department, or specialization may create barriers to the development of mentoring relationships and may limit women and minority members' access to high-power mentors. In a study of 229 female and 281 male employees in three research and development organizations, Ragins and Cotton (1991) found that women reported less access to mentoring relationships than men, even when controlling for gender differences in mentorship experience, age, rank, and organizational tenure. Of particular interest is that for both men and women, perceived barriers to mentoring were greater at lower than higher ranks. Given that women and minorities are disproportionately found at lower ranks (Brown & Ford, 1977; Fierman, 1990), this research suggests that structural segregation may constitute a significant barrier to the development of mentoring relationships among women and minorities in organizations.

Structure and Composition of Relationship. Structural segregation not only might influence barriers to mentoring, it might also influence the composition of the relationship. Existing research indicates that women are more likely than men to be in cross-sex mentoring relationships (Korn/Ferry International, 1992; Ragins & Cotton, 1991), and that Blacks are more likely than Whites to be in cross-race relationships (Atkinson, Neville, & Casas, 1991; Murray, 1982; D. Thomas, 1990). White protégés with Black mentors are virtually nonexistent (Thomas & Alderfer, 1989), and the dearth of male protégés with female mentors often results in an exclusion of this gender combination from most studies of gender and mentoring (see, e.g., review by Ragins, 1989). This situation limits balanced contrasts of diversified and homogeneous mentoring relationships, and the low sample size for White male protégés in diversified relationships attenuates the statistical power needed to detect existing differences.

From a structural perspective, the prevalence of diversified relationships for women and minorities, and homogeneous relationships for White males, increases with rank and is influenced by department. In a study of 205 female executives, Gaskill and Sibley (1990) found that high-ranking women were more likely to have male mentors and older mentors than women at lower organizational ranks. In another study of 1,736 management employees in a health maintenance organization, Bachman and Gregory (1993) found that women were more likely to have female mentors in female-dominated departments than male-dominated departments. Finally, in a study of 63 middle-level managers, Ibarra (1994) found that compared with their Caucasian peers, minority protégés had lower ranking mentors with more restricted network contacts. This research yields the hypothesis that the proportion of homogeneous to diversified mentoring relationships for women and minorities will become more balanced as organizations achieve vertical and horizontal structural integration.

The gender and racial composition of the relationship is important, as it may influence mentorship outcomes and the development of power in organizations. In a study of 100 middle-class Black males, Murray (1982) found that protégés with White male mentors had greater incomes than protégés with Black male mentors. In another study of 89 female psychologists, Brefach (1986) reported that women perceived male mentors as having more power at work than female mentors. Given the gender and racial differences in power in organizations discussed earlier, majority mentors may provide more resources for power than minority mentors. The downside of this situation, which will be discussed later in this chapter, is that majority mentors are restricted in their ability to provide role modeling functions to minority protégés (Ragins, 1989; Ragins & McFarlin, 1990; Thomas & Alderfer, 1989).

In sum, structural segregation may increase the barriers to developing a mentoring relationship among women and minorities in organizations. Structural segregation, by definition, promotes the development of diversified mentoring relationships for women and minority protégés as well as the development of homogeneous relationships for White male protégés. This differential pattern of relationships increases with higher ranks in male-dominated organizations. Diversified mentoring relationships may provide greater access to power but more restricted role modeling for minority protégés. Although there are few empirical studies, outcomes associated with mentoring relationships may be influenced by the composition of the dyad. Finally, it should be noted that most research on race effects has been limited to African Americans and may not generalize to other minority groups in organizations.

Influence of Diversified Mentoring on Structure

Diversified mentoring relationships have the potential to influence the three structural indicators of unequal power relationships in organizations that were identified in the first part of this chapter: rank, career track, and positional power.

Rank. Mentoring relationships have been found to be related to promotion rates in organizations (Dreher & Ash, 1990; Scandura, 1992; Whitely et al., 1991), and these effects are equivalent for women and men (Dreher & Ash, 1990; Fagenson, 1989). While there is a need for future research to determine whether these outcomes hold for different racioethnic and minority groups, existing research suggests that mentors may facilitate the advancement and structural integration of women and minorities in organizations. Moreover, because mentoring generally occurs across all departments in organizations (Hunt & Michael, 1983; Kram, 1985), structural integration can occur horizontally as well as vertically.

Career Tracks and Departments. Mentoring relationships may also influence structural variables relating to career tracks and placement in powerful departments. As discussed earlier, women and minorities are often tracked into low-power career tracks with limited opportunities for advancement and are often segregated into staff support positions in departments with limited power. One of the primary functions of mentors is to provide career advice, coaching, and guidance for their protégés' advancement (Kram, 1985), and existing research has found that female protégés report receiving career guidance equivalent to that of their male counterparts (Dreher & Ash, 1990; Ragins & McFarlin, 1990; D. Thomas, 1990). Mentoring relationships often span departmental lines, and this provides the opportunity for women and minorities to make lateral moves into more powerful departments. As reviewed earlier, Dave Thomas (1990) found that Blacks were more likely than Whites to seek mentors in other departments in the organization, suggesting that minority members may use mentors to offset tracking into low-power career tracks.

Positional Power. Mentors may help compensate for gender and racial differences in positional power. As discussed earlier, even when women and minorities obtain promotions, they are less likely than their White male counterparts to obtain the power associated with the position. Because the presence of a mentor has been found to be associated with reports of positional power (Fagenson, 1988), it is reasonable to hypothesize that women and minorities are more likely to obtain positional power when they have a mentor than when they lack a mentor.

In short, mentors have the capacity to influence structural access to power by facilitating the advancement of women and minorities into high-power career tracks and powerful positions. Advancement into higher ranks increases the number of minority mentors available for both minority and majority protégés. An increase in high-ranking minority mentors would create a shift in the type of mentoring relationships found in organizations— an increase in homogeneous relationships for women and minorities and an increase in diversified relationships for White males. As discussed earlier, the diversification of mentoring relationships is a tool for changing organizational culture with respect to diversity.

Behavioral Influences
of Mentoring on Diversity

Behavioral factors influence the initiation and effectiveness of diversified mentoring relationships. The reciprocal relationship between protégé and mentor behaviors and the development of diversified mentoring relationships in organizations is explored in this section.

Influence of Behavior
on Diversified Mentoring

Overcoming Barriers to Mentoring. In addition to the structural barriers to mentoring discussed earlier, behavioral barriers may also impede the development of mentoring relationships among minority protégés. Ragins and Cotton (1991), in their study of 229 female and 281 male employees, found that women were more likely than men to report that mentors were unwilling to mentor them, that supervisors and coworkers would disapprove of the relationship, and that the initiation of the relationship might be misconstrued as sexual in nature by either the mentor or others in the organization. In short, while structural barriers influence access, behavioral barriers reflect interpersonal factors that may impede the development of the relationship.

While behavioral and structural barriers to obtaining a mentor may increase the difficulty of establishing a relationship, individuals may still overcome barriers to gaining a mentor. The women in the Ragins and Cotton (1991) study reported more barriers to gaining a mentor than their male counterparts, but they were as likely as their male counterparts to report the presence of a mentor, suggesting that they overcame the real or perceived barriers to obtaining a mentor. In a survey of 1,736 male and female management employees in a female-dominated, health maintenance organization, Bachman and Gregory (1993) found that women expressed greater motivation for gaining a mentor than men and actually were more likely to have a mentoring relationship. Similarly, no gender differences in the presence of a mentor were found among samples of 800 accountants (Scandura & Ragins, 1993), 518 health care employees (Fagenson, 1989), and 320 business school graduates (Dreher & Ash, 1990).

There is in fact some empirical evidence that minorities exert extra effort to establish a mentoring relationship. In a study of 88 Black and 107 White managers, Dave Thomas (1990) found that Blacks were more likely than Whites to go outside their departments and formal lines of authority to develop mentoring relationships with mentors of the same race. Future research should directly investigate the hypothesis that women and minorities exert greater effort to establish mentoring relationships than majority members of organizations.

Research on the presence of mentors suggests that race and gender may have independent effects on mentoring. While research on gender has found no support for the idea that men are more likely to have mentors than women (e.g., Bachman & Gregory, 1993; Dreher & Ash, 1990; Fagenson, 1989; Ragins & Cotton, 1991; Swerdlik & Bardon, 1988), research on race has been less consistent. Studies comparing Blacks and Whites found no race differences in the presence of a mentor (Greenhaus et al., 1990; Ibarra, 1994; D. Thomas, 1990), and studies of Black samples found that the majority of respondents reported having at least one mentor during the course of their careers (Ford & Wells, 1985; Malone, 1982; Murray, 1982). However, a lack of mentors was reported in two interview studies based on small samples of African Americans (Gooden, 1980; Herbert, 1990). There is clearly a need for more comparative research that assesses the presence of a mentor and barriers to developing mentoring relationships among a variety of racioethnic and other minority groups.

Initiation of Mentoring Relationships. Although there has been relatively little research on the topic of the decision to mentor, there are a number of factors that may lead majority mentors to choose majority over minority protégés. One factor is that majority mentors have restricted informal and social interactions with minority protégés and may therefore be less comfortable interacting with minority than with majority protégés (Thomas, 1989). Cross-sex relationships face similar barriers; the potential for sexual involvement or unfounded rumors of sexual relationships with female protégés may result in male mentors selecting male over female protégés (Ragins, 1989).

Another potential barrier to the development of diversified relationships is the nature of the selection process. According to existing theory, a primary factor guiding selection is the mentor's identification with the protégé as a younger version of him- or herself (Kram, 1985; Levinson et al., 1978), which places minority protégés at a disadvantage (see, e.g., Ilgen & Youtz, 1986). However, protégé performance has been found to be a primary factor in mentors' selection of protégés (Olian, Carroll, & Giannantonio, 1993) and may compensate for "like-me" biases in the selection process.

A final potential barrier to the development of diversified relationships is the potential cost associated with mentoring a minority protégé. Jones (1986) observed that White managers may be uncomfortable sponsoring Black protégés for promotion or high-visibility assignments for fear of ostracism from other Whites. Majority mentors may be reluctant to mentor minority protégés because the high visibility of tokens amplifies both the success and the failures of the protégé and the relationship (Kanter, 1977). Given that the protégé's performance is a reflection of the mentor's competence (Levinson et al., 1978), the risk of negative exposure may therefore be greater with a minority protégé than a majority protégé.

Minority mentors may also face barriers to developing diversified relationships. As in the case of majority mentors, identification and perceived similarity may lead minority mentors to prefer minority protégés over majority protégés. Ford and Wells (1985), in a study of 134 Black administrators, found that 60% were mentors, with 92% mentoring Black protégés. A 1992 Korn/Ferry study of 439 female executives found 88% reported that they served as a mentor to lower level women. While minority mentors may prefer minority protégés, members of the organization's minority may face greater barriers to becoming mentors than members of the organizations' majority. Ragins and Cotton (1993) investigated gender differences in willingness to mentor in a matched sample of 229 women and 281 men in three research and development organizations. When controlling for gender differences in factors relating to decisions to mentor (age, rank, tenure, and mentorship experience), women anticipated more drawbacks to becoming a mentor and were less likely to be mentors than men, even though they expressed equivalent intentions to mentor. Drawbacks included such factors as being put in a bad light by their protégés' failures, lacking the time to be a mentor, and feeling unqualified in assuming a mentorship role. In an extension of this study to a national matched sample of 80 male and 80 female executives above the glass ceiling, Ragins and Scandura (1994a) found that women were as likely to be mentors as men and reported equivalent costs and benefits to the relationship as well as intentions to mentor others in the future. Moreover, female mentors mentored same-sex protégés with greater frequency than their male counterparts, thus dispelling the "queen bee" notion that senior women are unwilling to help junior women (Gallese, 1993). This research suggests that rank may influence barriers to becoming a mentor; while women below the glass ceiling reported barriers to becoming a mentor and might not have been in a position to withstand the increased visibility of a same-gender mentoring relationship, those above the ceiling were as willing and more able to mentor female protégés. Future research should investigate the relationship among rank, opportunity, and willingness to mentor among other minority groups in organizations.

In short, compared with their majority counterparts, minority mentors face greater barriers to mentoring minority and majority protégés. Many of the barriers are due to rank and may therefore be dissolved with structural integration. However, minority mentors are more visible than majority mentors, and their relationships are more "high stakes" with respect to risks and benefits. The risks are greatest in homogeneous relationships of minority mentors and protégés, the most visible of all mentoring combinations. Finally, protégés may prefer majority over minority mentors for the reduced visibility associated with the relationship (Ragins, 1989) and for their real or perceived ability to provide resources for power (Brefach, 1986; Erkut & Mokros, 1984). As discussed earlier, stereotypes and attributions may lead to distortions in the perception of a minority member's power, and the eventual attenuation of power. Even when holding similar positions with equivalent positional power, minority mentors may be perceived as having less power than their majority counterparts.

In sum, a number of behavioral factors influence the selection of mentors and protégés. Perceived similarity, identification, level of comfort, and absence of sexual issues contribute to the selection of homogeneous mentors and protégés. Diversified mentoring relationships are more common with majority mentors than minority mentors; the factors that contribute to unequal power relationships among groups can also lead to the restriction of diversified mentoring relationships with minority mentors. One proposition that can be drawn from this perspective is that structural integration of women and minorities will increase the pool of high-power minority mentors and the number of diversified relationships with minority mentors. However, to achieve a balance of homogeneous and diversified mentoring relationships, structural integration must be accompanied by cultural and behavioral changes that allow minorities to be perceived as powerful mentors.

Influence of Mentoring on Behavior

Mentoring and Career Outcomes. There is mixed evidence that career outcomes associated with having a mentor may be influenced by the protégés' race. In a study of 456 White and 273 Black M.B.A.s, Cox and Nkomo (1991) found that Blacks were less likely than Whites to report that their career was aided by a mentor. Murray (1982), in a study of 100 middle-class Black males, found that protégés reported less satisfaction with their careers than nonprotégés. Similarly, in a study of 134 male and female Black administrators, Ford and Wells (1985) found that while half of the respondents had mentors, the presence of a mentor was unrelated to promotion or compensation. Mentoring was, however, found to be positively related to reports of social support and negatively related to job stress, stress-related health symptoms, frustration, and burnout. These studies of Black respondents directly contradict other research with primarily Caucasian samples, which found greater career satisfaction, advancement, and promotion among protégés than nonprotégés of both sexes (Bachman & Gregory, 1993; Dreher & Ash, 1990; Fagenson, 1989). In contrast, in a study of 57 Black and 48 White protégés, Alleman, Newman, Huggins, and Carr (1987) found that Black protégés rated the career benefits of the relationship higher than White protégés.

Although Black protégés may obtain fewer career benefits from their mentoring relationships than their White counterparts, one study found no differences in protégé reports of the mentor's behaviors and functions in the relationship. In a study of 88 Black and 107 White managers, Dave Thomas (1990) found no race or gender differences in reports of mentor behaviors involving career development and psychosocial functions. However, in a study of 63 middle-level managers, Ibarra (1994) found that compared with their majority counterparts, minority protégés reported less intimate relationships with their mentors. Moreover, in spite of the fact that mentoring was unrelated to promotion or compensation, Ford and Wells (1985) found that 87% of the protégés indicated that their mentors had a positive impact on their careers. One explanation for these results is that protégé reports of a mentor's behavior may differ from the actual ability of the mentor to sponsor the protégé to high-ranking positions. Mentors may engage in equivalent career development behaviors for their White and Black protégés, but their ability to provide power-related outcomes may be less for minority than majority protégés. One reason for this is that structural segregation may contribute to differential access to high-ranking, powerful mentors; Black protégés may obtain mentors with fewer resources for power than White protégés. Another possible explanation is that mentors may be less willing to actively sponsor Black protégés, for fear of diversity backlash and negative reactions by others in the organization.

In contrast to the research on race and mentorship outcomes, most studies on gender have found that women obtain career benefits from mentoring relationships equivalent to men's. Dreher and Ash (1990), in a study of 147 female and 173 male business school graduates, found that female protégés did not significantly differ from their male counterparts in outcomes associated with the relationship, such as promotions, compensation, and satisfaction with compensation. Similarly, in a study of 518 high- and low-level men and women in a large health care organization, Fagenson (1989) found that, irrespective of gender, mentored individuals reported more mobility/opportunity, recognition, satisfaction, and promotions than nonmentored individuals. In contrast, Hill, Bahniuk, and Dobos (1989), in a study of 258 business professionals, found that while having a mentor was associated with such outcomes as job satisfaction, positive self-perception, rank, and income, female protégés reported fewer of these outcomes than male protégés and male nonprotégés. Combined, the research reviewed above suggests that race and gender may operate independently with respect to outcomes associated with mentoring relationships. Future research should also include the mentor's rank and positional power in comparative analyses of outcomes associated with mentoring relationships for majority and minority protégés.

Composition of Relationship. The composition of the relationship may be more important than race or gender in influencing mentorship behaviors and outcomes. While somewhat inconsistent, the literature generally suggests that homogeneous mentoring relationships provide more role modeling and psychosocial functions than diversified mentoring relationships. In a study of 88 Black and 107 White managers, Dave Thomas (1990) found that protégés in same-race relationships reported more psychosocial support than those in cross-race relationships, and protégés in same-sex relationships reported more trust and mutuality than protégés in cross-sex relationships. Similarly, in a study of 181 male and female protégés, Ragins and McFarlin (1990) found that, although mentor and protégé gender was unrelated to mentorship functions, protégés in same-gender mentoring relationships were more likely than protégés in cross-gender relationships to report engaging in after-work social activities with their mentors. In addition, compared with other gender combinations, female protégées with female mentors were significantly more likely to report that their mentor provided role modeling functions. In contrast, a study of 57 male and 44 female psychologists of African, Asian, and Hispanic descent revealed that ethnic similarity of mentor was unrelated to career development and psychosocial functions (Atkinson et al., 1991). However, among those who had mentors when they were novice professionals, as opposed to graduate students, same-ethnicity mentors received higher global evaluations of effectiveness than cross-ethnicity mentors. This study did not assess role modeling functions and did not have sufficient sample size to assess gender and ethnicity main or interaction effects.

Research investigating the influence of the protégé's and mentor's gender, without considering the composition of the relationship, has been inconsistent. Some studies have found that women are as likely as men to report that their mentors provided both psychosocial and career development functions (Dreher & Ash, 1990; Ragins & McFarlin, 1990; D. Thomas, 1990), whereas other studies have found that mentors report providing more psychosocial support to female protégés (Burke, McKeen, & McKenna, 1993) and that psychosocial functions are more likely to occur when the mentor is a woman (Gaskill, 1991), when the protégé is a woman (Noe, 1988), or when women are involved in the relationship as either a mentor or a protégé (Burke et al., 1993). It is important to note that the inconsistency of these findings may be due to variations in the gender compositions of the relationships across these studies.

Moderators. Two factors may moderate the relationship between diversified relationships and outcomes. The first is socioeconomic class. Whitely et al. (1991) found that career-oriented mentoring had a stronger relationship with promotion rates for protégés from higher socioeconomic backgrounds than protégés from lower socioeconomic backgrounds. In explaining these results, the researchers postulated that class either may have a direct impact on outcomes or may operate indirectly through the mentor's position in the organization. That is, individuals from higher socioeconomic backgrounds may have greater access to powerful mentors than individuals from lower socioeconomic backgrounds. To the extent that class correlates with race (Dovidio & Gaertner, 1986), this line of reasoning suggests that class is an important variable, and that the impact of class on mentoring outcomes needs to be studied and disentangled from race and socioethnic status in future research.

The second factor that may moderate the relationship between mentoring relationships and their outcomes is attitudes toward diversity. In a qualitative field study of 22 cross-race mentoring relationships, Thomas (1993) found that mentors provided both career development and psychosocial functions when mentors and protégés shared similar attitudes and strategies for dealing with racial differences in the relationship; that is, both members either denied racial differences or discussed them openly. However, mentoring relationships lacked psychosocial support when the members differed in their attitudes and approaches toward dealing with the racial differences in the relationship.

Future research should provide a comparative analysis of the influence of race and gender on mentorship outcomes while controlling for such potential confounds as rank, age, tenure in organization, and mentorship experience, which are related to mentorship outcomes but may differ by race and gender (Fagenson, 1989; Scandura, 1992; Whitely et al., 1991).

Summary of Mentorship and Diversity

Due to structural segregation and behavioral barriers, minority protégés are more likely to be in diversified relationships than majority protégés. This can have a positive impact on organizational culture; minority protégés can sensitize majority mentors to diversity issues and can change corporate culture. Alternately, diversified relationships can promote assimilation of minority protégés to the dominant culture and can undermine the preservation of independent cultures in organizations. Nevertheless, because mentoring is strongly related to advancement and the development of power, minority protégés need to develop mentoring relationships. Moreover, in spite of encountering greater barriers to developing mentoring relationships, minority members are as likely as their majority counterparts to actually obtain a mentor. Future research should investigate the behavioral and career outcomes associated with diversified and homogeneous mentoring relationships, and whether these outcomes differ by characteristics of the mentor, characteristics of the protégé, and the composition of the relationship.

Conclusion

Effective diversity efforts in organizations require a multilevel approach to change that involves organizational culture, structure, and behavior. Cultural, structural, and behavioral factors synergistically combine to support inequitable and exclusionary power relationships among groups in organizations. These factors create a culture that defines power in terms of majority attributes; promotes structural segregation of power by rank, department, and position; constrains minorities' power behaviors and distorts perceptions of their power; and promotes negative reactions and backlash to the use of power among minority members in organizations.

Mentoring is a key resource for the development of power in organizations, and has the potential to create cultural, structural, and behavioral change with respect to diversity and the development of power among minority groups. The relationships are reciprocal; cultural, structural, and behavioral factors limit the development of mentoring relationships among minorities, but mentoring also influences all three of these factors. Mentoring is a tangible method for the advancement of minorities; it promotes cultural change, structural integration, and the development of power. An effective intervention into this cycle is for organizations to develop a critical mass of minority mentors in high-ranking positions. This intervention would create a climate that supports the balanced development of diversified and homogeneous mentoring relationships for both minority and majority protégés and their mentors.

Note

1. The term *minority* refers to power rather than numerical status and includes race, ethnicity, gender, physical abilities, age, religion, and sexual/affectional orientation.

References

Acker, J. (1990). Hierarchies, jobs, bodies: A theory of gendered organizations. *Gender & Society, 4*, 139-158.

Acker, J., & Van Houten, D. R. (1974). Differential recruitment and control: The sex structuring of organizations. *Administrative Science Quarterly, 19*, 152-163.

Alderfer, C. P., & Smith, K. K. (1982). Studying intergroup relations embedded in organizations. *Administrative Science Quarterly, 27*, 35-65.

Alleman, E., Newman, I., Huggins, H., & Carr, L. (1987). The impact of race on mentoring relationships. *International Journal of Mentoring, 1*(2), 20-23.

Atkinson, D. R., Neville, H., & Casas, A. (1991). The mentorship of ethnic minorities in professional psychology. *Professional Psychology: Research and Practice, 22*, 336-338.

Ayers-Nachamkin, B., Cann, C. H., Reed, R., & Horne, A. (1982). Sex and ethnic differences in the use of power. *Journal of Applied Psychology, 67*, 464-471.

Bachman, S. I., & Gregory, K. (1993, April). *Mentor and protege gender: Effects on mentoring roles and outcomes.* Paper presented at the Society for Industrial and Organizational Psychology conference, San Francisco.

Beehr, T. A., & Juntunen, D. L. (1990). Promotions and employees' perceived mobility channels: The effects of employee sex, employee group, and initial placement. *Human Relations, 43*, 455-472.

Belk, S. S., Snell, W. E., Garcia-Falconi, R., Hernandez-Sanchez, J. E., Hargrove, L., & Holtzman, W. H. (1988). Power strategy use in the intimate relationships of women and men from Mexico and the United States. *Personality and Social Psychology Bulletin, 14*, 439-447.

Bell, E. L., Denton, T. C., & Nkomo, S. (1993). Women of color in management: Toward an inclusive analysis. In E. Fagenson (Ed.), *Women in management: Trends, issues, and challenges in managerial diversity* (Vol. 4, pp. 105-130). Newbury Park, CA: Sage.

Bendick, M., Jackson, C. W., Reinoso, V. A., & Hodges, L. E. (1991). Discrimination against Latino job applicants: A controlled experiment. *Human Resource Management, 30*, 469-484.

Blackburn, R. T., Chapman, D. W., & Cameron, S. M. (1981). "Cloning" in academe: Mentorship and academic careers. *Research in Higher Education, 15*, 315-327.

Bohan, J. S. (1993). Regarding gender: Essentialism, constructionism, and feminist psychology. *Psychology of Women Quarterly, 17*, 5-21.

Brass, D. J., & Burkhardt, M. E. (1993). Potential power and power use: An investigation of structure and behavior. *Academy of Management Journal, 36*, 441-470.

Brefach, S. M. (1986). *The mentor experience: The influences of female/male mentors on the personal and professional growth of female psychologists.* Unpublished doctoral dissertation, Boston University.

Brown, H. A., & Ford, D. L. (1977). An exploratory analysis of discrimination in the employment of Black MBA graduates. *Journal of Applied Psychology, 62,* 50-56.

Burke, R. J., McKeen, C. A., & McKenna, C. (1993). Correlates of mentoring in organizations: The mentor's perspective. *Psychological Reports, 72,* 883-896.

Burns, T., & Stalker, G. M. (1961). *The management of innovation.* London: Tavistock.

Cartwright, D. (Ed.). (1959). *Studies in social power.* Ann Arbor: University of Michigan, Research Center for Group Dynamics, Institute for Social Research.

Clark, K. B. (1966). Social power. *American Psychologist, 21,* 5.

Cox, T. (1991). The multicultural organization. *Academy of Management Executive, 5*(2), 34-47.

Cox, T. (1993). *Cultural diversity in organizations: Theory, research, and practice.* San Francisco: Berrett-Koehler.

Cox, T., & Finley-Nickelson, J. (1991). Models of acculturation for intra-organizational cultural diversity. *Canadian Journal of Administrative Sciences, 8*(2), 90-100.

Cox, T., & Nkomo, S. M. (1986). Differential performance appraisal criteria: A field study of Black and White managers. *Group & Organization Studies, 11,* 101-119.

Cox, T., & Nkomo, S. M. (1991). A race and gender-group analysis of the early career experience of MBAs. *Work and Occupations, 18,* 431-446.

Dahl, R. A. (1957). The concept of power. *Behavioral Science, 2,* 201-215.

Dansereau, F., Graen, G., & Haga, W. J. (1975). A vertical dyad linkage approach to leadership within formal organizations: A longitudinal investigation of the role-making process. *Organizational Behavior and Human Performance, 13,* 46-78.

Davis, J., & Rodela, E. S. (1992). Mentoring for the Hispanic: Mapping emotional support. In S. B. Knouse, P. Rosenfeld, & A. L. Culbertson (Eds.), *Hispanics in the workplace* (pp. 151-169). Newbury Park, CA: Sage.

Davis, R. C. (1951). *Fundamentals of top management.* New York: Harper.

DeFreitas, G. (1991). *Inequality at work: Hispanics in the U.S. labor force.* New York: Oxford University Press.

Dipboye, R. L. (1987). Problems and progress of women in management. In K. S. Koziara, M. H. Moskow, & L. D. Tanner (Eds.), *Working women: Past, present, future* (pp. 118-153). Washington, DC: Bureau of National Affairs.

Dovidio, J. F., & Gaertner, S. L. (1986). Prejudice, discrimination, and racism: Historical trends and contemporary approaches. In J. F. Dovidio & S. L. Gaertner (Eds.), *Prejudice, discrimination, and racism* (pp. 1-34). Orlando, FL: Academic Press.

Dreher, G. F., & Ash, R. A. (1990). A comparative study of mentoring among men and women in managerial, professional, and technical positions. *Journal of Applied Psychology, 75,* 539-546.

Eagly, A. H., Makhijani, M. G., & Klonsky, B. G. (1992). Gender and the evaluation of leaders: A meta-analysis. *Psychological Bulletin, 111,* 3-22.

Erkut, S., & Mokros, J. R. (1984). Professors as models and mentors for college students. *American Educational Research Journal, 21*(2), 399-417.

Fagenson, E. A. (1988). The power of a mentor: Protégés' and nonprotégés' perceptions of their own power in organizations. *Group & Organization Studies, 13,* 182-192.

Fagenson, E. A. (1989). The mentor advantage: Perceived career/job experiences of protégés vs. non-protégés. *Journal of Organizational Behavior, 10,* 309-320.

Faludi, S. (1991). *Backlash: The undeclared war against American women.* New York: Crown.

Ferdman, B. M. (1992). The dynamics of ethnic diversity in organizations: Toward integrative models. In K. Kelley (Ed.), *Issues, theory, and research in industrial/organizational psychology* (pp. 339-384). Amsterdam: North Holland.

Fierman, J. (1990, July 30). Why women still don't hit the top. *Fortune,* pp. 40-62.

Ford, D. L., & Wells, L. (1985). Upward mobility factors among Black public administrators: The role of mentors. *Centerboard, 3*, 38-48.

Galen, M., & Palmer, A. T. (1994, January 31). White, male, and worried. *Business Week*, pp. 50-55.

Gallese, L. R. (1993). Do women make poor mentors? *Across the Board, 30*(6), 23-26.

Gaskill, L. R. (1991). Same-sex and cross-sex mentoring of female proteges: A comparative analysis. *Career Development Quarterly, 10*(1), 48-63.

Gaskill, L. R., & Sibley, L. R. (1990). Mentoring relationships for women in retailing: Prevalence, perceived importance, and characteristics. *Clothing and Textile Research Journal, 9*(1), 1-10.

Gooden, W. E. (1980). *The adult development of Black men.* Unpublished doctoral dissertation, Yale University.

Greenhaus, J. H., & Parasuraman, S. (1993). Job performance attributions and career advancement prospects: An examination of gender and race effects. *Organizational Behavior and Human Decision Processes, 55,* 273-297.

Greenhaus, J. H., Parasuraman, S., & Wormley, W. M. (1990). Effects of race on organizational experiences, job performance evaluations, and career outcomes. *Academy of Management Journal, 33*, 64-86.

Griscom, J. L. (1992). Women and power: Definition, dualism, and difference. *Psychology of Women Quarterly, 16*, 389-414.

Gruber, K. J., & White, J. W. (1986). Gender differences in the perceptions of self's and others' use of power strategies. *Sex Roles, 15*, 109-118.

Haberfeld, Y., & Shenhav, Y. (1990). Are women and Blacks closing the gap? Salary discrimination in American science during the 1970s and 1980s. *Industrial and Labor Relations Review, 44*, 68-82.

Hare-Mustin, R. T., & Marecek, J. (1990). Gender and the meaning of difference: Postmodernism and psychology. In R. T. Hare-Mustin & J. Marecek (Eds.), *Making a difference: Psychology and the construction of gender* (pp. 22-64). New Haven, CT: Yale University Press.

Heilman, M. E., Block, C. J., & Lucas, J. A. (1992). Presumed incompetent? Stigmatization and affirmative action efforts. *Journal of Applied Psychology, 77*, 536-544.

Herbert, J. I. (1990). Integrating race and adult psychosocial development. *Journal of Organizational Behavior, 11*, 433-446.

Hill, S. E. K., Bahniuk, M. H., & Dobos, J. (1989). The impact of mentoring and collegial support on faculty success: An analysis of support behavior, information adequacy, and communication apprehension. *Communication Education, 38*, 15-33.

Hinnings, C. R., Hickson, D. J., Pennings, J. M., & Schneck, R. E. (1974). Structural conditions of intraorganizational power. *Administrative Science Quarterly, 16*, 216-229.

Hofstede, G., Neuijen, B., Ohayv, D. D., & Sanders, G. (1990). Measuring organizational cultures: A qualitative and quantitative study across twenty cases. *Administrative Science Quarterly, 35*, 286-316.

Horwitz, T. (1993, September 20). Not home alone: Jobless male managers proliferate in suburbs, causing subtle malaise. *Wall Street Journal*, pp. 1, 6.

Hunt, D. M., & Michael, C. (1983). Mentorship: A career training and development tool. *Academy of Management Review, 8*, 475-485.

Ibarra, H. (1993). Personal networks of women and minorities in management: A conceptual framework. *Academy of Management Review, 18*, 56-87.

Ibarra, H. (1994, August). *The structure of mentoring: A network perspective on race and gender differences in developmental relationships.* Paper presented at the annual meeting of the National Academy of Management, Dallas, TX.

Ibarra, H., & Andrews, S. B. (1993). Power, social influence, and sense making: Effects of network centrality and proximity on employee perceptions. *Administrative Science Quarterly, 38*, 277-303.

Ilgen, D. R., & Youtz, M. A. (1986). Factors affecting the evaluation and development of minorities in organizations. In K. M. Rowland & G. R. Ferris (Eds.), *Research in personnel and human resources management: A research annual* (Vol. 4, pp. 307-337). Greenwich, CT: JAI Press.

Johnson, P. (1976). Women and power: Toward a theory of effectiveness. *Journal of Social Issues, 32*, 99-110.

Jones, E. W. (1986). Black managers: The dream deferred. *Harvard Business Review, 64*, 84-93.

Jones, J. M. (1972). *Prejudice and racism*. Reading, MA: Addison-Wesley.

Kanter, R. M. (1977). *Men and women of the corporation*. New York: Basic Books.

Kaplowitz, S. A. (1978). Towards a systemic theory of power attribution. *Social Psychology, 41*, 131-148.

Kipnis, D., Schmidt, S. M., & Wilkinson, I. (1980). Intraorganizational influence tactics: Exploration in getting one's way. *Journal of Applied Psychology, 65*, 440-452.

Korn/Ferry International & UCLA Anderson Graduate School of Management. (1992). *Decade of the executive woman*. New York: Korn/Ferry International.

Kossek, E. E., & Zonia, S. C. (1993). Assessing diversity climate: A field study of reactions to employer efforts to promote diversity. *Journal of Organizational Behavior, 14*, 61-81.

Kraiger, K., & Ford, J. K. (1985). A meta-analysis of ratee race effects in performance ratings. *Journal of Applied Psychology, 70*, 56-65.

Kram, K. E. (1985). *Mentoring at work*. Glenview, IL: Scott, Foresman.

Lachman, R. (1989). Power from what? A reexamination of its relationships with structural conditions. *Administrative Science Quarterly, 34*, 231-251.

Landy, F. J., & Farr, J. L. (1980). Performance rating. *Psychological Bulletin, 87*, 72-107.

Lee, J. A., & Brown, R. G. (1993). Hiring, firing, and promoting. In L. Diamant (Ed.), *Homosexual issues in the workplace* (pp. 45-62). Washington, DC: Taylor & Francis.

Levinson, D. J., Darrow, C. N., Klein, E. B., Levinson, M. H., & McKee, B. (1978). *The seasons of a man's life*. New York: Knopf.

Malone, B. L. (1982). *Relationship of Black female administrators' mentoring experience and career satisfaction*. Unpublished doctoral dissertation, University of Cincinnati.

Mechanic, D. (1962). Sources of power of lower participants in complex organizations. *Administrative Science Quarterly, 7*, 349-364.

Miller, C. L., & Cummins, A. G. (1992). An examination of women's perspectives on power. *Psychology of Women Quarterly, 16*, 415-428.

Moch, M. K. (1980). Racial differences in job satisfaction: Testing four common explanations. *Journal of Applied Psychology, 65*, 299-306.

Molm, L. D. (1985). Gender and power use: An experimental analysis of behavior and perceptions. *Social Psychology Quarterly, 48*, 285-300.

Morrison, A. M. (1992). *The new leaders: Guidelines on leadership diversity in America*. San Francisco: Jossey-Bass.

Morrison, A. M., & Von Glinow, M. A. (1990). Women and minorities in management. *American Psychologist, 45*(2), 200-208.

Morrison, A. M., White, R. P., & Van Velsor, E. (1987). *Breaking the glass ceiling: Can women reach the top of America's largest corporations?* Reading, MA: Addison-Wesley.

Murray, M. M. (1982). *The middle years of life of middle class Black men: An exploratory study*. Unpublished doctoral dissertation, University of Cincinnati.

Nedd, A. (1989). Cultural bases of individual differences in compliance gaining strategies: An exploratory study of Chinese in Singapore. In A. Nedd, G. R. Ferris, & K. Rowland (Eds.), *Research in personnel and human resources management* (Suppl. 1, pp. 79-95). Greenwich, CT: JAI Press.

Nkomo, S. (1992). The emperor has no clothes: Rewriting "race in organizations." *Academy of Management Review, 17*, 487-513.

Noe, R. A. (1988). Women and mentoring: A review and research agenda. *Academy of Management Review, 13*, 65-78.

Olian, J. D., Carroll, S. J., & Giannantonio, C. M. (1993). Mentor reactions to proteges: An experiment with managers. *Journal of Vocational Behavior, 43*, 266-278.

Ostroff, C., & Kozlowski, S. W. J. (1993). The role of mentoring in the information gathering processes of newcomers during early organizational socialization. *Journal of Vocational Behavior, 42*, 170-183.

Pettigrew, T. F. (1979). The ultimate attribution error: Extending Allport's cognitive analysis of prejudice. *Personality and Social Psychology Bulletin, 5*, 461-476.

Pettigrew, T. F., & Martin, J. (1987). Shaping the organizational context for Black American inclusion. *Journal of Social Issues, 43*, 41-78.

Pfeffer, J. (1981). *Power in organizations.* Boston: Pitman.

Phillips-Jones, L. L. (1983). Establishing a formalized mentoring program. *Training and Development Journal, 37*(2), 38-42.

Powell, G. N. (1988). *Women and men in management.* Newbury Park, CA: Sage.

Ragins, B. R. (1989). Barriers to mentoring: The female manager's dilemma. *Human Relations, 42*, 1-22.

Ragins, B. R., & Cotton, J. (1991). Easier said than done: Gender differences in perceived barriers to gaining a mentor. *Academy of Management Journal, 34*, 939-951.

Ragins, B. R., & Cotton, J. (1993). Gender and willingness to mentor in organizations. *Journal of Management, 19*, 97-111.

Ragins, B. R., & McFarlin, D. (1990). Perception of mentor roles in cross-gender mentoring relationships. *Journal of Vocational Behavior, 37*, 321-339.

Ragins, B. R., & Scandura, T. (1994a). Gender differences in expected outcomes of mentoring relationships. *Academy of Management Journal, 37*, 957-971.

Ragins, B. R., & Scandura, T. (1994b). Gender and the termination of mentoring relationships. In D. P. Moore (Ed.), *Academy of Management Best Paper Proceedings* (pp. 361-365). Dallas: Academy of Management.

Ragins, B. R., & Sundstrom, E. (1989). Gender and power in organizations: A longitudinal perspective. *Psychological Bulletin, 105*, 51-88.

Ragins, B. R., & Sundstrom, E. (1990). Gender and perceived power in manager-subordinate relations. *Journal of Occupational Psychology, 63*, 273-287.

Ragins, B. R., Sundstrom, E., & Thomas, J. B. (1993). Gender differences in attributions of power in manager-subordinate pairs. In D. P. Moore (Ed.), *Academy of Management Best Paper Proceedings* (pp. 368-372). Atlanta: Academy of Management.

Redmond, S. P. (1990). Mentoring and cultural diversity in academic settings. *American Behavioral Scientist, 34*, 188-200.

Rodriguez, A. M. (1987). Institutional racism in the organisational setting: An action-research approach. In J. W. Shaw, P. G. Nordlie, & R. M. Shapiro (Eds.), *Strategies for improving race relations: The Anglo-American experience* (pp. 128-148). Manchester, UK: Manchester University Press.

Rowe, M. P. (1990). Barriers to equality: The power of subtle discrimination to maintain unequal opportunity. *Employee Responsibilities and Rights Journal, 3*(2), 153-163.

Sagrestano, L. M. (1992). Power strategies in interpersonal relationships: The effects of expertise and gender. *Psychology of Women Quarterly, 16,* 481-495.

Scandura, T. A. (1992). Mentorship and career mobility: An empirical investigation. *Journal of Organizational Behavior, 13,* 169-174.

Scandura, T. A., & Ragins, B. R. (1993). The effects of sex and gender role orientation on mentorship in male-dominated occupations. *Journal of Vocational Behavior, 43,* 251-265.

Schein, E. H. (1985). *Organizational culture and leadership.* San Francisco: Jossey-Bass.

Schneider, B., & Reichers, A. (1983). On the etiology of climates. *Personnel Psychology, 36,* 19-39.

Schockett, M. R., & Haring-Hidore, M. (1985). Factor analytic support for psychosocial and vocational mentoring functions. *Psychological Reports, 57,* 627-630.

Stewart, L. P., & Gudykunst, W. B. (1982). Differential factors influencing the hierarchical level and number of promotions of males and females within an organization. *Academy of Management Journal, 25,* 586-597.

Stroh, L. K., Brett, J. M., & Reilly, A. H. (1992). All the right stuff: A comparison of female and male managers' career progression. *Journal of Applied Psychology, 77,* 251-260.

Swerdlik, M. E., & Bardon, J. I. (1988). A survey of mentoring experiences in school psychology. *Journal of School Psychology, 26,* 213-224.

Taps, J., & Martin, P. Y. (1990). Gender composition, attributional accounts, and women's influence and likability in task groups. *Small Group Research, 21,* 471-491.

Thomas, D. A. (1989). Mentoring and irrationality: The role of racial taboos. *Human Resource Management, 28,* 279-290.

Thomas, D. A. (1990). The impact of race on managers' experiences of developmental relationships (mentoring and sponsorship): An intra-organizational study. *Journal of Organizational Behavior, 11,* 479-492.

Thomas, D. A. (1993). Racial dynamics in cross-race developmental relationships. *Administrative Science Quarterly, 38,* 169-194.

Thomas, D. A., & Alderfer, C. P. (1989). The influence of race on career dynamics: Theory and research on minority career experiences. In M. B. Arthur, D. T. Hall, & B. S. Lawrence (Eds.), *Handbook of career theory* (pp. 133-158). Cambridge, MA: Cambridge University Press.

Thomas, R. R., Jr. (1990, March-April). From affirmative action to affirming diversity. *Harvard Business Review,* pp. 107-117.

Thomas, R. R., Jr. (1991). *Beyond race and gender: Unleashing the power of your total work force by managing diversity.* New York: Amacom.

Triandis, H. C. (1989). The self and social behavior in differing cultural contexts. *Psychological Review, 96,* 506-520.

Triandis, H. C., Bontempo, R., Villareal, M. J., Asai, M., & Lucca, N. (1988). Individualism and collectivism: Cross-cultural perspectives on self-ingroup relationships. *Journal of Personality and Social Psychology, 54,* 323-338.

Trompenaars, F. (1993). *Riding the waves of culture: Understanding cultural diversity in business.* London: Economist Books.

U.S. Department of Labor. (1990). *Breaking the glass ceiling in the 1990's.* Washington, DC: Author.

Weber, M. (1947). *The theory of social and economic organization* (A. M. Henderson & T. Parsons, Eds. and Trans.). New York: Free Press.

Whitely, W., Dougherty, T. W., & Dreher, G. F. (1991). Relationship of career mentoring and socioeconomic origin to managers' and professionals' early career progress. *Academy of Management Journal, 34,* 331-351.

Wiley, M. G., & Eskilson, A. (1982). The interaction of sex and power base on perceptions of managerial effectiveness. *Academy of Management Journal, 25,* 671-677.

Wilson, J. A., & Elman, N. S. (1990). Organizational benefits of mentoring. *Academy of Management Executive, 4*(4), 88-94.

Wolf, W. C., & Fligstein, N. D. (1979). Sex and authority in the workplace: The causes of sexual inequality. *American Sociological Review, 44,* 235-252.

5

Diversity in Decision-Making Teams
All Differences Are Not Created Equal

VALERIE I. SESSA
SUSAN E. JACKSON

D iversity is a fundamental fact in today's business organizations. Even in the most traditional U.S. company, employees differ from each other by tenure, technical and business backgrounds, educational background and level, organizational level, and socioeconomic status. And now, diversity is increasing in terms of ethnicity, sex, and age (Jackson & Alvarez, 1992). During the late 1980s, the term *workforce diversity* suddenly gained currency as a way to refer to these many types of differences among employees. Since then, in some of the more progressive firms, attention to issues of workforce diversity has had a profound impact on many areas of the organization. Personnel policies, benefits packages, career paths, work schedules, training programs, and even office parties are now being examined for the potentially negative consequences they may have for those who differ from "traditional" employees—that is, the ones who have usually been in positions of power.

By changing their official policies and many personnel practices, employers are addressing some of the previously unquestioned biases that can interfere with effective organizational functioning. But such changes are only a first step. Organizations also need to develop a much better understanding of exactly how workforce diversity affects interpersonal dynamics among employees as they work at various types of tasks.

Because businesses are rapidly restructuring around work teams (versus individual contributors), understanding the dynamics of diversity within work teams is especially important. In today's business environment, work teams often bring together diverse organization members in hopes of reaping the potential benefits of having people with different points of view address the same problem. From top management teams (e.g., see Hambrick, 1994) to self-managed work teams (e.g., see Lawler, Mohrman, & Ledford, 1992), in offices and on the factory floor, organizations are intentionally creating situations where people can argue about their differences of opinion. At the same time, managers are realizing that harnessing diversity in a synergistic manner is difficult (Sessa, Jackson, & Rapini, in press). Managing the assets and liabilities of diversity effectively requires a thorough understanding of how and why diversity affects the behaviors of teams and their members.

To date, much of the literature on workforce diversity has implicitly assumed that different types of diversity (e.g., in age, gender, or ethnicity) are more or less equal in their consequences. For example, in many organizations, the argument has been made that organizations should value diversity because, in general, diversity should improve the performance of decision-making and problem-solving teams. The assumption behind this argument is that diversity of all kinds is associated with differing ideas, perspectives, skills, and abilities (see Jackson, 1992), and that when all of these differences are brought to bear on a problem, there is a performance benefit. In organizational settings, the argument that diversity results in improved problem solving within teams often is assumed to hold regardless of the dimensions of diversity under consideration.

While organizations recognize the potential value of diversity, they also recognize that diversity creates its own problems. Indeed, the current interest in managing diversity grew out of the recognition that people often do not get along as well with other organizational members who are dissimilar as they do with people who are similar. Here again, broad generalizations are assumed to apply. Thus in-groups and out-groups might be based on sex, race, age, tenure, occupational specialty, and so on, but regardless of which of these characteristics might be relevant in a setting, the same dynamics are assumed to unfold.

We refer to this view of diversity, which assumes that characteristics such as race, gender, age, and so on are all more or less equal in their consequences, as the "horizontal" perspective (Blau, 1977). In the horizontal perspective, it is the fact of difference alone that is viewed as central. Based on our knowledge of a wide range of psychological literature, we assert that the horizontal perspective is implicitly assumed by many psychologists. In contrast, in the sociological literature, the explicit assumption underlying much of the research related to issues of diversity is that differences among people are the basis for "vertical" differentiation (Blau, 1977). That is, differences serve as a cue that is used to assign people to positions in a hierarchy of asymmetrical power relationships.

To understand how diversity affects the dynamics of work teams and the longer term outcomes of these teams, we believe that both perspectives must be used. Perhaps because the two perspectives are rooted in two different disciplines, however, research that incorporates the two dimensions is scarce. Therefore a major objective of this chapter is to consider how the psychological study of decision making in work teams might be enriched if it were to incorporate the vertical perspective.

A Framework for
Understanding the Consequences of Diversity

Based on a review of literatures in social psychology, organizational psychology, management, and sociology, Jackson, May, and Whitney (in press) proposed a theoretical framework for considering the complex consequences of diversity within decision-making teams. Because it provides a broad overview of the literature, we use this framework to guide our discussion.

Jackson et al.'s framework includes two components: a general causal model and a taxonomy of relevant constructs. These two components are shown in Figures 5.1 and 5.2, respectively.

As shown in Figure 5.1, Jackson et al.'s framework organizes constructs into four general categories that are linked as follows:

aspects of diversity → mediating states and processes → short-term behavioral
manifestations → longer term consequences

Furthermore, constructs are arrayed vertically to reflect three levels of analysis: individual, interpersonal, and team. The framework assumes that

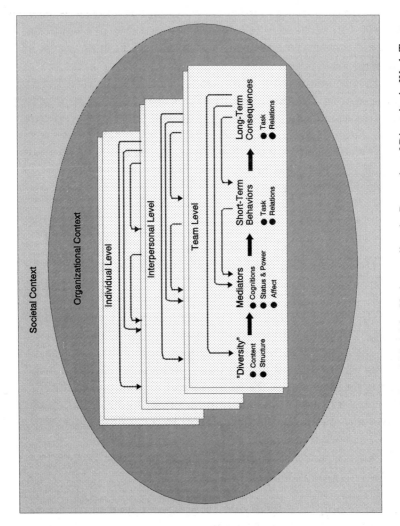

Figure 5.1. General Causal Model for Understanding the Dynamics of Diversity in Work Teams

SOURCE: S. E. Jackson, K. E. May, and K. Whitney. Copyrighted material, used with permission of authors.

phenomena are best understood by a consideration of the dynamics that arise at all of these levels of analysis.

As shown in Figure 5.2, the framework also recognizes some fundamental distinctions that can be made among the types of diversity that might characterize a work team. Specifically, aspects of diversity that are most directly associated with a team's acknowledged objectives are labeled task related, while those that form the context of more general social relationships are labeled relations-oriented. For example, in a product design team, work experiences and educational background would probably be task related, whereas age would be relations oriented. Within each of these two broad categories, the framework further distinguishes personal characteristics (attributes) that are readily detectable from those that are underlying. This distinction reflects the fact that some characteristics are more subject to construal and more psychological in nature. Underlying attributes are often used as explanations for the effects of diversity that are found when diversity is operationalized using readily detectable attributes (e.g., people who differ in educational level, a readily detectable attribute, are assumed to differ in their knowledge, skills, and abilities, which are attributes underlying educational level).

Although Jackson et al.'s presentation of the task versus relations-oriented attribute categories and the detectable versus underlying attribute categories implies dichotomous distinctions, many attributes are likely to be somewhat mixed or ambiguous. For example, ethnicity is often (but not always) readily detectable as well as being socially constructed by both self and others. Furthermore, for some tasks (e.g., developing a marketing campaign for a new cosmetic product), ethnicity may be a task-related attribute as well as an attribute that affects social relations. Thus these features of attributes should be recognized as partially dependent on the situational context.

In presenting their framework, Jackson et al. did not elaborate the distinction we are drawing out here between horizontal and vertical differentiation. Such differentiation is implied by terms such as *power* and *status,* however, included in Figure 5.2. We turn next to a discussion of the distinction between horizontal and vertical differentiation.

To illustrate how our understanding of team decision making can be enhanced by considering the joint effects of horizontal and vertical differentiation, we must first review what is known about the consequences of each type of diversity, beginning with the horizontal dimension.

1. Aspects of Diversity: Content and Structure	2. Mediating States and Processes	3. Short-term Behavioral Manifestations	4. Longer-term Consequences
		Level of Analysis: Individual	
Readily detectable attributes:	Task-related:	Task-related:	Task-related:
•Task-related: organizational tenure, team tenure, dep't./unit membership, memberships in task-relevant external networks, formal credentials, educational level •Relations-oriented: sex, culture (race, ethnicity, national origin), age, memberships in formal organizations (e.g., religious and political), physical features Underlying attributes: •Task-related: knowledge, skills, abilities (cognitive and physical), experience •Relations-oriented: social status, attitudes, values, personality, behavioral style, extra-team social ties	•Information processing (e.g., attention, recall) •Learning (e.g., discovery, creativity) •Task-based information •Power to control tangible resources •Power to control human resources Relations-oriented: •Social cognitive processes: operation of stereotypes and schema-based expectancies •Affective responses: attraction, anxiety, fear, guilt, frustration, discomfort	•Seeking/offering/receiving work-related information, tangible resources, or human resources •Initiating/responding to influence attempts Relations-oriented: •Seeking/offering/receiving social information and/or support	•Personal performance (speed, creativity, accuracy) •Satisfaction w/ performance of self and team •Acquisition of knowledge and skills re: technical aspects of task, managing human and tangible resources •Establishment of position in work communication networks Relations-oriented: •Acquisition of interpersonal knowledge and skills re: interpersonal aspects of task, •Establishment of position in social communication networks (within team and in external environment) •Satisfaction with social relationships

Level of Analysis: Interpersonal			
•Interpersonal (dis)similarity in terms of readily detectable and underlying attributes: Dyadic Individual-to-subgroup Individual-to-team	Task-related: •Differences in task-based cognitions •Expertise-based status differentials •Differences in power over tangible and/or human resources Relations-oriented: •Social familiarity •Diffuse status differentials •Differences in social cognitions •Differences in affective responses	Task-related: •Exchanges/negotiations/consolidation of task-related information, tangible resources, or human resources Relations-oriented: •Exchanges/consolidation of social information and/or support	Task-related: •Power balance Relations-oriented: •Status hierarchy •Balance of interpersonal accounts (e.g., political debts and credits) •Solidification of friendship coalitions

Level of Analysis: Team			
•Team composition: heterogeneity versus homogeneity of readily detectable and underlying attributes •Special configurations: Presence of "tokens" Presence of small minority faction Bipolar team composition	Task-related: •Shape of expertise-based status hierarchy •Patterns of task-based cognitions •Shape of power distributions for control of tangible and/or human resources Relations-oriented: •Stage of team socialization •Shape of diffuse social status hierarchy •Patterns of social cognitions •Patterns of affective responses across team members	Task-related: •Task-related communication networks •Allocation and use of tangible and human resources •Influence networks Relations-oriented: •Friendship communication networks	Task-related: •Team performance (speed, accuracy, creativity) •Team satisfaction with performance •Team learning about technical aspects of task, and management of tangible and human resources Relations-oriented: •Membership stability •Adoption of social structures (e.g., norms & roles, influence networks, friendship networks)

Figure 5.2. Primary Constructs in a Framework for Understanding the Dynamics of Diversity in Work Teams
SOURCE: S. E. Jackson, K. E. May, and K. Whitney. Copyrighted material, used with permission of authors.

Horizontal Perspective

Diversity and Long-Term Consequences

Discussions of the effects of diversity within task teams often seem to begin with the assumption that "all differences are created equal." That is, categories for classifying people are considered nominal; differences between people are treated as horizontal and symmetrical; and attention is focused on the possible benefits of approaching a problem from diverse perspectives. This perspective is clearly evident in discussion of decision aids, such as brainstorming methods, devil's advocacy, and dialectical inquiry (Schweiger, Sandberg, & Rechner, 1989; Schwenk, 1983). Within the horizontal perspective, diversity within a decision-making team is recognized as important primarily because it is associated with the resources available during the decision-making process—especially task-related cognitive resources. For example, in creative and decision-making tasks, demographic diversity often is assumed to be associated with differences in the perspectives, attitudes, skills, and abilities of team members. Differences in experiences and perspectives lead team members to approach problems and decisions drawing on different information, from different angles, and with different attitudes. Therefore teams composed of people with diverse backgrounds and characteristics are expected to produce a wider variety of ideas, alternatives, and solutions—and thus perform better—than teams composed of people who are similar in terms of demographic characteristics.

Empirical evidence from both laboratory and field settings indicates that team composition is related to longer term team consequences such as performance of individuals within the team (e.g., Nemeth, 1992) and the team as a whole on some tasks (e.g., Jackson, 1992). Although the link is more complex, there is also evidence that management team diversity predicts organizational outcomes, including innovation and strategic direction (e.g., Bantel & Jackson, 1989; Finkelstein & Hambrick, 1990; Michel & Hambrick, 1992; Murray, 1989; Wiersema & Bantel, 1992).

Interestingly, although research and theory based in the horizontal approach suggest that diversity has a positive impact on performance, diversity is hypothesized to have the opposite effect on cohesion. Why? Theory suggests that greater diversity leads to lower satisfaction and higher turnover because interpersonal similarity is one of the most important determinants of interpersonal attraction (Byrne, 1971), which in turn creates a social context for relationships among organizational members. Further, theory suggests that through processes of attraction, selection, and attrition, similar others are invited to and are more likely to join teams, while pressures are formed to encourage dissimilar others to leave (Schneider, 1987).

Empirical evidence tends to support these theoretical arguments. Thus individuals who differ from their teammates or work unit members on sex and race are more likely to report a lower commitment to their organization, less intent of staying, and more absences than those who are in teams that are similar in terms of these variables. Although some evidence suggests that being different in sex has a more negative effect on organizational attachment for men than for women and that being different in race has a more negative effect on attachment for Whites than for non-Whites (Tsui, Egan, & O'Reilly, 1992), other evidence demonstrates that minorities are slightly less committed to the group than nonminorities (Kirchmeyer & Cohen, 1992). In terms of turnover, several studies have shown that age and tenure diversity decrease organizational commitment and increase turnover (Jackson et al., 1991; McCain, O'Reilly, & Pfeffer, 1983; O'Reilly, Caldwell, & Barnett, 1989; Wagner, Pfeffer, & O'Reilly, 1984). In addition, in top management teams, diversity in terms of college alma mater, curriculum studied, and industry experiences is associated with higher rates of turnover (Jackson et al., 1991). This association between diversity and turnover has also been noted in non-U.S. settings (Wiersema & Bird, 1993).

Diversity and Short-Term
Behavioral Manifestations

In the Jackson et al. (in press) framework, short-term behavioral manifestations of diversity involve observable phenomena, such as communications and the exercising of influence, which might explain how diversity influences longer term consequences. Communications among team members are viewed as particularly important. In the broadest sense, communications involve the management of task- and relations-oriented information. They involve producing, transmitting (sending), and interpreting (receiving) symbols (Roloff, 1987)—through verbal as well as nonverbal channels, directly and indirectly, passively and actively (e.g., see Miller & Jablin, 1991). Presumably, employees engage in work-related communications which involve descriptive and evaluative task information, primarily for instrumental purposes. In contrast, friendship communications, which involve social information (e.g., support), carry their own intrinsic value (Brass, 1984; Ibarra, 1990). Although communications often involve relatively benign exchanges, influence communications engaged in for the purpose of changing the attitudes, values, beliefs, and behaviors of others are particularly potent, which is why they are highlighted in the taxonomy presented by Jackson et al. (in press). Through their communications, work teams manage information, tangible resources (e.g., equipment, tools, money), and human resources (e.g., skills, effort).

When differences in perspectives, expertise, and attitudes are conceptualized as horizontal differentiation, the assumption made is that all team members will communicate more or less equally with each other and express their differing views. Presumably, the eventual solution agreed to by the team simply reflects the team's best efforts to understand and integrate these diverse views and find a solution that is acceptable to everyone.

Actually, however, the short-term behavioral manifestations that account for observed longer term consequences are not yet well understood, because few studies of team diversity have included observations of behavior within the team. Instead, diversity is treated as the causal variable, outcomes are assessed, and then inferences are made about the likely behaviors that account for the observed outcomes.

Contradictory Evidence

Associated with the horizontal perspective is an assumption that decision making in teams is a relatively rational process that is driven primarily by a concern for finding the best solution. While cognitive biases and errors in information processing may interfere with good decision making, presumably it is the human cognitive apparatus that is the major source of such interference—interpersonal factors often are assumed to be of less consequence. The assumption is that team members who have different viewpoints and perspectives will actively discuss these and perhaps generate conflict among the members, resulting eventually in a good team decision.

Contrary to this scenario, however, studies of communication patterns in work organizations indicate that demographic diversity has an impact on communication patterns among coworkers. For example, a study of communication networks in five organizations found that demographic homogeneity (on the dimensions of authority, education, sex, race, and organization branch) consistently affected work-communication chains, suggesting that diversity decreases communication overall (Lincoln & Miller, 1979). Other studies of communication patterns have shown that informal networks are segregated along demographic lines (Brass, 1984), that formal and informal meetings among peers and with immediate subordinates are fewer in racially diverse groups (Hoffman, 1985), and that age and tenure similarities between coworkers predict levels of communication among project teams of engineers (Zenger & Lawrence, 1989). Consistent with these findings for teams and larger work units, similarity among friendship pairs has been found for a variety of readily detectable and underlying attributes, including age, sex, race, education, prestige, social class, attitudes, and beliefs (e.g., Berscheid, 1985; Brass, 1984; Byrne, 1971; Cohen, 1977; Ibarra, 1992; McPherson & Smith-Lovin, 1987).

It seems likely that diversity would affect influence patterns as well as friendship patterns. This notion is supported by research on attitude change and persuasion, which shows that people are more likely to be influenced by the opinions of demographically and ideologically similar others (McGuire, 1985). Conversely, influence attempts may be more likely to be directed toward others who are dissimilar. In the latter case, diverse teams would be characterized by relatively more, and relatively less effective, influence communications.

Diversity as Vertical Differentiation: Status Characteristics

Theory

In contrast to an approach that considers diversity to represent horizontal differentiation, when attention is focused on the construct of status, the initial assumption is that differences among team members create a rank ordering within the team, which we refer to as vertical differentiation. This perspective acknowledges that observed decision-making processes seldom fit the idealized, rational model of decision-making. Instead, available resources may not be fully identified and used by the team (Bottger & Yetton, 1988; Stasser

& Titus, 1985), and the final decision may be shaped by irrelevant and unintentional dynamics among team members. In other words, the texture of interactions observed within decision-making teams is not a function of task-based cognitions alone. Observed behaviors also reflect differential status and hence differential power over tangible and human resources. For example, in one recent study of groups engaged in face-to-face interactions, researchers demonstrated that (a) more ideas were generated in groups characterized by low (versus high) status differentiation, and (b) in the status differentiated groups, even ideas that were generated and discussed were censored and not entered into the written record (Silver, Cohen, & Crutchfield, 1994). Such effects reflect the "process losses" identified by Steiner (1972).

Much of the research relevant to understanding the consequences of diversity for the nature of communications has been conducted to test hypotheses about the formation and consequences of status characteristics (Berger, Cohen, & Zelditch, 1966). A theory of status organizing processes that has been extensively tested is status characteristics theory (SCT; Berger, Rosenholtz, & Zelditch, 1980). SCT specifies the processes through which evaluations of and beliefs about the characteristics of team members become the basis of observable inequalities in face-to-face social interactions.

A status characteristic is any characteristic that influences one's own and others' evaluations and beliefs about oneself. Status characteristics can be specifically relevant to the task at hand (e.g., mathematical ability in a mathematical problem-solving group), or people may judge each other based on characteristics that have little to do with actual competence. Such characteristics, called diffuse characteristics, include physical attractiveness, gender, race, and age. SCT posits that status characteristics become apparent in the context of a collective task, that is, for tasks defined by a team goal as opposed to individual goals. Team goals have four essential properties: There are two or more possible outcomes; contributions from team members influence the final outcome; one solution is better than another; and there can be only one outcome.

According to SCT, task-specific and diffuse characteristics lead to unequal interactions through a three-step process: activation, establishing relevance, and translation.

Activation. If team members differ on status characteristics and the differences are salient, then the beliefs and evaluations associated with those status characteristics become activated or operative. More than one characteristic may become activated at a time. For example, when interacting with a male clerk regarding the most efficient way to install drywall, a female carpenter would be ranked low on gender status characteristic and high on occupational status.

Relevance. SCT assumes that status characteristics are used as cues in interactions unless a characteristic is demonstrated not to be relevant. Thus, for collective tasks that require team members to estimate their own and others' abilities, even diffuse status cues, such as gender, may be used. The more direct the linkage between a status characteristic and the task, however, the more important the status cue is likely to be. In this example, carpentry should have a closer link to drywalling than gender, although both characteristics may be activated in the interaction.

Translation. Activation and relevance provide team members with information that enables them to define their immediate task situation. On the basis of this information, specific expectations about relative levels of required task ability are formed for both the self and others in the interaction. These expectations determine the power and prestige order in that group in that particular situation. Power and prestige rankings, in turn, are translated into interaction patterns. Specifically, relative levels of participation, influence attempts, influence acceptance, and evaluations follow from the power and prestige rankings (e.g., see Cohen & Silver, 1989).

Vertical Differentiation and Short-Term Behavioral Manifestations

Substantial evidence indicates that demographic cues trigger status assignments quickly, and that unfairly low (nontask) status assignments prove difficult to undo (Ridgeway, 1982), in part because the behavioral effects of initial status attributions are so pervasive. Compared with those with lower status, higher status persons display more assertive nonverbal behaviors during communication; speak more often, criticize more, state more commands, and interrupt others more often; have more opportunity to exert influence, attempt to exert influence more, and are actually more influential; and they are evaluated more positively and have higher self-esteem (Levine & Moreland, 1990). Evidence supporting SCT has most often been generated in laboratory settings. As is typical for laboratory studies, most of the evidence comes from observations of dyads (not teams) of students who do not know each other, and often the effects of only one status characteristic have been considered. Less research has been conducted on long-standing work teams in which multiple status characteristics are operative, and the team may work on a variety of different tasks (with the exception of Cohen & Zhou, 1991). Thus there is much opportunity to add to our knowledge by conducting more research in field settings.

Vertical Differentiation and Long-Term Consequences

Findings such as those cited above indicate that participation and input on task-related decision-making activities is likely to be unequal among members of teams characterized by greater status differentiation, with lower status members participating less. Given that demographic characteristics are the cues used in the initial assignments of status, such evidence suggests that status differentiation may translate into long-term consequences for both individuals and team members. Some evidence is available to support this notion. Specifically, in one experiment, subjects given arbitrarily high status indicators outperformed subjects given arbitrarily low status indicators (Jemmott & Gonzalez, 1989). Attributions about the reasons that account for the high performance of team members are also associated with their status. High status leads to attributions of high skill across both easy and difficult tasks, but low status results in attributions to luck during difficult tasks and skill during easy tasks (Zimmer & Sheposh, 1975).

Less research has assessed the influence of vertical differentiation on the team as a whole. However, theoretically, to the extent that status hierarchies do not match distributions of task-relevant expertise, unequal participation rates are likely to interfere with team performance because available resources will not be fully used. Teams may assign roles that are consistent with stereotypes rather than attending to the actual underlying attributes of team members, potentially leading to inappropriate assignments of roles and responsibilities. Thus vertical differentiation would have a negative impact on team performance, because team members believe that the ideas voiced by higher status members (who are also attributed greater skill or ability) are superior. Lower status members may never voice their own ideas, alternatives, or opinions, or disagree with the alternatives proposed by the higher status members. If they do voice them, the ideas may be discounted because they come from lower status (and therefore lower ability) members (e.g., see

Cohen & Silver, 1989; Silver, Cohen, & Rainwater, 1988; Silver et al., 1994). The differences in experiences and perspectives arising from the diversity of the team members that lead team members to approach problems and decisions drawing on different information, from different angles and with different attitudes, are never allowed or brought out in the team.

Recent theory and research suggests that status characteristics also affect individual satisfaction and comfort. Initially, group members behave more positively toward higher status members (Zander & Cohen, 1955), perhaps because higher status newcomers contribute to a positive group identity (Turner, 1987). Newcomers, in turn, are able to detect a group's affective reaction to them, and newcomers then reflect this reaction back to the group. This process is aptly referred to as a "two-way mirror" by some researchers (Davis, 1963, 1971) and as "perceptual reciprocity" by others (Ibrahim, 1970). Thus positive affect appears to operate like a lubricant that smooths the adjustments that must occur during socialization. In addition, due to the social exchange value of high status, old-timers may be more willing to adjust their own behavior to accommodate higher status newcomers than they are for lower status newcomers.

On the other hand, Ridgeway and Johnson (1990) argued that low-status team members often elicit negative responses from others (disagreement), but because of their low status they must absorb the negative reactions rather than respond and defend their positions. A team member who receives disagreement from another is, in turn, more likely to experience negative affect or dissatisfaction. This reasoning suggests that lower status members will be more dissatisfied with the team, compared with higher status members, and there is some evidence to support this logic (Kirchmeyer & Cohen, 1992). Little research has assessed the influence of vertical differentiation on the cohesion of the team as a whole. More theory and research are needed in this area to determine whether and how vertical differentiation affects the team as a whole.

Future Research Issues

In this chapter, we have suggested that considering vertical differentiation of team members in addition to horizontal differentiation is worthwhile and necessary to fully understand the influence of diversity on work teams. To date, however, little research has been designed to explore simultaneously the impact of both horizontal and vertical dimensions of diversity on team effectiveness. However, our own exploratory research (Sessa & Jackson, 1994) supports the general view that this distinction is worthy of future attention. In a study of medical decision-making teams, we found that these different types of diversity were differentially useful in predicting team performance and team satisfaction. Additionally, this field study of intact groups found that, consistent with laboratory research, diffuse status characteristics (i.e., status based on race, age, highest degree, and level in the hospital) that were not clearly related to a team's decision task nevertheless predicted many aspects of interactions among team members, including frequency and timing of participation in the discussion, contributions to the task, and the probability of initiating conflict with other team members. Our research supported our initial belief about the value of conducting research that draws the distinction between horizontal and vertical differentiation. But perhaps more important, it alerted us to several difficulties other researchers are likely to experience as they conduct research of this type. In closing, we address three of these: construct measurement, the multidimensionality of status profiles, and the development of theory.

Measurement Issues

Perhaps the most significant issue that arises in the field studies concerns the conceptualization and operationalization of vertical differentiation or status. As we have mentioned, most research on SCT has relied on dyads as the unit for study. In laboratory studies of dyadic relationships, status conceptualization and measurement can be a simple matter. An experimental manipulation is introduced so that one person has high status on one salient status indicator while the other person is assigned to a low-status position. Through random assignment to status conditions, all other status characteristics are held constant.

Use of work teams in organizations renders the conceptualization and measurement of status more complex. Much complication is introduced simply by the fact that in work teams typically more than two people are involved. This has several consequences. First, status now has more levels than simply lower and higher, which means that multiple patterns of status orderings become possible, depending in part on the size of the team. Second, in the real world, status characteristics are likely to be correlated, not independent. Third, each person's status can now be conceptualized in relation to (a) the team as a whole and (b) each other person or subgroup of people within the team. Fourth, when more than two people are included for observation, a decision must be made about how to calibrate the status metric. Previous research has implicitly treated the degree of differences in status levels as equivalent. Thus such research might lead one to expect that interactions between a team member with a Ph.D. and a team member with an M.A. would be the same as the interactions between a team member with a Ph.D. and one with a high school degree. However, interactions between members with large status differences may not be the same as interactions between members with small status differences. Finally, in different teams, different levels of the status indicator may represent high or low status. For example (again using educational status indicators), in some teams members with a Ph.D. might be ranked the highest. In other teams where there are no members with Ph.D.s, a member with an M.A. or a B.A. might be ranked highest. Because of issues such as these, calibrating status across teams is difficult. Furthermore, comparing results across different studies may be problematic.

One way to address some of these measurement problems is by computing status as a within-team standardized score. In this way, the team member (or members) with the highest status indicator in the team automatically receives the highest score and the member(s) with the lowest status indicator receives the lowest score. Each other member on the team is placed on the underlying continuum that links these two status positions. We recognize, however, that this is only a partial solution because standardized scores fail to reflect the pattern of a team's status hierarchy. That is, standardizing scores does not differentiate between teams that are polarized into two extreme status subgroups and those that include a more or less continuous and smooth distribution of status gradations. Yet such differences in team composition may have important consequences for team interactions. To the extent such patterns are as important as relative status, more sophisticated statistical indicators may be needed.

Multidimensionality of Attribute Profiles

A second issue in developing operationalizations of status in long-standing work teams is the question of whether teams as a whole develop a single status hierarchy based on the many different and possibly conflicting status indicators within the team. Previous research has assumed that a single status hierarchy emerges within a team in a relatively short period of time and that once this hierarchy emerges it is stable over time. This suggests that each team member receives a unique position in the status hierarchy and the best way to measure this is by deriving a single status indicator for each team member. Yet, as we know, demography-based status rankings in society (e.g., sex and race) are not always consistent with organizationally derived status rankings (e.g., hierarchical rank), and both may be different than task-derived status rankings (e.g., technical expertise).

There are at least two options to empirically creating a single status indicator for each team member. First, the researcher could ask team members to delineate the status hierarchy in their team by having them rank or rate team members. Second, status could be operationalized empirically as multidimensional, with no attempt being made to develop a single status hierarchy within the team. Initially, the best option may be a combination of these two approaches. In combination, having both types of data would allow researchers to establish both which types of diversity have observable consequences and which types of diversity research participants attend to in forming their own subjective status hierarchies. Such information could further inform us about the mediating processes through which team diversity is translated into behavior.

Developing More Theory

On a related issue, this chapter alludes to the need for and importance of further theory development. While research continues to demonstrate that diversity does have an impact on the outcomes of work teams, less work has been done to understand why diversity has an impact. To develop our understanding of diversity, scientists must determine which kinds of diversity really matter. (For example, is it race that causes team members to interact in certain ways, or is it an underlying construct such as status that causes such an interaction, in which case race is only one possible operationalization?)

Second, better theories are needed to understand what outcomes are affected by different types or dimensions of diversity and when. The taxonomy reviewed here (Jackson et al., in press) lists both short-term behavioral manifestations and longer term consequences, and it also includes both potentially positive and potentially negative outcomes. Whereas researchers tend to focus on one or two outcomes, teams must deal with and perhaps actively manage multiple outcomes. This suggests that teams may proceed through phases, with the consequences of diversity varying across the phases. For example, while diversity may initially create conflict and feelings of dissatisfaction, teams that are able to use their diversity effectively during the early stages of task performance may subsequently show increased cohesiveness and openness to new ideas (see Watson, Kumar, & Michaelson, 1993).

Implications for Organizations

The framework developed by Jackson et al. (in press) and the analysis described in this chapter suggest that practitioners interested in the topic of diversity need to consider the consequences of both vertical differentiation and horizontal differentiation to fully understand the influence of workforce diversity on work team interactions and to ensure the team capitalizes on the benefits of diversity.

Recently, a television advertisement for a razor featured a man shaving with a voice-over saying "sometimes to be different is to be better." This statement would only make sense, and people would only understand it, if the common assumption were the opposite: To be different is often considered to be worse (Morrison, Ruderman, & Hughes-James, 1993, p. 11). In U.S. society, and particularly in the business community, the standard for comparison often is a White, middle-class, middle-age or older, male manager. As predicted by SCT, in the context of work teams, those who look different or have a different background are often viewed as less able or less qualified. Thus they may hold back before joining discussions, offer fewer performance outputs, verbalize fewer negative evaluations, initiate fewer conflicts, and participate less overall. These actions often are legitimized in the team by all members, including those with both high and low status. To ameliorate these tendencies, organizations may wish to consciously create decision-making and problem-solving teams that are less stratified in terms of status. They may also find it useful to familiarize team members with the causes and effects of the status hierarchies within a team. And, finally, they may want to create situations that will cause status hierarchies to arise due to expertise and not due to nonrelevant status characteristics (e.g., see Heilman, 1994).

Equalizing Hierarchy and
Status Differences in Teams

One option available to the practitioner who is developing a team-based organization is to equalize the hierarchy and status differences within the team. Organization change efforts targeted at establishing an egalitarian corporate culture may accomplish this in the long run, but in the short run it may be expedient to limit the team to members who are at a similar level in the organization. Other possibilities include dividing the team into equal-status subgroups and then training a team leader to integrate the output of the subgroups.

Diversity Training

In many cases, creating teams that are more equal in status along some status-based characteristics is inconvenient, impossible, or even illegal. Another mechanism to improve the benefits of diversity, while mitigating potential liabilities, is through training the team to be aware of and to guard against the influence of vertical diversity. One implication suggested by SCT theory is that practitioners who are concerned with using what we know about SCT to promote change should be certain to seek to change the behaviors of all parties involved. Because status hierarchies affect the behaviors of everyone, training will not be effective if it focuses, for example, only on training low-status members to behave like high-status members or, conversely, if it focuses only on training high-status members to be more sensitive to their impact on low-status members. Additionally, it is not enough for a lower status member to learn to be assertive and say in a team meeting that he or she was interrupted or has not been able to make a point. Higher status members must also actively ask for and legitimately consider performance outputs from lower status members.

Technology Mediated Teams

A third possibility that is rising in popularity in organizations is designing teams and team meetings to make use of the myriad choices of technology available. Thus teams may work in meetings using Electronic Meeting Support Systems (Kranz & Sessa, 1994). Or they may rarely meet face-to-face, depending instead on such technologies as whiteboards, video- or teleconferencing, electronic mail, and facsimile machines. Technology helps ensure anonymity so that when an idea is put forth, it is judged on its own merit, not by the location on the status hierarchy of the team member who put it forth (e.g., also see Armstrong & Cole, 1994; Poole, Holmes, & DeSanctis, 1991; Sproull & Kiesler, 1986).

The objective of this chapter was to induce both the scientist and the practitioner to broaden how they think about diversity to include both horizontal and vertical differentiation. From the researchers, we called for theory and research designed to give us a better understanding of how diversity affects short-term behavior manifestations and longer term consequences, without assuming that all diversity has the same impact on the team. This means gaining a better comprehension of the mediating states and processes that arise due to diversity. From the practitioners, we called for procedures that will help teams gain the benefits of diversity as well as help them deal with some of the liabilities of diversity. We offered three possibilities, including creating teams that are equal vertically, training teams to recognize and impede the influence of vertical diversity, and creating situations that actually hinder the development of a status hierarchy based on irrelevant characteristics. We hope this chapter encourages such changes and infuses the field with creative ideas to take our understanding of diversity to a more mature level.

References

Armstrong, D. J., & Cole, P. (1994). *Managing geographic, temporal and cultural distances in distributed work groups.* Cambridge, MA: Armstrong & Cole.

Bantel, K. A., & Jackson, S. E. (1989). Top management and innovations in banking: Does the composition of the top team make a difference? *Strategic Management Journal, 10* (Special issue), 107-124.

Berger, J., Cohen, B. P., & Zelditch, M., Jr. (1966). Status characteristics and expectation states. In J. Berger, M. Zelditch Jr., & B. Anderson (Eds.), *Sociological theories in progress* (pp. 47-73). Boston: Houghton-Mifflin.

Berger, J., Rosenholtz, S. J., & Zelditch, M., Jr. (1980). Status organizing processes. *Annual Review of Sociology, 6,* 479-508.

Berscheid, E. (1985). Interpersonal attraction. In G. Lindsey & E. Aronson (Eds.), *The handbook of social psychology* (Vol. 2, pp. 413-484). New York: Random House.

Blau, P. M. (1977). *Inequality and heterogeneity*. New York: Free Press.

Bottger, P. C., & Yetton, P. W. (1988). An integration of process and decision scheme explanations of group problem solving performance. *Organizational Behavior and Human Decision Processes, 42*, 234-249.

Brass, D. J. (1984). Being in the right place: A structural analysis of individual influence in an organization. *Administrative Science Quarterly, 29*, 518-539.

Byrne, D. (1971). *The attraction paradigm*. New York: Academic Press.

Cohen, B. P., & Silver, S. D. (1989). Group structure and exchange: Introduction to a theory. *Sociological Theories in Progress, 3*, 160-181.

Cohen, B. P., & Zhou, X. (1991). Status processes in enduring work groups. *American Sociological Review, 56*, 179-188.

Cohen, J. M. (1977). Sources of peer group homogeneity. *Sociology of Education, 50*, 227-341.

Davis, F. J. (1963). Perspectives of Turkish students in the United States. *Sociology and Social Research, 48*, 47-57.

Davis, F. J. (1971). The two-way mirror and the U-curve: America as seen by Turkish students returned home. *Sociology and Social Research, 56*, 29-43.

Finkelstein, S., & Hambrick, D. C. (1990). Top management team tenure and organizational outcomes: The moderating role of managerial discretion. *Administrative Science Quarterly, 35*, 484-503.

Hambrick, D. C. (1994). Top management groups: A conceptual integration and reconsideration of the "Team" label. *Research in Organizational Behavior, 16*, 171-213.

Heilman, M. E. (1994). Affirmative action: Some unidentified consequences for working women. *Research in Organizational Behavior, 16*, 125-169.

Hoffman, E. (1985). The effect of race-ratio composition on the frequency of organizational communication. *Social Psychology Quarterly, 48*, 17-26.

Ibarra, H. (1990, August). *Differences in men and women's access to informal networks at work: An intergroup perspective*. Paper presented at the Academy of Management National Meeting, San Francisco.

Ibarra, H. (1992). Homophily and differential returns: Sex differences in network structure and access in an advertising firm. *Administrative Science Quarterly, 37*, 422-447.

Ibrahim, S. E. M. (1970). Cross-cultural interaction and attitude formation before and after a major crisis. *Sociological Forces, 4*, 1-16.

Jackson, S. E. (1992). Team composition in organizational settings: Issues in managing an increasingly diverse work force. In S. Worchel, W. Wood, & J. A. Simpson (Eds.), *Group process and productivity* (pp. 138-176). Newbury Park, CA: Sage.

Jackson, S. E., & Alvarez, E. B. (1992). Working through diversity as a strategic imperative. In S. E. Jackson et al. (Eds.), *Diversity in the workplace: Human resources initiatives* (pp. 13-35). New York: Guilford.

Jackson, S. E., Brett, J. F., Sessa, V. I., Cooper, D. M., Julin, J. A., & Peyronnin, K. (1991). Some differences make a difference: Individual dissimilarity and group heterogeneity as correlates of recruitment, promotions, and turnover. *Journal of Applied Psychology, 76*, 675-689.

Jackson, S. E., May, K. E., & Whitney, K. (in press). Understanding the dynamics of diversity in decision making teams. In R. A. Guzzo & E. Salas (Eds.), *Team decision making effectiveness in organizations*. San Francisco: Jossey-Bass.

Jemmott, J. B., III, & Gonzalez, E. (1989). Social status, the status distribution, and performance in small groups. *Journal of Applied Social Psychology, 19*, 584-598.

Kirchmeyer, C., & Cohen, A. (1992). Multicultural groups: Their performance and reactions with constructive conflict. *Group & Organization Management, 17*, 153-170.

Kranz, M. E., & Sessa, V. I. (1994). Electronic meeting support systems. *PC Magazine, 13*(11), 205-212.

Lawler, E. E., III, Mohrman, S. A., & Ledford, G. E. (1992). *Employee involvement and total quality management: Practices and results in Fortune 1000 companies*. San Francisco: Jossey-Bass.

Levine, J. M., & Moreland, R. L. (1990). Progress in small group research. *Annual Review of Psychology, 41*, 585-634.

Lincoln, J. R., & Miller, J. (1979). Work and friendship ties in organizations: A comparative analysis of relational networks. *Administrative Science Quarterly, 24*, 181-199.

McCain, B. R., O'Reilly, C. A., III, & Pfeffer, J. (1983). The effects of departmental demography on turnover. *Academy of Management Journal, 26*, 626-641.

McGuire, W. J. (1985). Attitudes and attitude change. In G. Lindzey & E. Aronson (Eds.), *Handbook of social psychology* (Vol. 2, pp. 233-346). New York: Random House.

McPherson, J. M., & Smith-Lovin, L. (1987). Homophily in voluntary organizations: Status distance and the composition of face-to-face groups. *American Sociological Review, 52*, 370-379.

Michel, J. G., & Hambrick, D. C. (1992). Diversification posture and top management team characteristics. *Academy of Management Journal, 35*, 9-37.

Miller, V. D., & Jablin, F. M. (1991). Information seeking during organizational entry: Influences, tactics, and a model of the process. *Academy of Management Review, 16*(1), 92-120.

Morrison, A. M., Ruderman, M. N., & Hughes-James, M. (1993). *Making diversity happen: Controversies and solutions* (Report number 320). Greensboro, NC: Center for Creative Leadership.

Murray, A. I. (1989). Top management group heterogeneity and firm performance. *Strategic Management Journal, 10*, 125-141.

Nemeth, C. J. (1992). Minority dissent as a stimulant to group performance. In S. Worchel, W. Wood, & J. A. Simpson (Eds.), *Group process and productivity* (pp. 95-111). Newbury Park, CA: Sage.

Poole, M. S., Holmes, M., & DeSanctis, G. (1991). Conflict management in a computer-supported meeting environment. *Management Science, 37*, 926-953.

O'Reilly, C. A., III, Caldwell, D. F., & Barnett, W. P. (1989). Work group demography, social integration, and turnover. *Administrative Science Quarterly, 34*, 21-37.

Ridgeway, C. L. (1982). Status in groups: The importance of motivation. *American Sociological Review, 47*, 76-88.

Ridgeway, C., & Johnson, C. (1990). What is the relationship between socioemotional behavior and status in task groups? *American Journal of Sociology, 95*, 1189-1212.

Roloff, M. E. (1987). *Interpersonal communication: The social exchange approach*. Newbury Park, CA: Sage.

Schneider, B. (1987). The people make the place. *Personnel Psychology, 40*, 437-453.

Schweiger, D. M., Sandberg, W. R., & Rechner, P. L. (1989). Experiential effects of dialectical inquiry, devil's advocacy, and consensus approaches to strategic decision making. *Academy of Management Journal, 32*, 745-772.

Schwenk, C. R. (1983). Laboratory research on ill-structured decision aids: The case of dialectical inquiry. *Decision Sciences, 14*, 140-144.

Sessa, V. I., & Jackson, S. E. (1994, October). *Diversity in work teams: Horizontal and vertical dimensions*. Paper presented at the Conference on Work Team Dynamics and Productivity in the Context of Diversity, Center for Creative Leadership, Greensboro, NC.

Sessa, V. I., Jackson, S. E., & Rapini, D. T. (in press). Workforce diversity: The good, the bad, and the reality. In G. R. Ferris (Ed.), *Handbook of human resources management.* Cambridge, MA: Blackwell.

Silver, S. D., Cohen, B. P., & Crutchfield, J. H. (1994). Status differentiation and information exchange in face-to-face and computer-mediated idea generation. *Social Psychology Quarterly, 57*(2), 108-123.

Silver, S. D., Cohen, B. P., & Rainwater, J. (1988). Group structure and information exchange in innovative problem solving. *Advances in Group Processes, 5*, 22-40.

Sproull, L. S., & Kiesler, S. (1986). Reducing social context cues: Electronic mail in organizational communication. *Management Science, 32*, 1492-1512.

Stasser, G., & Titus, W. (1985). Pooling of unshared information in group decision making: Biased information sampling during discussion. *Journal of Personality and Social Psychology, 48*, 1467-1478.

Steiner, I. D. (1972). *Group processes and productivity.* New York: Academic Press.

Tsui, A. S., Egan, T. D., & O'Reilly, C. A., III. (1992). Being different: Relational demography and organizational attachment. *Administrative Science Quarterly, 37*, 549-579.

Turner, J. C. (1987). *Rediscovering the social group: A self-categorization theory.* New York: Blackwell.

Wagner, W., Pfeffer, J., & O'Reilly, C. A., III. (1984). Organizational demography and turnover in top-management groups. *Administrative Science Quarterly, 29*, 74-92.

Watson, W. E., Kumar, K., & Michaelson, L. K. (1993). Cultural diversity's impact on interaction process and performance: Comparing homogenous and diverse task groups. *Academy of Management Journal, 3,* 590-602.

Wiersema, M. F., & Bantel, K. A. (1992). Top management team demography and corporate strategic change. *Academy of Management Journal, 35,* 91-121.

Wiersema, M. F., & Bird, A. (1993). Organizational demography in Japanese firms: Group heterogeneity, individual dissimilarity, and top management. *Academy of Management Journal, 36,* 996-1025.

Zander, A., & Cohen, A. R. (1955). Attributed social power and group acceptance: A classroom experimental demonstration. *Journal of Abnormal and Social Psychology, 51,* 490-492.

Zenger, T. R., & Lawrence, B. S. (1989). Organizational demography: The differential effects of age and tenure distributions on technical communications. *Academy of Management Journal, 2,* 353-376.

Zimmer, J. L., & Sheposh, J. P. (1975). Effects of high status and low status actor's performance on observer's attributions of causality and behavioral intentions. *Sociometry, 38,* 395-407.

6

Leadership and Diversity in Groups and Organizations

MARTIN M. CHEMERS
SUSAN E. MURPHY

M ost organizational theorists agree that the quality of leadership is a powerful contributor to organizational success (Chemers, 1993; Fiedler & House, 1988; Lord & Maher, 1991). Leaders serve to coalesce, coordinate, and deploy the collective resources of the group to achieve a mission or reach a goal. Organizational diversity adds additional challenges to the already considerable demands on leaders.

Our concern in this chapter is with diversity defined in demographic terms. We focus on the increased prevalence in organizations, both as leaders and as followers, of individuals whose gender, ethnic background, sexual orientation, age, physical status, or other characteristics make them different than those who have traditionally held the positions and roles in which they find themselves. Although our main attention is on such demographic factors, much of what we discuss is also relevant to other diversity characteristics, such as functional specialization or organizational level.

Questions surrounding leadership and organizational diversity have two forms, which might be characterized as "diverse leaders" versus "leadership of a diverse workforce." The first question asks whether differences in sex or ethnicity are associated with differences in the styles, patterns, or effects of leadership. The second question asks what types of leadership are necessary or desirable for the effective use of the talents and energies of a diverse work-force. In essence we are examining the critical issues of diversity for both leadership and followership in this chapter.

Diverse Leaders

Do men and women, and African, Latino, Asian, and European Americans, differ in the ways that they approach the responsibilities of leadership? Does it make sense to talk about "masculine leadership" as opposed to "feminine leadership"? Many people think so. Assumptions that such differences exist and explanations for why they might exist arise from several perspectives.

Conceptual Explanations for Sex Differences in Leadership

Why should there be sex differences in leadership? Several possibilities have been raised. In this section of the chapter, we will discuss three major interpretations of differences, and in subsequent sections, we will evaluate the evidence in support of these interpretations.

The *cultural* approach suggests that differences in the socialization of men and women for their respective gender roles might result in different values, attitudes, and motivations. Such differences could be carried over into organizational life and affect leadership style. This notion is referred to as "gender role spillover" (Nieva & Gutek, 1980).

The cultural view holds that because of their roles as family caretakers, women are socialized to be sensitive, nurturant, and caring. When they carry that socialization over into organizational roles, women are likely to be warm, considerate, and democratic leaders.

Alternative explanations for potential sex differences in leadership find the causes rooted not in real differences between the sexes but in expectations that limit the expression, and bias the interpretation, of the behavior of men and women in leadership roles. For example, the *structural* explanation holds that behavioral differences observed between men and women in organizations are caused by differences in their relative positions in the structure of the organization. A social structure is a "persisting and bounded pattern of social relationships among units in a social system" (House, 1981, p. 542). One's position in a social structure and the status, power, and norms attendant to that position largely determine one's feasible and likely behaviors. Thus status and power rather than gender are assumed to be the causes of observed differences.

For example, research on influence (Kipnis & Schmidt, 1982; Yukl & Falbe, 1990; Yukl & Tracey, 1992) suggests that strategies used in upward influence attempts (i.e., attempts of a less powerful person to influence a more powerful person) are likely to be different than those used in downward influence attempts. Upward influence attempts more often apply indirect or ingratiating influence tactics. If there are more women (or minority group members) in low-power positions in an organization, they might be more likely to use such tactics. Observers might ignore the situational power differences between men and women and make the "fundamental attribution error," inferring that women use different influence tactics from men. The structural explanation illuminates why people with similar internal beliefs, attitudes, and motivation might act very differently if their positions in a social system are different.

The *social category* approach (Deaux, 1984) argues that male-female differences are more apparent than real and largely the result of attributions that are influenced by stereotypes and expectations. For example, Deaux reports that attributions for success and failure by both actors and observers are affected by expectations such that unexpected outcomes, whether successes or failures, are more likely to be ascribed to external causes, and expected outcomes ascribed to internal causes. Thus, when a woman performs well on a stereotypical masculine sex-typed task, the unexpectedness of the outcome can result in external attributions by all parties.

Furthermore, expectations and reactions based on stereotypes set up confirmatory sequences (Darley & Fazio, 1980). For example, a woman student who attempts to exercise leadership influence in a small group working on a classroom project might meet with unsupportive reactions from other students who may not expect or approve of leadership behaviors from a woman. The negative reactions of her followers may lead the woman to withhold or become tentative in her subsequent attempts to lead, reinforcing unfavorable expectations about women's leadership motivation or capacity. In this example, the reactions of the actor and others in the situation are guided by the stereotypes they hold about women in general rather than by their reactions to the specific behaviors of the actor.

The research emphasis in the social category approach focuses less on identifying differences in the behaviors of men and women than on the differences in categorical perceptions, cognitive processes, and resultant effects. This approach suggests that observed differences in leadership style between men and women are more a function of biases in the observation process than the result of true differences. If we are more likely to notice and remember behaviors that are consistent with our categorical stereotypes, our observations of male and female leaders may be biased in attention, selection, memory, and recall.

In summary, these three explanations make quite different predictions about the likelihood of gender differences in leadership. The cultural approach assumes that behavioral and performance differences are real, and their causes are rooted in the differences in values, attitudes, and behaviors between men and women or between European Americans and others. The structural approach allows that some differences in behavior may exist, but sees these differences as caused by variation in the social context rather than by differences in the inclinations of the different actors. The social category approach accentuates the role of stereotypical expectations in creating or exaggerating the perception of differences between members of different groups. Can the available empirical evidence help us to choose from among these interpretations?

The Research Evidence:
Gender Differences in Leadership Style,
Emergence, Evaluation, and Performance

In the early 1970s, Virginia Schein (1973, 1975) asked business school students to describe the characteristics of men, women, and managers. She found that these descriptions showed much greater similarity between the stereotypes of men and the stereotypes of managers than they did between women and managers. Fifteen years later, Heilman and her associates found similar results (Heilman, Block, Martell, & Simon, 1989; Heilman, Martell, & Simon, 1988). Heilman et al. (1989) also found considerable divergence in the stereotypes of "male managers" and "female managers," although somewhat more convergence was found for "successful male" and "successful female" managers.

Of course, the fact that laypeople think there are differences between men and women in leadership roles does not mean that such differences really exist. However, a number of recent books written by management theorists for nonscientific audiences extol the beneficial differences of "feminine" leadership styles (Helgesen, 1990; Loden, 1985; Rosener, 1990). These books argue that while male leaders are competitive, controlling, and analytical, female leaders are nurturant, participative, and intuitive. While this comparison is much more favorable to women than those of 30 or 40 years ago, which presented men as logical, rational, and decisive and women as emotional, illogical, and passive, the question remains as to the scientific validity of these assertions.

In the last 20 years, empirical research on the relationship between gender and leadership motivation, behavior, and decision styles has begun to appear (Bartol, 1976; Brief & Aldag, 1975; Brief & Oliver, 1976; Terborg, 1977). In 1981 Bass summarized the extant literature and concluded: "The preponderance of available evidence is that no consistently clear pattern of differences can be discerned in the supervisory style of female as compared to male leaders" (p. 499).

Interest in gender and leadership remained strong throughout the 1980s, and a comprehensive meta-analysis by Eagly and Johnson (1990) reviewed data from 162 studies. The extent of differences between men and women in leader behavior, leadership style, and decision-making style was examined. Studies were further segmented on the basis of the research venue, that is, organizational settings, assessment centers, and laboratory experiments. Consistent with the cultural or gender role explanation, women were hypothesized to be more relationship-oriented than task-oriented in their behaviors and leadership styles, and more democratic than autocratic in their decision style.

Further analyses revealed that leader behavior and leadership style differences between men and women were very slight, with no differences at all found in the data from organizational studies. Some differences were found in studies of decision style, with women appearing to be more democratic, but these effects were moderated by a number of variables. For example, among lower level managers, men were more directive than women, but the effect was reversed at the middle management level. Furthermore, when women functioned in settings that were supportive (i.e., organizations or fields in which females traditionally hold leadership positions), gender differences disappeared.

Employing a similar meta-analytic approach, Eagly and Karau (1991) performed a review of studies of gender differences in leadership emergence to ask whether women are more or less likely than men to assume the leadership position in a formerly leaderless group. The emergence phenomenon shifts the focus somewhat from how men and women are behaving (i.e., style) to how their leadership attempts are received by others.

Emergence studies, almost none of which are conducted in organizational settings, are of two types: ad hoc experimental groups brought together for one short meeting to discuss an issue or solve a problem, and ongoing class project groups completing a specific task such as writing a report or participating in a business simulation. Eagly and Karau hypothesized that women would be more likely to emerge as leaders (i.e., to be rated by other group members as making leadership contributions or to display high levels of participation in group discussions) when measures of contribution focused on social issues (a stereotypical feminine strength), rather than on task issues, and in longer term, task-focused groups where true competence would be more evident and more important in determining leadership. The results of the analysis supported their hypotheses. Men tended to emerge as leaders more frequently on measures of task than of social leadership, and differences in rates of emergence were reduced in situations with longer interaction time.

Gender differences have also been studied in evaluations of leaders by others, usually superiors or subordinates. Like the measures of acceptance of emergent leadership, the evaluation of leaders reflects less on what the leader actually does than on how the leader is perceived. Two methodologies have been used to study evaluations: (a) experimental approaches employing written vignettes or confederates as stimuli (these, while artificial, do control for any real differences between leaders) and (b) organizational surveys in which functioning leaders are rated by superiors and subordinates.

Like much of the research in this area, individual studies yield mixed results that are not explained by methodological differences. Some field studies have failed to find gender differences (e.g., Day & Stogdill, 1972; Osborn & Vicars, 1976; Rice, Instone, & Adams, 1984), but other field studies have reported differences (e.g., Petty & Lee, 1975; Petty & Miles, 1976). The same confusion holds true in laboratory studies, with some studies showing differences (e.g., Bartol & Buttterfield, 1976; Rosen & Jerdee, 1973) and others not (e.g., Bartol, 1974; Cohen, Bunker, Burton, & McManus, 1978; Lee & Alvares, 1977).

In a conceptual review of this literature, Nieva and Gutek (1980) emphasized theoretical differences between the various studies. They argued that evaluation biases are likely to be strongest when judgments of the leader require a great deal of inference rather than simple reporting of behaviors or performance. Terborg and Ilgen (1975) have also suggested that biases, stereotypes, and expectations are likely to be most potent when little information about the target is known.

Nieva and Gutek (1980) also concluded that evaluations of male and female leaders are affected by sex role congruence. Women in stereotypically "female" positions and men in "male" jobs are more likely to receive positive evaluations than persons whose position and gender are incongruent.

The third moderator identified by Nieva and Gutek is consistent with Deaux's (1984) conclusions about the role of expectations. Expectations for men to succeed and for women to fail become stronger the higher the level of qualification required for the position. Of interest, when expectations are disconfirmed, attributions to internal causes, such as ability, were greater for women than for men. In other words, because women are thought not as likely to succeed, their good performance may result in more positive evaluations unless observers find an external cause, such as a lucky occurrence or a supportive environment, to which to attribute the unexpected success.

Recently, Eagly, Makhijani, and Klonsky (1992) reported a meta-analysis of gender effects in leadership evaluation. They found that gender effects were quite small overall with only a slight tendency to undervalue women (i.e., men were favored in 56% of the studies—an effect not significantly greater than chance). However, there were a number of interesting moderators to the overall result. For example, women were more likely to be devalued when perceived as acting in a "masculine" (i.e., task-oriented or directive) style. Evaluative biases were greatest in settings that were traditionally male venues (e.g., sports coaching) and when ratings were made by certain individuals (e.g., high school basketball players as opposed to real managers in organizational settings). Eagly et al. concluded that gender bias in the evaluation of leadership is relatively weak.

Finally, the Eagly group (Eagly, Karau, & Makhijani, 1995) reported a meta-analysis of gender differences in leadership performance that arrived at conclusions similar to the earlier meta-analyses. Overall differences between men and women in leadership performance were very minimal, but there were some moderator variables that increased the difference. For example, some organizational settings, such as the military, disadvantage women leaders, whereas women perform better in settings more congenial to female leaders.

In several of the meta-analyses (Eagly et al., 1992; Eagly et al., 1995), an index was developed assessing the "congeniality" of various leadership positions for men or women. The indices were created by asking college student men and women to rate how comfortable or easy a position might be to perform in for themselves or for the average man or woman. In the recent study (Eagly et al., 1995), those ratings revealed an interesting commentary on stereotypical expectations. When the subjects in that study were rating the congeniality of various positions for themselves, no gender differences were found. However, when the ratings were made from the perspective of an "average" man or woman, strong differences were found. This seems to indicate that even though individuals may not themselves experience gender-related differences in preferences or proclivities, they assume them to exist for others, creating biased expectations that have the power to affect performance.

Evidence on Minority Leaders

Ann Morrison and Mary Ann Von Glinow (1990) have reported strong evidence that the upward mobility of managers with certain ethnic minority heritages (e.g., African, Hispanic, Asian, Native, and Jewish American leaders) may be even worse than that for women. In his article on the prospects of African American managers, E. W. Jones Jr. (in Bass, 1981) concluded that there has been "almost no progress at all."

A culturally oriented explanation of the problems of minority managers would conclude that members of these groups have values, attitudes, traits, or behaviors that are inimical to successful leadership and managerial performance. How good is the evidence in support of that assertion? In reviews of the available literature (which is quite limited), both Riger and Galligan (1980) and Bass (1990) concluded that there is very little support for the notion that culture plays an important role in the outcomes for these groups.

Most of the research in this area focuses on African American leaders or subordinates. While African American leaders tend to be less satisfied with their jobs (Jennings, 1980; O'Reilly & Roberts, 1973; Slocum & Strawser, 1972), there is little evidence of differences in motivation (Miner, 1977; Thomas, 1982; Vinson & Mitchell, 1975), in values (Watson & Barone,

1976), aspirations and expectations for success (Allen, 1975), or in preferred leadership style (Barati, 1981) or leader behavior (Schott, 1970).

On the other hand, a number of studies have shown systematic biases in the perceptions of and attributions about the performance of African American leaders (Hammer, Kim, Baird, & Bigoness, 1974; Pettigrew, Jemmott, & Johnson, 1984). In some studies, African American leaders are rated higher than Whites, and in other studies lower, or they are seen more positively or less positively by African American subordinates or by White subordinates. Such contradictory findings led Bass (1990) to conclude that individual differences or organizational context probably override any possible broader generalizations.

When we turn to the admittedly sparse research findings on Hispanics, Asian Americans, Jewish Americans, or older workers, the patterns are similar. The more collectivist cultural backgrounds of Hispanic and Asian peoples are generally expected to make those leaders somewhat more likely to emphasize cooperation and assistance over competition and rivalry (Hsu, 1981; Ross, Triandis, Chang, & Marin, 1982; Triandis, Ottai, & Marin, 1982). However, there is little direct evidence linking these tendencies to leadership performance. In other studies, Quinn, Kahn, Tabor, and Gordon (1968) found that a substantial portion of Gentile executives held discriminatory attitudes toward Jewish managers, and Waldman and Avolio (1986) reported that, although they found no differences in actual job performance between younger and older workers, subjective performance appraisals by supervisors were biased in favor of the younger workers.

Conclusion. The literature on leadership styles, emergence, evaluation, and performance would seem to suggest that biological or cultural factors generate few important differences in the ways that men and women behave in the leadership role, but culturally based stereotypes and expectations may influence the way that others react to men and women in leadership positions. An examination of the literature that approaches the question from a structural point of view is quite illuminating.

Status, Gender, Minority Group Membership, and Leadership

A structural analysis argues that an individual's behavior in any social system is largely determined by his or her position in that system. This analysis would further suggest that gender or ethnic differences observed in leadership behavior are caused by differences in the distribution of these groups in positions in the social and organizational structure.

Starting from an examination of women's access to power in organizations, Ragins and her associates (Ragins, 1989, 1991, this volume; Ragins & Scandura, 1994; Ragins & Sundstrom, 1989, 1990) have employed methodologies that match men and women leaders on power, status, and other important organizational variables. These studies indicate that, while it is much more difficult for women to gain power in organizations than it is for men (Ragins & Sundstrom, 1989), men and women of equal power act in very similar ways with very similar effects (Ragins, 1991; Ragins & Sundstrom, 1990). Men and women use similar bases of power in attempts to influence their subordinates, and their subordinates respond similarly in evaluation of the use of that power regardless of gender.

Recently, Ragins and Scandura (1994) studied men's and women's intentions to be mentors and their evaluations of the costs and benefits of mentoring. Earlier work had suggested that women are less willing to act as mentors because of the costs involved, and are especially less willing to mentor other women, because of their feeling of competitiveness with other women, the so-called "queen bee syndrome." They found, however, that when women and men are matched for level in the organization, there are no differences in their willingness to mentor protégés of either sex. Ragins and Scandura conclude that earlier findings that women mentor less may be attributable to fewer women being in positions where mentoring was feasible.

A series of studies by Snodgrass and her associates (Snodgrass, 1985; Snodgrass, Hecht, & Ploutz-Snyder, 1994) add an interesting twist to the structural analysis. Snodgrass was interested in testing the hypothesis that women are more interpersonally sensitive and empathically accurate than men, a belief consistent with cultural views of women as relationship-oriented, nurturant, and attentive to others. In a series of studies conducted with college students, men and women were given the roles of leader and follower in a work simulation. After a period of dyadic interaction, subjects were asked to rate their own emotions and thoughts, the thoughts and emotions of the other person, and the other person's thoughts and emotions about them.

The findings indicated no differences between men and women in their ability to predict the other person's thoughts and feelings, but a strong effect for assigned role. Leaders were better able to predict how their subordinates felt about their own task performance (a perception important to the leader's responsibilities), but the leaders were not very sensitive to how the subordinate felt about them as leaders. On the other hand, the students in the subordinate role were very sensitive to how the leader felt about them (a perception of great concern to a subordinate), but were not sensitive to how the leader felt about him- or herself. Each member of the dyad, regardless of gender, was *most sensitive to the aspects of the interpersonal exchange that were important for his or her own role.* In one study, people showed this pattern even when the experimental manipulation did not assign them to roles, but only suggested that they might be in such roles in the future.

The studies by Ragins and by Snodgrass reveal that much of a person's behavior may be dictated by a role in a social structure, by the normative expectations and social responsibilities, or by the freedoms or limitations of status and power. However, the influence of such external factors is frequently ignored, and attributions are made to an actor's character, ability, or culture. Sometimes the character, ability, or cultural style of an individual is already inferred from the social category (e.g., woman, African American, elder) to which he or she belongs.

Social Category Approaches
to Women's Leadership

The research presented so far in this chapter suggests that real differences between the sexes or ethnic groups in leadership behavior are very slight. Nonetheless, stereotypical beliefs and their attendant expectations persist. Such beliefs and expectations and the biases in perception and evaluation to which they give rise may be important contributors to organizational barriers to success for women and other nontraditional leaders.

Lord and Maher (1991) have presented an information processing approach to leadership perception and evaluation. They argue that leaders are judged through both behavior and performance. When a leader's behavior is consistent with an observer's prototypical expectations for a leader, the actor is more likely to be judged a good leader. Also, if the leader is associated with successful outcomes (such as high productivity in her work group), an attributional inference will be made that the leader is responsible for the group's performance and therefore is an effective leader. The judgments of leaders may be made automatically, with the perceiver paying little attention to the processing of information, or they may be made in a more careful and effortful manner.

Lord and Maher (1991) hypothesized a number of ways in which stereotypes about women disadvantage them in the context of leadership judgments. As we reported earlier in this chapter, stereotypes of females are relatively incompatible with stereotypes of effective managers; thus the prototypes evoked have little overlap. This makes it much harder for a woman to be seen as acting like a leader even when she acts in the same way as a male counterpart. Biases in expectations, attention, and memory militate against women.

These stereotypes will be especially pernicious for women in the early stages of their managerial careers, when little information about the person is available and judgments are more likely to be stereotypical. In the middle stages of a woman's career when more information about her work history is available, stereotypical judgments are likely to be replaced by fairer, more effortful, information-based analyses. However, at the highest levels of organizational life, both the fact that the prototype of a CEO is almost exclusively male and the fact that direct performance information is very ambiguous again put women at a serious disadvantage. Of course, all of these processes are equally true for members of minority groups that traditionally have been excluded from leadership positions.

Roya Ayman (1993) has discussed the effects of the salience of situationally inappropriate social categories. As long as the managerial situation is defined in appropriate terms (i.e., a focus on work roles and responsibilities), women and other nontraditional managers (e.g., African Americans, Latinos, Asian Americans) can function in role-appropriate ways. However, if the salience of inappropriate categories is raised (for example, by referring to a woman's clothes or appearance, or by reminding an ethnic minority manager of his divergence from the managerial norm), double binds are created. Role behavior appropriate to being a woman or an ethnic minority within a group is inimical to the behaviors appropriate to the managerial role. For example, if others expect a woman or minority manager to be deferent and submissive, such managers will find it very difficult to act in accordance with those expectations while still fulfilling role-appropriate behavior for a manager. Such double binds result in anxiety and tentativeness that inhibit the very behaviors necessary for effective functioning.

A program of research by Heilman and her associates (Heilman, Kaplow, Amato, & Stathatos, 1993; Heilman, Rivero, & Brett, 1991; Heilman, Simon,

& Repper, 1987) reveals the way in which biases and expectations surrounding certain social categories can be very problematic for nontraditional leaders. In a series of laboratory analogues of affirmative action issues in organizations, findings have shown that implying that a person was chosen for a position on the basis of preference rather than merit can have subtle negative effects on the person's thoughts and behaviors. For example, male and female college students were told that they had received a managerial position in a simulation either due to merit or because of their sex, and were then asked to judge the portfolios of a number of other job applicants, both male and female. Women subjects who were ostensibly chosen because of their sex were significantly more critical of female applicants than were "merit"-selected women or men. When the subjects were told that they got their job because of their sex, but that they also had the appropriate level of merit, the differences disappeared.

Some Conclusions About
the "Diversity of Leadership"

The evidence is fairly clear and strong that men and women and minority group members in real leadership positions in real organizations are probably quite similar in the ways that they approach their responsibilities. When subordinates interact with leaders over a long period of time, in close associations that allow for judgments of competence and performance, evaluations of men and women leaders differ little. Nonetheless, stereotypes about gender and leadership persist, sometimes reinforced by popular books extolling the superiority of masculine or feminine leadership. Even when women are described as superior to male leaders, the dangers of invoking cultural explanations are present. The "queen bee syndrome" and other negative stereotypes of female leaders lurk just below the surface and are easily evoked.

Raising the salience of inappropriate social categories in leadership situations can create anxiety and rob nontraditional role occupants of confidence. Recent research (Chemers, 1994; Murphy, 1992) indicates that confidence, and especially perceptions of self-efficacy for leadership, are highly related to performance in the leadership role. Such feelings of confidence arise partly from the actors' perceptions that they possess the appropriate skills, knowledge, and personal characteristics for the role. Factors that make individuals feel that they are not appropriate for the leadership role arouse self-doubt and anxiety. It is likely, then, that inappropriate expectations for nontraditional leaders can leech confidence and result in poorer behaviors and performance outcomes, which are then incorrectly interpreted as evidence in support of those stereotypical expectations.

Leading a Diverse Workforce

This section addresses the challenges faced by leaders who find themselves leading a diverse workforce. Specifically, what factors should a leader consider in leading a group of subordinates who may be of a different gender or ethnic background than him- or herself? Pertinent issues may involve the motivational needs and values of diverse work groups, communication practices, or expectations for authority in an organization.

Many books in the popular business literature have attempted to address the required skills for leaders of a diverse workforce. While these sources provide examples of where and how issues of diversity might be addressed in the workplace, most do not cite experimental research in the area, nor do they discuss how contemporary leadership theories might address the topic of diversity.

After a brief review of issues surrounding the leadership of diversity, the remainder of this chapter discusses the role of subordinate diversity in various theories of leadership as well as issues requiring future research. It is our contention that the leadership of diversity is a two-pronged issue: First, leaders of diverse work groups need to be sensitive to real differences *when they exist*, and, second, they must find ways to reduce the negative impact of stereotypes. Finally, it is our thesis that good leadership includes the orientations and behaviors appropriate to the successful coordination of these situations whether characterized by real or stereotypical differences, because effective leadership is based on the establishment of authentic and open relationships between leaders and followers, and for such relationships to exist, the leader must be sensitive to the needs, expectations, and perceptions of followers *whatever the origin of those states*. Effective organizations hold leaders accountable for the development of all subordinates.

Brief Overview
of Popular Literature

The current interest in managing diversity results from demographic changes that indicate that 85% of new market entrants will be women and minorities and that, by the year 2000, only 45% of the workforce will be White males (Johnston & Packer, 1987). Roosevelt Thomas wrote one of the earliest books outlining the issues associated with the diversity of this new workforce. According to Thomas (1991), managing diversity is defined as a comprehensive managerial process for developing an environment that works well for all employees, including dominant-culture employees. In addition to race and ethnic diversity, an effective environment accommodates diversity with respect to age, personal and corporate background, education, functional specialization, and personality, as well as lifestyle, sexual preference, geographic location, tenure within the organization, and management or nonmanagement status.

Previous initiatives in the area of diversity, however, had as their main goal the valuing of differences. These efforts were designed to encourage awareness of and respect for diversity within the workplace by increasing acceptance, tolerance, and understanding of diversity. However, according to critics such as Thomas (1991), efforts at valuing diversity do not go far enough. Instead, *managing* diversity is needed to empower a diverse group of employees to reach their full potential. Managing diversity begins by looking at the system within an organization. A number of basic questions must be asked by an organization's management to assess whether diversity is being effectively managed: Are we getting the highest productivity possible? Does our system work as smoothly as it could? Is morale as high as we would wish? And are those outcomes as strong as they would be if all the people who worked here were the same sex and race and had the same lifestyle and value system and work expectations?

According to Thomas, if the answer to any one of these questions is no, then the solution is to change the system and modify the core culture. Thomas also believes that the primary barrier to managing diversity is that managers in many organizations have been taught to be "doer" managers, that is, doing the work. He believes that for effective leadership to occur in a diverse organization, an empowerment model of leadership must exist. *Empowerment* is defined as the process of enabling and motivating subordinates by increasing their personal efficacy (Conger, 1989). Thus it becomes the leader's responsibility to help each subordinate reach his or her full potential. The process of empowerment becomes even more challenging when dealing with subordinates of diverse backgrounds.

Recently, Morrison (1992) extensively studied diversity management practices through surveys and in-depth interviews with 196 managers in 16 organizations. Her findings revealed that a leader's role in developmental activities such as coaching and mentoring becomes very important for managers of a diverse workforce. A major part of the leader's developmental role is ensuring that minority subordinates receive feedback. Managers are often reluctant to give employees meaningful feedback, especially if it is critical. With a diverse workforce, it becomes even more important that a leader's role includes mentoring, coaching, and providing accurate feedback to encourage minority development. Diversity consultants and researchers also stress the importance of leaders increasing their tolerance of diverse viewpoints and learning to deal effectively with groups that have different values.

Theories of diversity management emphasize the *goals*, such as empowerment, that good leadership would ensure for minority employees, but these approaches tend to be relatively silent on the *specific leadership behaviors* that can achieve these goals. Contemporary leadership theory, on the other hand, focuses on the characteristics of effective leadership but makes no special statements about how such leadership needs to be modified under conditions of organizational diversity (Ayman, Chemers, & Fiedler, in press). We hope to bridge the gap between these two approaches by reviewing what good leadership is in the general case and what factors must be accommodated for the specific case of diversity leadership.

Critical Functions
of Effective Leadership

The last 50 years of research have produced a number of findings as to what makes for effective leadership. Fiedler and House (1988) outlined the best established findings in the study of leadership, including (a) the identification of two major categories of leader behavior, one directed toward interpersonal relations and the other toward task accomplishment; (b) the recognition of a set of personality characteristics reliably associated with effective leaders, such as intelligence, competence, social skill, and the need for power to influence others; (c) demonstration that the effectiveness of different leadership styles is dependent upon situational variables, such as the clarity and predictability of the leader's and followers' task environment (e.g., Fiedler & Chemers, 1974; House, 1971); and (d) documentation of the important role of attributions in the determination of leaders' actions toward subordinates (Mitchell & Wood, 1980). These research findings can provide a basis for understanding how diversity issues are related to effective leadership.

In an integration of the literature on effective leadership, Chemers (1993) outlined three pervasive leadership functions. The first function of leadership is *image management*, through which leaders must establish credibility by projecting an image consistent with observers' expectations of how effective leaders appear. The second function is *relationship development*, which addresses the interpersonal relationship between leader and followers that affects subordinate motivation, task-related efficacy, and perceptions of justice and fairness. Finally, the third function of effective leadership is *team coordination and deployment,* which concerns the leader's ability to successfully coordinate the intellectual, material, and emotional resources available in the group to accomplish the organizational mission.

Applications of Leadership Functions to Issues of Diversity

Image Management

Leadership is a process of social influence in which the leader induces followers to apply their energies and resources to a collective objective. The perceptions of the leader by followers and other observers are the bases on which the leader's credibility and correspondent influence are built. These perceptions may be affected by differences in the assumptions and expectations about leadership that different people bring to the leadership situation.

Early social psychological research on influence processes and attitude change (Hovland, Janis, & Kelley, 1953) made it clear that a key basis of social influence was credibility. The two most important contributors to communicator credibility were found to be expertise and trustworthiness.

Edwin Hollander (1964) has shown us that the same principles apply to leadership credibility. Research using the idiosyncrasy credit model revealed that the factors that contribute to a leader's status and influence are expertise, in the form of task-related competence, and trustworthiness, manifested as loyalty to the group's goal or mission. Leaders who demonstrate competency and trustworthiness are accorded greater legitimacy on which to base their influence.

One way that diversity might affect a leader's ability to establish legitimacy is by creating barriers to trust. Some research has addressed how trust levels differ in cross-gender and cross-race dyads. Scott (1983) reported that cross-gender dyads had lower trust than same-gender dyads. Jeanquart-Barone (1993) extended this research and examined cross-race and cross-gender dyads, finding that the highest level of trust was for female subordinates reporting to male supervisors, but that there were no significant differences in trust between males reporting to males as compared with females reporting to females. Significant differences in trust were also found for cross-race pairs. Specifically, Blacks reporting to Blacks expressed higher levels of mutual trust than did Blacks reporting to Whites, Whites reporting to Blacks, or even Whites reporting to other Whites.

Another potential effect of diversity on leadership perceptions arises from the possibility that there are ethnic or gender differences in the characteristics that are considered appropriate or prototypical for effective leaders. The adaptation of social cognitive theory to leadership studies by researchers like Robert Lord (Lord & Maher, 1991) and James Meindl (1990) and their associates has illuminated the processes by which judgments of competency and trustworthiness are made. For example, it is clear that observers of leadership, whether superiors, followers, or so-called objective observers, hold prototypes about the traits and behaviors that characterize effective leaders. These prototypical expectations for leadership can affect whom we see as effective leaders and what we notice and remember about leadership actions.

Managing a group of employees from diverse ethnic backgrounds may become problematic if these subordinates hold prototypes of leadership that differ from what is "traditional" or from the norm for a particular organization. Hofstede (1981) has shown that cultures vary greatly in their work-related values, which, in part, determine what leader behaviors are seen as prototypical. Diverse subordinates may have diverse prototypes for judging leaders.

Relationship Development

The quality of the relationship between leader and follower is a major determinant of the followers' motivation and commitment to organizational goals. A major component of the relationship involves the leader's attempts to provide coaching and guidance to subordinates. The relative effectiveness of these efforts is determined by the leader's ability to understand and react to the follower's particular needs and desires. High-quality relationships result in a sense of equity and fairness that is satisfying and motivating to followers. Cultural differences may affect (a) followers' reactions to leader behavior, (b) the leader's accuracy in assessing subordinate needs, and (c) the resultant feelings of equity and satisfaction.

Coaching and Guidance: Reactions to Leader Behavior. Research indicates that the effectiveness of the two general classes of leader behavior (i.e., task-oriented, directive behavior versus relationship-oriented, considerate behavior) is determined by the characteristics of the task and the preparedness and/or willingness of the subordinate. For example, Path-Goal Theory (House & Mitchell, 1974) suggests that directive leadership is more appropriate when the subordinate is faced with a complex and difficult task, and especially when the subordinate lacks experience and expertise. Supportive leadership is more appropriate when a boring, highly structured task frustrates a subordinate's need for growth and autonomy.

However, in addition to task and preparedness issues, a subordinate's personality also mediates the effects of leader behavior. For example, Griffin (1981) found that subordinates who were high in the need for growth and development reacted negatively to a leader's directive behavior even when confronted with a task that was highly complex. Similar ideas about matching leader behavior to subordinate characteristics are present in other models such as Hersey and Blanchard's (1977) Situational Leadership theory.

Work-related values and the needs and expectation to which they give rise, however, can vary dramatically across cultures. Hofstede (1983) has explored cross-cultural differences in attitudes and values and has identified four work-related values that account for a large proportion of cultural differences. The four values were labeled *power distance*, referring to the degree of centralization of authority in organizations and acceptance of autocratic leadership; *uncertainty avoidance*, representing the degree to which individuals seek to avoid unpredictable situations by establishing structured environments and formal rules; *individualism-collectivism*, reflecting the relative emphasis in the culture on personal motivation and individual achievement versus collective responsibility, harmony, and loyalty; and *masculinity-femininity*, indicating the degree to which the culture values "masculine" traits such as assertiveness, competitiveness, and independence as opposed to more "feminine" emphases, such as sensitivity to others and concern about the quality of life.

These work-related values can determine subordinate reactions to leader behavior and coaching. For example, a follower high in power distance would, in general, be much more comfortable with authoritarian and directive leadership than would be a follower from a more egalitarian culture. Similarly, a need to avoid uncertainty might also give rise to more positive reactions to structuring and direction by a leader. Collectivist values would lessen a follower's need to gain autonomy and have personal achievements recognized.

Workers and managers in the United States have cultural heritages from all over the world. To the extent that value differences characterize American subcultures, a leader's behavior may have very different effects on different subordinates. In fact, studies indicate that many minority group members in the United States are bicultural, that is, having knowledge of dominant culture norms but also holding the norms of their own ethnic groups (Cox, Lobel, & McLeod, 1991).

A study by Thomas (1982) found that Black male and female business students were more task oriented than White students. In contrast, Triandis, Marin, Lisansky, and Betancourt (1984) found that Hispanics are more likely than non-Hispanics to expect high frequencies of positive social behaviors and low frequencies of negative social behaviors. These interpersonal communications are characterized by what Triandis et al. (1984) call the cultural script of *simpatía*—an ability to share in others' feelings. Murillo (1976) notes that Mexican Americans place a great emphasis on manners and courtesy in interpersonal relations. A significant issue in diversity leadership, then, depends on how strong and pervasive subcultural differences in work-related values are.

Judging Others: The Attribution Process. Appropriate direction and coaching depend on accurate judgments of the causes and meaning of subordinate behavior and performance. Most theories that emphasize coaching (such as Path Goal Theory) simply assume that leaders can make accurate judgments. However, research on leaders' attributions for poor subordinate performance (e.g., Brown, 1984: Mitchell & Wood, 1980) reveals that a number of biases threaten the validity of such perceptions, the chief culprits being defensiveness and self-protection. When subordinates' poor performance has strong implications for the supervisor's own performance evaluation, there is a tendency to blame the subordinate, even when other causes are reasonable or probable. Thus, when subordinates frequently perform poorly or perform poorly in ways that are very serious, the supervisor may be seen as responsible. This may enhance the supervisor's tendency to assign blame to the subordinates.

Regardless of the true level of cultural difference between members of various ethnic groups, leaders' stereotypes can affect judgments about their subordinates' performance or action. Rosen and Jerdee (1977) asked business students to evaluate the extent to which participative decision-making styles were appropriate for certain types of subordinates. The students felt that a more directive style would be necessary with minority subordinates. In another study, Greenhaus and Parasuraman (1993) found that managers judging African American subordinates were more likely to attribute good performance to external and unstable factors rather than to the subordinate's ability.

A recent review of issues facing women of color makes distinctions among even more specific stereotypes (Bell, Denton, & Nkomo, 1993). The authors point out that "model-minority" stereotypes of Asian American women emphasize passive behavior, while Latina women "are often depicted as passive and dominated by the 'machismo' of their men" (Horowitz, 1983). These stereotypes of subordinates can affect how a leader assigns tasks or makes attributions about performance.

Exchanges, Equity, and Relationship. Finally, effective relationship development depends on mutual perceptions of just and fair exchanges between leader and follower. One group of leadership theories stresses the idea that a leader's relationship with each subordinate is unique. Bass and colleagues (Bass, 1985; Bass & Avolio, 1993) argue that truly outstanding (i.e., transformational) leaders practice "individualized consideration," in which the leader recognizes and provides to each subordinate the kinds of challenges and opportunities that will result in maximum personal growth for that subordinate.

A similar focus on the unique relationship between leader and follower is the central tenet of Graen's (Graen & Scandura, 1986) theory of leader-member exchange (LMX). According to LMX theory, the quality of the relationship between the leader and follower can range from "true partnerships" to "overseer-peon" interactions. Research has shown that those followers who enjoy better relationships with their leaders also have higher levels of task performance and job satisfaction.

Both transformational leadership theory and leader exchange theory have implications for the leadership of diverse groups. Ethnic differences between leader and follower may result in expectations or working styles that threaten the development of high-quality exchanges. If perceived similarity between leader and follower is an important determinant of the initial quality of an exchange, differences between leader and follower may start the relationship off on the wrong foot. Liden, Wayne, and Stillwell (1993), however, found that demographic characteristics (such as gender, race, or age) did not affect perceived similarity in a study of managerial dyads.

In related research, D. Thomas (1993) specifically examined how relationships developed in mentor-protégé pairs. He found that one determinant of the quality of the mentoring relationship for cross-race pairs was the denial and/or suppression of race issues as compared with direct engagement of the topic. Ragins (this volume) provides an extensive review of the literature on the effects of demographic and ethnic differences on the mentoring process and concludes that such differences may, but do not always, result in poor exchanges.

Many minority group members in organizations do perceive that their opportunities for high-quality exchanges are more limited than those of dominant-culture persons. Greenhaus, Parasuraman, and Wormley (1990) found that African Americans perceived that some of their organizational experiences differed from those of Whites. African American managers reported having less job discretion and reported feeling less accepted than White managers, but race had no effects on sponsorship, supervisory support, or career strategies.

Inequity in exchanges may lead to less effort on the part of minority employees who feel that they are receiving inequitable or unfair exchanges for the amount or quality of work that they provide for an organization. Romero (1979) reported that Mexican American workers had low confidence that they could find employment that was both satisfying and rewarding. While young Mexican Americans consider their employment prospects good, their attitudes show a significant decline four years after high school.

A significant problem in drawing conclusions about Mexican Americans as subordinates is the diversity that exists within that subculture. Rates of assimilation and acculturation may differ as a function of generation. First-generation Mexican Americans are not only likely to hold different values and assumptions regarding leadership but also may have markedly different career aspirations than third-generation groups (Maldonado, 1985). These differences in generations hold true for many other ethnic groups as well. In summary, cultural differences in the needs of leaders and followers may have strong effects on the ways in which relationships are negotiated and developed.

Team Coordination and Deployment

Effective leadership means more than just looking like a leader and more than simply generating a group of motivated followers. Effective leadership also means using these group resources to accomplish the organizational mission. Coordination of group resources to achieve performance is one of the most complex areas in the contemporary leadership and management literature. Two important areas of study have focused on "environment-fit" or contingency models of leadership and on group process models.

Environment-Fit (Contingency) Models. In the recent past, contingency theories such as Fiedler's model (Fiedler, 1967; Fiedler & Chemers, 1974, 1984) have been the dominant perspectives in this area. These approaches diagnose the nature of the leadership or organizational environment, typically in terms of its complexity, stability, or certainty, and match leadership or organizational strategies to the environment. Implied in these theories are two assumptions that may, in fact, be problematic. One assumption is that it is the objective nature of the environment or situation that is most important. The second assumption is that there is only one correct match that will result in effectiveness.

Problems arise if we consider the possibility that subjective depictions of the situation may be more important than objective ones. For example, research by Ayman and Chemers and their colleagues (Ayman & Chemers, 1991; Chemers, Ayman, Sorod, & Akimoto, 1991) indicates that subjective definitions of the leadership situation may be more important than objective ones. Leadership match based on subjective appraisals was more predictive of high levels of confidence, satisfaction, and performance than was designation based on more objective analyses.

Triandis (1993) has suggested that a society's level of adaptation with respect to certain situational variables may influence its judgment of a particular situation. For example, if a culture is high on uncertainty avoidance (Hofstede, 1981) and therefore builds high levels of structure into most situations, members of that culture will have correspondingly high expectations for structure that will affect their judgments of new tasks or situations. When confronted with a moderately structured situation, they may see it as much less structured than would a person with a different adaptation level. Thus leaders and subordinates who are from different ethnic groups may encounter the same objective environment, but see differing levels of situational control or need for leader intervention. An important question, then, is whether performance will be determined by the match with objectively or subjectively defined situations.

A corollary question is whether a leader can redefine a situation for followers, affecting their confidence, motivation, and performance. If a leader is able to convince followers that they have the capability to be successful, how much can the resultant confidence that followers develop affect the performance of the group? The role of the leader in defining and giving meaning to the environment is an important one with profound implications.

Reconciling differences between group members' perceptions, needs, and expectations, whether caused by ethnic or other diversity factors (e.g., functional specialization), becomes a central issue in the role of diversity in group process.

Leadership and Group Process. Diversity concerns have important implications for research in the area of group dynamics and group decisions. Sessa and Jackson (this volume) make the point that much of the literature on group process asserts that groups with heterogeneous beliefs, backgrounds, and skills may be more creative in problem solving, by virtue of the increased breadth of information and perspectives held by group members. Unfortunately, this heterogeneity can also increase the difficulty of coordinating and maintaining cohesiveness. Tension may make communication more difficult, and if the relative status of group members is based on inappropriate criteria (such as race or gender), decision making may become inefficient.

Cox, Lobel, and McLeod (1991) studied ethnically homogeneous and diverse task groups and found that, at the individual level, Asian, African, and

Hispanic American individuals had a more collectivist, cooperative orientation to a task than did Euro-Americans, and that ethnically diverse groups acted more cooperatively than did homogeneous Euro-American groups.

Most contingency theories of leadership (e.g., Fiedler, 1967; Vroom & Yetton's Normative Decision Theory, 1973) include the quality of leader-follower relationships as a central variable in specifying the nature of the leadership environment. If coordination difficulties are created by ethnic diversity, such theories must incorporate diversity issues into their formulation.

Summary, Conclusions, and Directions

In the first half of this chapter, our analysis of gender and ethnic differences in leadership styles concluded that the bulk of the evidence indicated that few major differences existed between these demographic categories. However, stereotypical beliefs and expectations based on categorical membership still function to limit the opportunities of women and minorities to attain leadership positions, and they continue to bias evaluations of such persons in those positions. The implication of that conclusion is that diversity efforts might best be directed at diminishing stereotypes and reducing their impact on organizational functioning. That is, rather than emphasizing the differences between people, organizational leaders might emphasize their similarities in needs, values, and abilities.

When we turn to the question of the leadership of diverse followers, some of the same questions arise. If men and women, Blacks and Whites, and other subgroups do not differ when they occupy leadership roles, how likely is it that they will differ greatly when in the follower role? If differences are indeed significant, then those who would lead in a diverse society must be especially sensitive to the potential problems that such differences create. However, if diversity challenges in organizations are accounted for more by stereotypes and historical hostilities than by true differences, other courses of action are reasonable. In particular, it is important to make it clear that every manager is responsible for the development of all subordinates and must make whatever efforts are necessary to do so.

Directions for Research

Image management, relationship development, and effective team deployment are crucial to the success of every leader. However, the question of whether effective leadership for diversity requires highly specialized training programs and organizational interventions, or whether a broad-based and universally enforced emphasis on the basic principles of good leadership is sufficient, rests on research findings still unavailable. Some appropriate research questions follow:

(1) Image Management. Do prototypes and implicit theories of leadership differ across ethnic and gender groups? Is the leader-subordinate relationship one that is so situationally overdetermined (Weiss & Adler, 1984) that ethnic differences in responses to authority, motivational values, and communication practices are of little importance? Do all ethnic groups perceive transformational leaders in the same way?

(2) Relationship Development. What is the role of gender and ethnicity in the development of high-quality exchanges? Do ethnic differences in personalities, needs, and expectations affect whether a leader will be differentially effective with different subordinates? Are variables such as subordinate maturity (Hersey & Blanchard, 1988) or growth-need strength (Griffin, 1981; Hackman & Oldham, 1976) differentially distributed by ethnic group, affecting the appropriateness of leadership? Is transformational leadership, as a leadership style or set of behaviors, effective for increasing the performance of all ethnic and gender groups?

(3) Team Coordination and Deployment. How can diversity and the potential coordination difficulties of heterogeneous groups be integrated into situational specifications in various contingency formulations? Are leader personality traits (e.g., self-monitoring) related to effectiveness in the leadership of heterogenous groups? Can we benchmark from organizations that effectively use diversity (as defined in terms either of ethnic differences and functional specializations) as suggested by Cox in this volume?

The viability of American organizations, and even of American society, depends on our ability to make productive use of our diversity, rather than letting it remain an impediment to success. Leadership makes a difference in the success of groups and organizations and can be especially important in situations with high diversity. Ultimately, our ability to solve these problems will depend on a combination of collective goodwill and sound empirical research. Let's hope we can find our way to both of those objectives.

References

Allen, W. R. (1975). Black and White leaders and subordinates: Leader choice and ratings, aspirations, and expectancy of success. In D. Frederick & J. Guilinan (Eds.), *New challenges of the decision sciences*. Amherst, MA: Northeast Region of the American Institute for Decision Sciences.

Ayman, R. (1993). Leadership perception: The role of culture and gender. In M. M. Chemers & R. Ayman (Eds.), *Leadership theory and research: Perspectives and directions* (pp. 137-166). San Diego, CA: Academic Press.

Ayman, R., & Chemers, M. M. (1991). The effect of leadership match on subordinate satisfaction in Mexican organizations: Some moderating influences of self-monitoring. *International Review of Applied Psychology, 40*, 299-314.

Ayman, R., Chemers, M. M., & Fiedler, F. E. (in press). The contingency model of leadership effectiveness: Its levels of analyses. *Leadership Quarterly*.

Barati, M. E. (1981). Comparison of preferred leadership styles, potential leadership effectiveness, and managerial attitudes among Black and White, female and male management students. *Dissertation Abstracts International, 43*(4A), 1271.

Bartol, K. M. (1974). Male vs. female leaders: The effect of leader need for dominance on follower satisfaction. *Academy of Management Journal, 17*, 225-233.

Bartol, K. M. (1976). Relationship of sex and professional training area to job orientation. *Journal of Applied Psychology, 61*, 368-370.

Bartol, K. M., & Butterfield, D. A. (1976). Sex effects in evaluating leaders. *Journal of Applied Psychology, 61*, 446-454.

Bass, B. M. (1981). *Stogdill's handbook of leadership*. New York: Free Press.

Bass, B. M. (1985). *Leadership and performance beyond expectations*. New York: Free Press.

Bass, B. M. (1990). *Bass and Stogdill's handbook of leadership* (3rd ed.). New York: Free Press.

Bass, B. M., & Avolio, B. J. (1993). Transformational leadership: A response to critiques. In M. M. Chemers & R. Ayman (Eds.), *Leadership theory and research: Perspectives and directions* (pp. 49-80). San Diego, CA: Academic Press.

Bell, E., Denton, T. C., & Nkomo, S. (1993). Women of color in management: Toward an inclusive analysis. In E. A. Fagenson, (Ed.), *Women in management: Trends, issues, and challenges in managerial diversity* (pp. 105-130). Newbury Park, CA: Sage.

Brief, A. P., & Aldag, R. J. (1975). Male-female differences in occupational values within majority groups. *Journal of Vocational Behavior, 6*, 305-314.

Brief, A. P., & Oliver, R. L. (1976). Male-female differences in work attitudes among retail sales managers. *Journal of Applied Psychology, 61*, 526-528.

Brown, K. A. (1984). Explaining poor group performance: An attributional analysis. *Academy of Management Review, 9*, 54-63.

Chemers, M. M. (1993). An integrative theory of leadership. In M. M. Chemers & R. Ayman (Eds.), *Leadership theory and research: Perspectives and directions* (pp. 293-319). San Diego, CA: Academic Press.

Chemers, M. M. (1994, July). *Heavy mettle: Confidence and optimism in leadership effectiveness.* Paper presented at the meeting of the International Congress of Applied Psychology, Madrid.

Chemers, M. M., Ayman, R., Sorod, B., & Akimoto, S. (1991, July). *Self-monitoring as a moderator of leader-follower relationships.* Paper presented at the International Congress of Psychology, Brussels.

Cohen, S. L., Bunker, K. A., Burton, A. L., & McManus, P. D. (1978). Reactions of male subordinates to sex-role congruency of immediate supervision. *Sex Roles, 4,* 297-311.

Conger, J. A. (1989). *The charismatic leader.* San Francisco: Jossey-Bass.

Cox, T. H., Lobel, S. A., & McLeod, P. L. (1991). Effects of ethnic group cultural differences on cooperative and competitive behavior on a group task. *Academy of Management Journal, 34,* 827-847.

Darley, J. M., & Fazio, R. H. (1980). Expectancy confirmation processes arising in the social interaction sequence. *American Psychologist, 35,* 867-881.

Day, D. R., & Stogdill, R. M. (1972). Leader behavior of male and female supervisors: A comparative study. *Personnel Psychology, 25,* 353-360.

Deaux, K. (1984). From individual differences to social categories. *American Psychologist, 39,* 105-116.

Eagly, A. H., & Johnson, B. T. (1990). Gender and leadership style: A meta-analysis. *Psychological Bulletin, 108,* 233-256.

Eagly, A. H., & Karau, S. J. (1991). Gender and the emergence of leaders: A meta-analysis. *Journal of Personality and Social Psychology, 60,* 685-710.

Eagly, A. H., Karau, S. J., & Makhijani, M. G. (1995). Gender and the effectiveness of leaders: A meta-analysis. *Psychological Bulletin, 117,* 125-145.

Eagly, A. H., Makhijani, M. G., & Klonsky, B. G. (1992). Gender and the evaluation of leaders: A meta-analysis. *Psychological Bulletin, 111,* 3-22.

Fiedler, F. E. (1967). *A theory of leadership effectiveness.* New York: McGraw-Hill.

Fiedler, F. E., & Chemers, M. M. (1974). *Leadership and effective management.* Glenview, IL: Scott, Foresman.

Fiedler, F. E., & Chemers, M. M. (1984). *Improving leadership effectiveness: The Leader Match concept* (2nd ed.). New York: Wiley.

Fiedler, F. E., & House, R. J. (1988). Leadership theory and research: A report of progress. In C. L. Cooper & I. Robertson (Eds.), *International review of industrial and organizational psychology* (pp. 73-92). London: Wiley.

Graen, G. B., & Scandura, T. A. (1986). Toward a psychology of dyadic organizing. In B. M. Staw & L. L. Cummings (Eds.), *Research in organizational behavior* (Vol. 9, pp. 175-207). Greenwich, CT: JAI Press.

Greenhaus, J. H., & Parasuraman, S. (1993). Job performance attributions and career advancement prospects: An examination of gender and race effects. *Organizational Behavior and Human Decision Processes, 55,* 273-297.

Greenhaus, J. H., Parasuraman, S., & Wormley, W. M. (1990). Effects of race on organizational experiences, job performance evaluations, and career outcomes. *Academy of Management Journal, 33,* 64-86.

Griffin, R. N. (1981). Relationships among individual, task design, and leader behavior variables. *Academy of Management Journal, 23,* 665-683.

Hackman, J. R., & Oldham, G. R. (1976). Motivation through the design of work: Test of a theory. *Organizational Behavior and Human Performance, 16*, 250-279.

Hammer, W. C., Kim, J. S., Baird, L., & Bigoness, W. J. (1974). Race and sex as determinants of ratings by potential employers in a simulated work-sampling task. *Journal of Applied Psychology, 59*, 705-711.

Heilman, M. E., Block, C. J., Martell, R. F., & Simon, M. C. (1989). Has anything changed? Current characterizations of men, women, and managers. *Journal of Applied Psychology, 74*, 935-942.

Heilman, M. E., Kaplow, S. R., Amato, M. G., & Stathatos, P. (1993). When similarity is a liability: Effects of sex-based preferential selection on reactions to like-sex and different-sex others. *Journal of Applied Psychology, 78*, 917-927.

Heilman, M. E., Martell, R. F., & Simon, M. C. (1988). The vagaries of sex bias: Conditions regulating the undervaluation, equivaluation, and overvaluation of female job applicants. *Organizational Behavior and Human Decision Processes, 41*, 98-110.

Heilman, M. E., Rivero, J. C., & Brett, J. F. (1991). Skirting the competence issue: Effects of sex-based preferential selection on task choices of women and men. *Journal of Applied Psychology, 76*, 99-105.

Heilman, M. E., Simon, M., & Repper, D. (1987). Intentionally favored, unintentionally harmed? The impact of sex-based preferential selection on self-perceptions and self-evaluations. *Journal of Applied Psychology, 72*, 62-68.

Helgesen, S. (1990). *The female advantage: Women's ways of leadership.* New York: Doubleday.

Hersey, P., & Blanchard, K. H. (1977). *Management of organizational behavior* (3rd ed.). Englewood Cliffs, NJ: Prentice-Hall.

Hersey, P., & Blanchard, K. H. (1988). *Management of organizational behavior.* Englewood Cliffs, NJ: Prentice-Hall.

Hofstede, G. (1981). *Culture's consequences: International differences in work-related values.* Beverly Hills, CA: Sage.

Hofstede, G. (1983, Summer). Motivation, leadership, organization: Do American theories apply abroad? *Organizational Dynamics, 9*, 42-63.

Hollander, E. P. (1964). *Leaders, groups, and influence.* New York: Oxford University Press.

Horowitz, R. (1983). *Honor and the American dream.* New Brunswick, NJ: Rutgers University Press.

House, J. (1981). Social structure and personality. In M. Rosenberg & R. Turner (Eds.), *Social psychology: Sociological perspectives* (pp. 525-561). New York: Basic Books.

House, R. J. (1971). A Path Goal Theory of leader effectiveness. *Administrative Science Quarterly, 16*, 321-338.

House, R. J., & Mitchell, T. R. (1974). Path-Goal Theory of leadership. *Journal of Contemporary Business, 3*, 81-98.

Hovland, C., Janis, I., & Kelley, H. H. (1953). *Communication and persuasion.* New Haven, CT: Yale University Press.

Hsu, F. L. K. (1981). *American and Chinese: Passage to differences* (3rd ed.). Honolulu: University of Hawaii Press.

Jeanquart-Barone, S. (1993). Trust differences between supervisors and subordinates: Examining the role of race and gender. *Sex Roles, 29*, 1-11.

Jennings, E. E. (1980, April). Profile of a Black executive. *World of Work Report,* p. 28.

Johnston, W. B., & Packer, A. E. (1987). *Workforce 2000: Work and workers for the 21st century.* Indianapolis: Hudson Institute.

Jones, E. W. (1986). Black managers: The dream deferred. *Harvard Business Review, 64*, 84-93.

Kipnis, D. M., & Schmidt, S. M. (1982). *Profiles of organizational influence strategies (Form M)*. San Diego, CA: University Associates.

Lee, D. M., & Alvares, K. M. (1977). Effects of sex on descriptions and evaluations of supervisory behavior in a simulated industrial setting. *Journal of Applied Psychology, 62,* 405-410.

Liden, R. C., Wayne, S. J., & Stillwell, D. (1993). A longitudinal study on the early development of leader-member exchanges. *Journal of Applied Psychology, 78,* 662-674.

Loden, M. (1985). *Feminine leadership or how to succeed in business without being one of the boys*. New York: Times Books.

Lord, R. G., & Maher, K. J. (1991). *Leadership and information processing: Linking perceptions and performance*. Boston: Harper Collins.

Maldonado, L. (1985). Altered states: Chicanos in the labor force. In W. A. Van Horne (Ed.), *Ethnicity and the workforce*. Madison: University of Wisconsin System, Board of Regents.

Meindl, J. R. (1990). On leadership: An alternative to the conventional wisdom. In B. A. Staw (Ed.), *Research in organizational behavior* (Vol. 12, pp. 159-203). New York: JAI Press.

Miner, J. B. (1977). Motivational potential for upgrading among minority and female managers. *Journal of Applied Psychology, 62,* 691-697.

Mitchell, T. R., & Wood, R. E. (1980). Supervisors' responses to subordinate poor performance: A test of an attributional model. *Organizational Behavior and Human Performance, 25,* 123-128.

Morrison, A. M. (1992). *The new leaders: Guidelines on leadership diversity in America*. San Francisco: Jossey-Bass.

Morrison, A. M., & Von Glinow, M. A. (1990). Women and minorities in management. *American Psychologist, 45,* 200-208.

Murillo, N. (1976). The Mexican-American family. In C. A. Hernandez, M. J. Haug, & N. N. Wagner (Eds.), *Chicanos: Social and psychological perspectives* (pp. 15-25). St. Louis: Mosby.

Murphy, S. E. (1992). *The contribution of leadership experience and self-efficacy to group performance under evaluation apprehension*. Unpublished doctoral dissertation, University of Washington, Seattle.

Nieva, V. F., & Gutek, B. A. (1980). Sex effects on evaluation. *Academy of Management Review, 5,* 267-276.

O'Reilly, C. A., III, & Roberts, K. H. (1973). Job satisfaction among Whites and non-Whites: A cross-cultural approach. *Journal of Applied Psychology, 57,* 295-299.

Osborn, R. N., & Vicars, W. M. (1976). Sex stereotypes: An artifact in leader behavior and subordinate satisfaction analysis? *Academy of Management Journal, 19,* 439-449.

Petty, M. M., & Lee, G. K. (1975). Moderating effects of sex of supervisor and subordinate on the relationship between supervisory behavior and subordinate satisfaction. *Journal of Applied Psychology, 60,* 624-628.

Petty, M. M., & Miles, R. H. (1976). Leader sex-role stereotyping in a female dominant work culture. *Personnel Psychology, 29,* 393-404.

Pettigrew, T. F., Jemmott, J. B., & Johnson, J. T. (1984). *Race and the questioner effect: Testing the ultimate attribution error*. Unpublished manuscript, University of California, Santa Cruz.

Quinn, R. E., Kahn, R. K., Tabor, J. M., & Gordon, L. K. (1968). *The chosen few: A study of discrimination in executive selection*. Ann Arbor: University of Michigan, Institute for Social Research.

Ragins, B. R. (1989). Power and gender congruency effects in evaluations of male and female managers. *Journal of Management, 15,* 65-76.

Ragins, B. R. (1991). Gender effects in subordinate evaluations of leaders: Real or artifact? *Journal of Organizational Behavior, 12*, 258-286.

Ragins, B. R., & Scandura, T. (1994). Gender differences in expected outcomes of mentoring relationships. *Academy of Management Journal, 37*, 957-971.

Ragins, B. R., & Sundstrom, E. (1989). Gender and power in organizations: A longitudinal perspective. *Psychological Bulletin, 105*, 51-88.

Ragins, B. R., & Sundstrom, E. (1990). Gender and perceived power in manager-subordinate relations. *Journal of Occupational Psychology, 63*, 273-287.

Rice, R. W., Instone, D., & Adams, J. (1984). Leader sex, leader success, and leadership process: Two field studies. *Journal of Applied Psychology, 69*, 12-32.

Riger, S., & Galligan, P. (1980). Women in management: An explanation of competing paradigms. *American Psychologist, 35*, 902-910.

Romero, M. (1979). *Chicano workers: Their utilization and development* (Monograph No. 8). Los Angeles: University of California, Chicano Studies Center.

Rosen, B., & Jerdee, T. H. (1973). The influence of sex-role stereotypes on evaluations of male and female supervisory behavior. *Journal of Applied Psychology, 57*, 44-48.

Rosen, B., & Jerdee, T. H. (1977). Influence of subordinate characteristics on trust and use of participative decision strategies in a management simulation. *Journal of Applied Psychology, 62*, 628-631.

Rosener, J. B. (1990, November-December). Ways women lead. *Harvard Business Review*, pp. 119-125.

Ross, W., Triandis, H. C., Chang, B., & Marin, G. (1982). *Work values of Hispanics and mainstream Navy recruits* (ONR Tech. Rep. No. 8). Champaign: University of Illinois.

Schein, V. E. (1973). The relationship between sex role stereotypes and requisite management characteristics. *Journal of Applied Psychology, 57*, 95-100.

Schein, V. E. (1975). Relationship between sex role stereotypes and requisite management characteristics among female managers. *Journal of Applied Psychology, 60*, 340-344.

Schott, J. L. (1970). *The leader behavior of non-White principals in inner-city elementary schools with integrated teaching staffs under conditions of high and low morale.* Unpublished doctoral dissertation, Purdue University, Lafayette, IN.

Scott, W. (1983). Trust differences between men and women in superior-subordinate relationships. *Group and Organization Studies, 8*, 319-336.

Slocum, J. W., & Strawser, R. H. (1972). Racial differences in job attitudes. *Journal of Applied Psychology, 56*, 29-32.

Snodgrass, S. E. (1985). Women's intuition: The effect of subordinate role on interpersonal sensitivity. *Journal of Personality and Social Psychology, 49*, 146-155.

Snodgrass, S. E., Hecht, M., & Ploutz-Snyder, R. J. (1994, August). *Status, gender, and interpersonal sensitivity with ongoing interaction.* Paper presented at the meeting of American Psychological Association, Los Angeles.

Terborg, J. R. (1977). Women in management: A research review. *Journal of Applied Psychology, 62*, 647-664.

Terborg, J. R., & Ilgen, D. R. (1975). A theoretical approach to sex discrimination in traditionally masculine occupations. *Organizational Behavior and Human Performance, 13*, 352-376.

Thomas, D. A. (1993). Racial dynamics in developmental relationship. *Administrative Science Quarterly, 38*, 169-194.

Thomas, R. R., Jr. (1991). *Beyond race and gender: Unleashing the power of your total work force by managing diversity.* New York: Amacom.

Thomas, V. G. (1982). The relationship of race and gender of supervisor, subordinates, and organization to estimated stress and supervisory style in a simulated organization: A study of business administration and management students. *Dissertation Abstracts International, 44*(12B), 3970.

Triandis, H. C. (1993). The contingency model in cross-cultural perspective. In M. M. Chemers & R. Ayman (Eds.), *Leadership theory and research: Perspectives and directions* (pp. 167-188). San Diego, CA: Academic Press.

Triandis, H. C., Marin, G., Lisansky, J., & Betancourt, H. (1984). Simpatía as a cultural script of Hispanics. *Journal of Personality and Social Psychology, 47*, 1363-1375.

Triandis, H. C., Ottai, V., & Marin, G. (1982). *Social attitudes among Hispanic and mainstream Navy recruits* (ONR Tech. Rep. No. 10). Champaign: University of Illinois.

Vinson, E., & Mitchell, T. R. (1975, August). *Differences in motivation: Predictors and criterion measures for Black and White employees*. Paper presented at the meeting of Academy of Management, New Orleans.

Vroom, V. H., & Yetton, P. W. (1973). *Leadership and decision-making*. Pittsburgh, PA: University of Pittsburgh Press.

Waldman, D. A., & Avolio, B. J. (1986). A meta-analysis of age differences in job performance. *Journal of Applied Psychology, 71*, 33-38.

Watson, J. G., & Barone, S. (1976). The self-concept, personal values, and motivational orientations of Black and White managers. *Academy of Management Journal, 19*, 36-48.

Weiss, H. M., & Adler, S. (1984). Personality and organizational behavior. In B. M. Staw & L. L. Cummings (Eds.), *Research in organizational behavior* (Vol. 6, pp. 1-50). Greenwich, CT: JAI Press.

Yukl, G. A., & Falbe, C. M. (1990). Influence tactics and objectives in upward, downward, and lateral influence attempts. *Journal of Applied Psychology, 75*, 132-140.

Yukl, G. A., & Tracey, J. B. (1992). Consequences of influence tactics used with subordinates, peers, and the boss. *Journal of Applied Psychology, 77*, 525-535.

PART III

ORGANIZATIONAL PERSPECTIVES ON DIVERSITY

7

Diversity in Organizations
Lessons From Demography Research

ANNE S. TSUI
TERRI D. EGAN
KATHERINE R. XIN

The workforce of organizations is becoming increasingly diverse or heterogeneous in such demographic attributes as age, sex, race, ethnicity, and national origin. This fact is well accepted among practicing managers and management scholars alike. Consequently, both groups are interested in understanding the effect of such diversity on the organization and in developing insights on how best to manage this increasingly diverse workforce. Fortunately, such knowledge is accumulating. Within the past decade, two largely nonintersecting but related streams of work that deal with this topic have appeared in the organization and management literatures. One stream, referred to here as *diversity research*, developed largely in response to the Hudson Institute report on the U.S. workforce by the year 2000 (Johnston & Packer, 1987). A second stream, referred to as *demography research*, was inspired by Pfeffer's (1983) paper on organizational demography. These two publications stimulated a plethora of empirical and theoretical work

AUTHORS' NOTE: This chapter was partially completed in fall 1993 while Anne S. Tsui was a sabbatical visitor at the School of Business and Management, Hong Kong University of Science and Technology. An earlier version of this chapter was presented as a paper at the American Psychological Society meeting, June 1993, Chicago.

analyzing the nature and effects of workforce diversity or heterogeneity on individuals, groups, and organizations.

Diversity research studies the effects of heterogeneity in a variety of social and cultural attributes on the employment experiences of individuals, usually individuals who are in the minority categories of these attributes. Diversity research takes heterogeneity in a setting as given, and the research agenda is driven by the social objective of improving practices in managing a diverse workforce. In this research stream, at least six books were published in the early 1990s (Cox, 1993; Fernandez, 1991; Jackson & Associates, 1992; Jameison & O'Mara, 1991; Loden & Rosener, 1991; Thomas, 1991). These books share the dual purposes of documenting the effect of diversity on employment outcomes as well as suggesting solutions to minimize the negative effects and to enhance the benefits of diversity. Many empirical and theoretical articles have also appeared that address the issue of diversity in organizations and work groups (e.g., Cox, 1991; Cox & Blake, 1991; Cox, Lobel, & McLeod, 1991; Jackson, 1992; Jackson & Associates, 1992; Jackson, May, & Whitney, 1993; Jackson, Stone, & Alvarez, 1993; Nkomo, 1992; Watson, Kumar, & Michaelsen, 1993). In this stream of work, much of the knowledge about the effects of diversity is based on case studies (e.g., Jackson & Associates, 1992), qualitative interviews (e.g., Fernandez, 1991), or social psychological experiments using student samples (e.g., Hoffman, 1979; McGrath, 1984; Shaw, 1981).

Demography research, on the other hand, studies both the causes and the consequences of the composition or distribution of specific demographic attributes of employees in an organization or in units within it. In studying consequences, organizational demography researchers are interested in the effect of demography on everyone, not only on minority individuals. These researchers seek understanding of the demographic dynamics as a primary goal; deriving policy or practice implications is a secondary objective. Another major distinction from diversity research is that demography research uses entirely organizational samples.

Since Pfeffer's article in 1983, at least 15 empirical studies and one edited volume (Tolbert & Bacharach, 1992) were devoted to topics on intraorganization demographic issues.[1] Six studies analyzed the nature and effects of demography in top management teams (see Table 7.1 for study authors and description of samples). Five focused on departments, work units, or work groups. Two studies analyzed demographic effects in project or new product teams. One study focused on a sample of organizations, and another

Table 7.1
List of Demography Studies Using Organizational Samples

Study	Sample
Top management teams	
1. Wagner, Pfeffer, & O'Reilly, 1984	576 members in 31 teams (*Fortune* 500 companies)
2. Bantel & Jackson, 1989	199 teams (chartered and national banks in 6 states)
3. Murray, 1989	89 teams (*Fortune* 500 companies) (observed over the period 1967 to 1981)
4. Jackson et al., 1991	625 members in 93 teams (bank holding companies)
5. Michel & Hambrick, 1992	134 *Fortune* 500 firms
6. Wiersema & Bantel, 1992	87 *Fortune* 500 firms
Departments, work groups, or work units	
7. McCain, O'Reilly, & Pfeffer, 1983	32 academic departments (one large university)
8. Hoffman, 1985	2,083 supervisors in 96 installations (Federal Civil Service Commission)
9. O'Reilly, Caldwell, & Barnett, 1989	129 employees in 20 convenience stores (in a national chain)
10. Konrad, Winter, & Gutek, 1992	623 individuals in 89 work groups (49 Southern California organizations)
11. Tsui, Egan, & O'Reilly, 1992	1,705 individuals in 151 operating units (three large organizations)
Project or product teams	
12. Zenger & Lawrence, 1989	88 members in 19 project groups (one electronics firm)
13. Ancona & Caldwell, 1992	45 new product teams (five high-technology companies)
Organizations	
14. Pfeffer & O'Reilly, 1987	298 hospitals (national random sample) (nursing staffs only)
Supervisor-subordinate dyads	
15. Tsui & O'Reilly, 1989	272 dyads in a *Fortune* 500 firm

addressed demographic issues in supervisor-subordinate dyads. The primary focus of these empirical studies was on investigating the impact of demographic composition on a variety of outcomes at the individual, group, and organizational levels. In addition, several conceptual papers (in Tolbert & Bacharach, 1992) provide interesting discussions on different typologies of demographic structures as well as on determinants of demographic composition and change in firms.

Though there are merits and limitations both to field studies using organizational samples and to laboratory experiments using student subjects, it seems desirable to integrate the knowledge derived from these two largely independent streams of research that focus on essentially the same problems. The purpose of the current chapter is threefold. First, it reviews published empirical work on organizational demography, beginning with specification of the conceptual and operational definitions of organizational demography. The review describes the specific demographic attributes studied and the specific effects analyzed in these studies, treating demographic composition as an exogenous variable.[2] The second purpose is to discuss the lessons learned from these demography studies and their implications for understanding diversity in organizations and for future research. A third purpose of this chapter is to argue that diversity is a context-dependent phenomenon; hence an ecologically valid framework of diversity in general or of demography in specific must incorporate the context as a central variable. We propose an organizational demography framework that emphasizes the role of organizational culture in understanding demographic processes within firms. This framework relates organizational culture, demography, and social identity to intergroup relations and to outcomes at both the individual and the group levels. An obvious implication of this framework is that empirical tests ideally should use field designs with organizational samples and incorporate organizational context as a central variable.

A Review of Demography Research

The Nature of Organizational Samples Used

The focus of existing demography research in organizations has been to study the effect of heterogeneity on specific demographic attributes among a group of individuals who work within a particular unit. The unit can range in size from dyads to an entire organization. Table 7.1 describes samples used in 15 demography studies.

As shown in Table 7.1, the largest unit of analysis was the entire organization. In the only example of this type, a random sample of 298 community hospitals was studied (Pfeffer & O'Reilly, 1987). The smallest unit of analysis was supervisor-subordinate dyads, 272 of which were studied in a large corporation (Tsui & O'Reilly, 1989). Most studies focused on the work group or unit, such as top management teams, product teams, or functional departments. It is important to note that there was no comparative study of the demographic composition of an organization's entire workforce. The study by Pfeffer and O'Reilly (1987) used only the nursing staff in community hospitals. Given that most companies have computerized personnel information systems and that methods exist to index the demographic distribution of an employee population, the lack of research on organizational-level demography is a puzzle.

A second interesting observation from Table 7.1 is that, with the exception of new product or R&D teams (Ancona & Caldwell, 1992; Zenger & Lawrence, 1989), there was no study of demography using production or service work groups. Given the importance and increasing use of teams in organizations (Lawler, Mohrman, & Ledford, 1992), research on the effect of diversity in operating work groups beyond R&D teams is desirable.

Conceptual and Operational
Definitions of Organizational Demography

Two major approaches of demographic analysis can be identified in the demography research stream—compositional and relational. These two approaches involve different definitions of demography, different levels of analysis, and different operational measures. *Compositional demography*, according to Pfeffer (1983), "refers to the composition, in terms of basic attributes such as age, sex, educational level, length of service or residence, race, and so forth of the social entity under study" (p. 303). Thus organizations can be described in terms of their sex composition, their racial composition, and so forth. Pfeffer further argued that

> it is the distributional properties of demography of the organization, not merely
> single descriptive statistics such as the mean, median, or proportion of the work force
> with a given length of service, that can be crucial in understanding the effects of
> demography on organizational processes and outcomes. (p. 307)

Therefore, measures that reflect variations in the entire length-of-service distributions across organizations or organizational subunits are more appropriate than those, for example, that reflect only a specific category of length of service.[3]

It is this emphasis on distributions and variations in these distributions across units that distinguishes Pfeffer's composition theory of demography from approaches proposed by Kanter (1977) and Blau (1977). Kanter and Blau both focused on the impact of proportions of workers on individuals, using race and sex as primary examples for such categorization. For example, they both would predict that individuals in the numerical minority category would have different social experiences than those in the majority category. Pfeffer, on the other hand, focused on length-of-employment distributions in which the concept of majority or minority is less relevant.

Several operational definitions of compositional demography have been used in empirical studies following the Pfeffer definition. The most common index for measuring the distribution of continuous variables like age or tenure is the coefficient of variation, defined as the standard deviation divided by the mean. Allison (1978), in a thorough review of measures of inequality, observed that the coefficient of variation provides the most direct and scale-invariant measure of dispersion. All of the eight studies listed in Table 7.1 that included a demographic attribute measured on a continuous scale employed this index. For categorical variables, four indices were found. They are the Blau index (1977), the diversity or heterogeneity index (Teachman, 1980), the Gini index (Blau, 1977), and the Shannon index (Shannon & Weaver, 1949).[4] Among the four, the diversity index is the most widely accepted measure for providing information on a distribution (Allison, 1978). Table 7.2 summarizes studies that have employed the five compositional demography measures. Each measure captures the distributional pattern of the group and focuses on the group or organization as the unit of analysis.

A second approach in demographic analysis is the relational demography idea, originated by Wagner, Pfeffer, and O'Reilly (1984) and formalized by Tsui and O'Reilly (1989). *Relational demography* refers to "the comparative demographic characteristics of members of dyads or groups who are in a position to engage in regular interactions" (Tsui & O'Reilly, 1989, p. 403). The definition was subsequently revised (Tsui, Egan, & O'Reilly, 1992) simply to refer to an individual's similarity to or difference from others in a group on specific demographic attributes. Interpersonal interaction is no longer assumed to be necessary for demographic effects to occur. This approach is used to analyze demographic effects on individuals in the context of a group.

Table 7.2
Compositional Measures of Organizational Demography

Study	Compositional Demography Measures				
	C/V	*BI*	*DI/HI*	*GI*	*SI*
Wagner et al., 1984	x		x		
Pfeffer & O'Reilly, 1987			x	x	
Bantel & Jackson, 1989	x	x			
Murray, 1989	x	x			x
O'Reilly et al., 1989		x			
Jackson et al., 1991	x	x			
Ancona & Caldwell, 1992	x		x		
Michel & Hambrick, 1992	x		x		
Wiersema & Bantel, 1992	x	x			

NOTE: C/V = coefficient of variation; BI = Blau index; DI/HI = diversity index or heterogeneity index; GI = Gini index; SI = Shannon index.

Table 7.3
Relational Measures of Organizational Demography

Study	Relational Demography Measures		
	Total Group	*Subgroup*	*Dyad*
Wagner et al., 1984		x	
Zenger & Lawrence, 1989		x	
O'Reilly et al., 1989	x		
Tsui & O'Reilly, 1989			x
Jackson et al., 1991	x		
Tsui et al., 1992		x	

NOTE: The primary index is the Euclidian distance measure. Total Group = distance between one individual and all others in a prespecified unit; Subgroup = distance between one individual and a subset of other individuals in a prespecified unit; Dyad = distance between two individuals.

The most frequently used operational definition of relational demography is the Euclidean distance measure. Computationally, it is the square root of the individual's mean squared distance from the other members in the group on any given demographic attribute. It is a network analogue for representing social similarity or, conversely, isolation (Burt, 1982). It has the advantage of being applicable to groups of any size. For large groups, a subset of the group may be used in deriving the distance measure (e.g., Wagner et al., 1984). At the dyad level, the squared difference in the values of the demographic variable for the two individuals has been used (e.g., Tsui & O'Reilly, 1989). Table 7.3 shows the types of distance measures used in studies on relational demography.

An important observation concerning measurement in demography is that the measures are all related to a single demographic attribute. Thus studies (e.g., Jackson et al., 1991; Tsui et al., 1992) that used multiple demographic attributes treated them as independent effects in regression models. Only one study (Murray, 1989) attempted to develop an aggregate measure that combined the scores over multiple variables. Unfortunately, Murray did not fully describe how these aggregate scores were formed. Another study (Judge & Ferris, 1993), not a primary demography study, summed the standardized absolute differences on age and job tenure between supervisor and subordinate, but no logic was offered for this summation process. Developing an understanding of the relationship among multiple demographic measures (both compositional and relational) is a needed and fruitful avenue for future research.

Demographic Attributes Studied in the Field

Table 7.4 summarizes the attributes included in the 15 demography studies as well as the specific effects analyzed. The tenure or date of entry variable was the most often analyzed attribute, appearing in 13 studies. Ten studies focused on tenure with the entire company, while five measured tenure with the team or group. One study (Tsui & O'Reilly, 1989), in addition to company tenure, also analyzed the difference in job tenure between supervisor and subordinate. Age was the next most frequently studied demographic attribute, appearing in 9 of the 15 studies. Usually age and tenure were included as independent variables in the same study, and such studies were designed explicitly to test Pfeffer's (1983) tenure demography theory. Educational level and functional background or specialization were each included in six studies. Sex and race each appeared in three studies.

The attributes studied most often were age and company tenure. While these two variables are important, especially for outcomes such as turnover, the smaller number of studies on other attributes suggests the opportunity for more work. The major challenge with many attributes is the sampling issue. Most top management teams, for instance, are primarily Caucasian males. There is little, often no, variance on the sex and race variables. Many laboratory studies, on the other hand, have focused on diversity on these two attributes. Jackson (1992b), however, questioned the generalizability of results from diversity research based on student samples. Research using management teams at lower levels, where there is more variation in race and sex,

Table 7.4
Attributes and Effects Analyzed in 15 Organizational Demography Studies

Study	Attributes Studied	Outcomes Analyzed
1. Wagner et al., 1984	age, company tenure	turnover
2. Bantel & Jackson, 1989	age, company tenure, function, education	technical innovation, administrative innovation
3. Murray, 1989	age, company tenure, team tenure, educational major, occupation	firm performance
4. Jackson et al., 1991	age, company tenure, educational level, college alma mater, curriculum, experience outside industry, military experience	turnover, promotions
5. Michel & Hambrick, 1992	team tenure, function	firm performance
6. Wiersema & Bantel, 1992	age, organizational tenure, team tenure, functional specialization	change in diversification strategy
7. McCain et al., 1983	company tenure (gaps in cohort)	turnover
8. Hoffman, 1985	race	interpersonal communication, organizational communication, interorganizational communication
9. O'Reilly et al., 1989	age, group tenure	social integration, turnover
10. Konrad et al., 1992	sex	isolation, sexism, dissatisfaction
11. Tsui et al., 1992	age, company tenure, sex, race, education	psychological commitment, absenteeism, intent to stay
12. Zenger & Lawrence, 1989	age, company tenure	technical communication
13. Ancona & Caldwell, 1992	team tenure, function	team process, external communication, innovation, performance (rated), budget, and schedule
14. Pfeffer & O'Reilly, 1987	company tenure	turnover
15. Tsui & O'Reilly, 1989	age, gender, race, education, job tenure, company tenure	(rated) performance, supervisory affect, role ambiguity, role conflict

NOTE: Statistically significant effects were found on those attributes and outcomes printed in bold.

199

may be invaluable in providing insight into the effects of these demographic configurations on interpersonal dynamics and decision processes.

For example, Tsui et al. (1992), using a sample of 151 operating units, found gender and race heterogeneity to be associated with low psychological commitment, high absence behavior, and high intent to leave the organization. The interesting result, however, was in the nonsymmetrical findings on both the sex and the race variable. Males and Whites were found to respond more negatively than females and non-Whites to increasing degrees of sex and race heterogeneity, respectively. Organizational attachment of males and Whites declined as heterogeneity on gender and race increased. However, heterogeneity had no effect on females' and non-White employees' attachment to the organization. These results suggest that the social dynamic of heterogeneity may be quite complex in organizational settings, and they underscore the importance of studying demographic variables in addition to age and company tenure.

Demographic Effects Analyzed

The outcome that has been studied most often is turnover—the dependent variable in five studies. These studies provided robust findings on the positive effect of age and tenure heterogeneity on turnover in management teams (Jackson et al., 1991; McCain, O'Reilly, & Pfeffer, 1983; Pfeffer & O'Reilly, 1987; Wagner et al., 1984) and work units (O'Reilly et al., 1989). In addition to age heterogeneity, Jackson et al. (1991) also found that heterogeneity in educational level, curriculum, and experience outside industry predicted turnover of individuals in executive teams.

The hypothesized mediating process that links demographic heterogeneity to turnover is low social integration, and the relationship between demography and social integration was analyzed in four studies. O'Reilly et al. (1989) directly measured social integration in the work unit and found it to be negatively related to the group-level tenure distribution. Konrad, Winter, and Gutek (1992) found that women in the minority are more likely to experience isolation and dissatisfaction, two measures of low social integration. Tsui et al. (1992) found a larger demographic distance of sex and race to be associated with low levels of organizational attachment. Finally, at the dyad level, demographic dissimilarity on gender, education, and job tenure was associated with a low level of liking by the supervisor for the subordinate (Tsui & O'Reilly, 1989). Interpersonal liking may be considered a form of social integration at the dyad level.

Communication behavior was the focus of three studies. Hoffman (1985) analyzed frequency of communication as a function of race composition in 93 supervisory teams. He found that a higher race ratio in the group (i.e., more Blacks) was associated with higher organizational-level communication but lower within-team communication. Zenger and Lawrence (1989) found that project members who were of similar age to others on the project team tended to engage in more technical communication with insiders, while those who were similar to members outside the project team on both age and organizational tenure tended to communicate more with outsiders. Ancona and Caldwell (1992) found that the greater the functional diversity of the new product team, the more team members communicated outside the team's boundary. In the same study, they also found such external communication to be associated with managerial ratings of greater team innovation. Innovation was the dependent variable in one other study (Bantel & Jackson, 1989), which found that more innovative banks were managed by more educated teams, who were diverse with respect to functional areas of specialization. It is unclear, however, whether the innovativeness associated with diversity implies good performance. For example, Ancona and Caldwell (1992) found both tenure diversity and functional diversity to be negatively associated with team-rated performance. It is possible that, even though diversity may enhance creativity, it may impede implementation of innovations generated by that creativity, due to the lower coordination capacity in heterogeneous compared with homogeneous work teams.

While Ancona and Caldwell (1992) analyzed performance at the team level, other studies focused on performance at the individual and organization levels. Tsui and O'Reilly (1989) found differences in gender and job tenure between superior and subordinate to be associated with low performance ratings of the subordinate by the superior. Murray (1989) discovered a negative relationship between occupational heterogeneity and firm efficiency (earnings ratios) but a positive relationship between temporal heterogeneity (defined by age and tenure variance) and firm adaptiveness (stock price ratios). Michel and Hambrick (1992) hypothesized that top management team demography (indexed by tenure and functional heterogeneity) would interact with corporate strategy to affect firm performance, but they did not find support for this hypothesis. The importance of diversity in the functional background of top management teams for corporate strategy, and especially for strategic change, was shown in another study (Wiersema & Bantel, 1992).

Four other dependent variables were investigated, three of which were found to be related to demography. Jackson et al. (1991) did not find a relationship between demographic similarity among team members and promotion of the lower status team members. Ancona and Caldwell (1992) found tenure diversity to be associated with improved task processes such as clarifying group goals and setting priorities. Tsui and O'Reilly (1989) reported lower role ambiguity by subordinates who were similar to their superiors on gender. Finally, Konrad et al. (1992) reported that women in male-dominated groups experienced more sexist stereotyping than women in female-dominated groups.

From this list of dependent variables, it appears that the primary focus of organizational demography research has been on testing the effect of heterogeneity on communication, cohesion, and turnover. The theoretical logic is based on two related perspectives, similarity-attraction theory (Byrne, 1971) and social identity theory (Tajfel, 1982). Individuals tend to identify with those who are similar to them on some personal attributes. Such identification is proposed to increase attraction and enhance communication, both of which foster understanding and solidify cohesion, resulting in a high level of commitment to the group (or the other individuals) and a low likelihood of leaving the group, that is, turnover. Ten of fifteen studies focused on these relationships.

A secondary focus of organizational demography research has been on the effect of diversity on performance at individual, group, and organizational levels. Performance measures include the firms' financial returns (Michel & Hambrick, 1992; Murray, 1989), innovation at organizational (Bantel & Jackson, 1989) and team levels (Ancona & Caldwell, 1992), changes in diversification strategies (Wiersema & Bantel, 1992), and subjective performance evaluations of teams (Ancona & Caldwell, 1992) and individuals (Tsui & O'Reilly, 1989). The primary logic underlying this research is the assumption of distributed resources or expertise among individuals with different backgrounds. Tenure is considered a proxy for experience, and educational or functional diversity represents different types of knowledge bases or expertise. These relationships received support in terms of firm-level innovation (Bantel & Jackson, 1989) and financial performance in one study (Murray, 1989) but not in another (Michel & Hambrick, 1992). A negative effect of team heterogeneity was observed both on management ratings of new-product team innovation and on teams' ratings of their own overall performance (Ancona & Caldwell, 1992). This negative relationship may be due to conflict and low social integration in diverse teams.

Lessons From Demography Research

What have we learned about diversity in organizations from demography research using organizational samples? The first lesson involves the domain of demographic attributes. Attributes analyzed in demography research complement those studied in the diversity stream of research. However, multiattribute research is lacking in both streams. The second lesson relates to the effects of demographic diversity. Findings on process outcomes corroborate those discovered in the laboratory studies, while results on performance outcomes are as inconclusive as those found in diversity research. The third lesson involves the meaning of specific demographic attributes. Results from demography research suggest that demographic interpretations may be both individually determined and situationally induced. These three lessons lead to the overall conclusion that diversity is a situation-dependent issue and that our understanding of diversity in organizations in general and of demographic processes in specific will be incomplete without incorporating the context in the framework.

Domain of Demographic Attributes

Based on the review in the preceding section, we may conclude with some confidence that heterogeneity in age and tenure is positively related to turnover, and negatively related to communication and cohesion. Of interest, age and tenure diversity were seldom studied in the diversity research stream. Most of the case analyses and experimental studies have focused on gender and race composition. Experimental studies by diversity researchers have been conducted almost exclusively with college students, for whom the variance in age is limited. Except in the rare instances where a longitudinal research design was used, the idea of (group) tenure also has been irrelevant. Thus the findings on age and tenure distribution in organizations have provided important knowledge about aspects of diversity that have not been addressed sufficiently in diversity research.

Demography research also introduced the idea of the demographic profile, arguing that individuals are a composite of multiple attributes (e.g., Tsui & O'Reilly, 1989). The dynamics of interaction among individuals, and consequently the effect of demography on the group and on individuals, may differ in non-trivial ways in cases involving different compositions on multiple demographic attributes. Diversity research tends to focus on one or at most two attributes. However, a man is not only a man; he may be a White man, an old man, a well-educated man, a man of particular religious beliefs, or a man of distinguished family background. All these attributes may interact to influence his interactions with others or the perceptions of others about him. Demography and diversity researchers concur that multiattribute measures are needed to handle this complexity.

A related question involves the relationship among the multiple attributes or their reduced dimensions. Are their effects cumulative or interactive in nature? Are there nonlinear patterns or configurations of attributes that may be associated with different process and performance outcomes? We would encourage explorations on various configurations of demographic attributes and their consequences for individuals and groups (Meyer, Tsui, & Hinings, 1993). Developing creative methods to capture demographic configurations or profiles seems essential.

In addition to considering the importance of multiple attributes, organizational scholars may find that the dynamics associated with particular patterns of demographic heterogeneity differ depending on the level of analysis. For example, there might be a different dynamic associated with age diversity in supervisor-subordinate dyads, in work teams, and in the organization as a total entity. In supervisor-subordinate relationships, superiors are generally expected to be older than subordinates. A large age difference in a dyad may lead to different interactional patterns and outcomes compared with dyads having a small age difference. However, in work teams, power is generally equally distributed and the correlation between power and age may be less strong. Therefore societal norms regarding power distance and age heterogeneity may not be a critical issue at the work team level. At the organizational level, age could have different connotations for different organizations. In a young, innovative, high-technology firm where the majority of workers are young, youth may be taken as a proxy for creativity. A middle-aged or old employee in this company might be viewed negatively by young employees.

When assessing the dynamics of demographic attributes, the level-of-analysis issue should not be ignored.

Results on the Effects
of Demographic Diversity

Most demography research focuses on process outcomes such as communication, cohesion and commitment, or turnover. Findings from these studies corroborate conclusions derived from social psychological research in laboratory settings. According to Jackson (1992b), evidence from laboratory studies is quite conclusive regarding the influence of attitudinal and demographic homogeneity on group cohesiveness. Less conclusive, however, are results on performance outcomes, though diversity research has focused substantially on group performance. Jackson (1992b) reviewed this stream of research and concluded that the only clear finding is that groups with heterogeneity on personal attributes and ability outperform homogeneous groups on tasks requiring creativity or judgmental decision making. There is no strong or conclusive evidence concerning the influence of heterogeneity on production or intellectual tasks, that is, tasks with known solutions. A similar conclusion may be drawn from demography research. Heterogeneity on certain dimensions, especially functional background, is associated with innovation (e.g., Ancona & Caldwell, 1992; Wiersema & Bantel, 1992), but there is no strong evidence on performance effects.

The lack of conclusive findings on performance outcomes may be due to inadequate specification of the relationships among the variables of demography, group process, and performance. A recent diversity study provides a good illustration of the complex relationships among these three variables. Watson et al. (1993) conducted a longitudinal study using student subjects, comparing both process and performance outcomes between teams that were racially heterogeneous or homogeneous (comprising all Caucasians), over 17 weeks divided into four time periods. The authors found that there was greater process and performance improvement over time in heterogeneous teams than in homogeneous teams. Initially, homogeneous teams outperformed the heterogeneous teams on all the measures. By the end of the fourth period, however, the heterogeneous teams outperformed the homogeneous teams on two of the five performance measures, and there were no differences on the remaining performance measures and one process measure. These results suggest that heterogeneous teams may require more time to work out process issues, but they may have greater promise for overall performance once those process issues are resolved. Thus time, a context variable, can play an important role in explaining and analyzing both process and performance outcomes. This study demonstrates the importance of research design in studying ongoing dynamic social systems, such as organizations. Results from research using a snapshot approach or cross-sectional design do not provide the total picture.

Another unique feature of this experimental design was that students received both performance and process feedback throughout the 17 weeks. This feedback may have played a critical role in individual and team learning concerning process issues as well as in the overall adjustment and cohesion of team members. With the increasing prevalence of work teams (e.g., Lawler et al., 1992), opportunities should be explored for conducting quasi-experiments that incorporate feedback and communication features. Such designs will allow tracking of the intricate relationship among heterogeneity, process, and performance outcomes.

Another design that could be used more often is the type of field experiment conducted by Aronson, Blaney, Stephan, Sikes, and Snapp (1978) in analyzing the effect of integration on children's performance in the "jigsaw classroom." These researchers found that ethnic minority children in mixed racial groups performed better when they were assigned to cooperative or interdependent learning tasks than when they worked on individual or independent learning tasks in group settings. The increased use of work team structures in contemporary organizations makes it possible to study the relationship between team heterogeneity and performance, moderated by different degrees of task interdependence.

In summary, the results on the dependent variables from demography research have provided confirming evidence on the effect of heterogeneity on process outcomes, but they have not produced knowledge about performance outcomes beyond that described in the diversity literature based primarily on laboratory studies using student subjects. These results suggest that understanding of diversity in organizations would be improved by demography research using quasi-experiments with ongoing organizational work groups and using a longitudinal design that permits the tracking of process and performance changes over time.

The Meaning of Demography

Findings from demography research also suggest systematic and subjective differences in the meaning of different demographic attributes. Jackson, May, and Whitney (1993) distinguished between readily detectable attributes and underlying attributes, and further organized the readily detectable attributes into task-related and relation-oriented categories. While such distinctions are a useful first step toward providing some clarity on the meaning of demography, categorizing an attribute as either task-related or relation-oriented may restrict rather than expand our understanding of the issue. For example, it is possible that an attribute (e.g., being a lawyer or an accountant) may convey both task-related and relation-oriented information. In some people's eyes, lawyers not only possess specialized expertise but also hold particular values. Occupation conveys information that may be potentially relevant for both task performance and relationships in the group. It is possible that most attributes may have both task and relationship implications. This may be part of the reason that demography researchers often use the same set of variables, such as age, sex, race, or education, to predict both relation-oriented outcomes (e.g., turnover, cohesion) and task-related outcomes (e.g., performance, innovation).

Demographic variables may differ in terms of their relationship to various outcome variables, depending on their underlying meaning to or subjective interpretation by team members. For example, demographic variables that convey attitudes and values but not ability and skills may be more strongly associated with conflict and cohesion than with performance. On the other hand, demographic variables that convey abilities and skills but not attitudes or values may be more strongly associated with performance than with cohesion and conflict. Probably the outcome will be less predictable if the attribute conveys both types of information.

Some research suggests that different people may subjectively ascribe different meanings to the same demographic attributes. For example, in the study by Tsui et al. (1992), sex appeared to be a more important social category for males than for females, and race appeared to be a more important source of identity for Whites than for people of color. In addition to individual differences on the subjective meaning of demography, its meaning may also be affected by situational cues. For instance, a young person may not recognize his or her youth when among a group of middle-aged individuals but may be very cognizant of difference in age when among a group of senior citizens. Research has shown that males reacted differently when in the minority than when in the majority (Wharton & Baron, 1987), implying that the situation modified the salience of the attribute.

Currently, researchers (e.g., Jackson et al., 1993) seem to assume that individuals attach the same meaning to a specific demographic attribute. This fundamental assumption may be problematic. Based on social identity and self-categorization theories (Tajfel, 1982; Tajfel & Turner, 1986; Turner, 1987), individuals derive self-identity from social categories, and different social categories are meaningful for different individuals. Future research on the effect of demography in small groups ideally should assess the cognitive processing of demographic information as well as potential subjective interpretations of demographic attributes by individuals in that social unit.

Summary

Based on lessons learned from demographic research, we conclude that the issue of demography is much more complex than suggested by most previous research. Demographic attributes are multiple and interdependent, with potentially differing results depending upon the level of analysis. In addition, organizations are dynamic social systems. Results from snapshot demographic research may be nonconclusive and nongeneralizable. Further, the preliminary results from this stream of research suggest that a demographic attribute may mean different things to different people and that its meaning may be affected by situational cues.

In essence, demography is about the relationship between a particular context and the demographic elements within it. Similarly, diversity is about the experience of being different from others in a specific setting that has a particular set of social structural features. Therefore analysis of specific demographic effects or of organizational diversity issues in general must incorporate the influence of the context in situ. The organization and its associated cultural attributes represent a context variable that may be particularly relevant for understanding the dynamics of demographic diversity in organizations.

We propose that the organization itself is a social category that comprises a set of unique cultural attributes conveying different meanings to different individuals. The organization as a cultural entity may be a source of social identity for some individuals. As a cultural entity, it may also modify the meaning or salience of other demographic attributes as well as the importance of these demographic patterns to individuals and groups. In the next section, we use the culture metaphor and two of the three perspectives proposed by Martin (1992) for analyzing an organization's culture, to illustrate how analysis and understanding of demographic effects may change depending on the cultural manifestations of an organization.

Understanding Demographic Diversity in Organizations: The Role of the Organization and Organizational Culture

Political scientist Robert Presthus (1978) suggested that we now live in an "organizational society," surrounded by organizations of all sorts. The employed population in particular spend two thirds of their waking hours in organizations. Organizations, however, are more than places where people work. For some people, organizations are a source of self-identity and emotional support. They are a "cultural phenomenon" in themselves, argued Morgan (1986)—"mini-societies that have their own distinctive patterns of culture and subculture" (p. 112). Martin (1992) elaborated further:

> As individuals come into contact with organizations, they come into contact with dress norms, stories people tell about what goes on, the organization's formal rules and procedures, its informal codes of behavior, rituals, tasks, pay systems, jargon, and jokes only understood by insiders, and so on. These elements are some of the manifestations of organizational culture. (p. 3)

The employing organization therefore has the potential of offering cultural meanings to its members much as do demographic variables of ethnicity, gender, or national origin.

In other words, the organization where people work potentially has the same social psychological significance for its employees' social identity as do these individuals' social or ethnic backgrounds. In this vein, Kramer (1991) referred to the organization as a "superordinate" category for deriving self-identity and proposed that intergroup relations would be more harmonious if members identified more with the organization than with the various units within it. Similarly, Tsui et al. (1992) considered the organization to be a potentially attractive psychological group for individuals. It appears that one critical question in understanding the role of the organization in demographic analysis is to determine when an organization as a social category will supersede other social categories in the social identification process.

The Organization as a Social Category

Social identity refers to the notion that individuals have some collective awareness of themselves as belonging to various groups that share some common identity (Tajfel & Turner, 1986). Social identity theory maintains that people derive their identity in great part from the social categories to which they belong. People belong to many different social categories and thus they potentially have a repertoire of many different identities to draw upon. To simplify perception and to reduce the infinite variability of stimuli into a more manageable number of distinct categories, people also engage in a process of categorization, by which objects and people are classified on the basis of similarities and differences. Through social categorization, others are perceived either as members of the same category as the self or as members of a different category. Groups that contain the self are likely to be perceived as special and regarded positively. This in-group bias or accentuation effect has been observed even in groups with minimal or near-minimal categorizations (Tajfel, 1982). Brewer (1979) showed that categorizing people, even on the basis of arbitrary criteria, can lead group members to perceive out-group members as less trustworthy, honest, or cooperative than members of their own (arbitrary) groups.

Social identity theory (Tajfel, 1982) and self-categorization theory (Turner, 1987) therefore place great importance on the group as a source of identity for the individual. The group, however, is not a constant phenomenon. As Abrams and Hogg (1990) explained:

> People do not experience the self-concept in its entirety but rather as relatively discrete self-images which are dependent on the "context." This means that different times, places, and circumstances may render different self-identifications "salient" self-images. The self is thus both enduring and stable, and also responsive to situational or exogenous factors. (p. 25)

The organization as a context provides an almost infinite number of possible categories that individuals may use to classify themselves and others. Further, it is a dynamic context in that its membership composition may change due to attraction and attribution processes. However, regardless of the extent of diversity, organizations need to gain cooperative efforts from their members. Citing work from numerous social psychologists spanning several theoretical schools, Turner (1985) suggested that

> there is a strong implication that the general process underlying mutually cooperative intentions and expectations is the extent to which players come to see themselves as a collective or a joint unit, to feel a sense of "we-ness," of being together in the same situation facing the same problems. (p. 34)

One implication of increasing diversity in organizations is its potential impact on the extent to which organizational members categorize themselves as "we" rather than as "us versus them." In general, it appears that self-categorization theory would predict that increasing diversity would make it more difficult to maintain a sense of organizational "we-ness."

Increasing diversity may also increase the likelihood of organizational subgroups forming and intergroup conflict and competition increasing. In fact, much of the empirical evidence reported in the previously cited field studies of organizational demography would support this general proposition. Clearly, however, organizations are not composed entirely of factions based on demographic or other social categories. Organizations are more than the composition of their members. One way of conceptualizing this "gestalt-like" quality of organizations is the concept of organizational culture. The nature of different cultural manifestations may provide insight into how the dynamics of demographic diversity may play out, and it may suggest when the organization will become a social category that supersedes other social categories as the primary source of social identity for its members versus when it will be subsumed by other perhaps less organizationally functional categories.

The Organization as a Cultural Entity

Martin (1992) proposed a three-perspective approach to analyzing an organization's culture. She argued that "when any single organization is viewed from all three perspectives, a greater understanding emerges than if it were viewed from any single perspective" (Martin, 1992, p. 4). Our purpose here is not to conduct a cultural analysis, but to explore the implications of organizational culture for demographic diversity when the organization is analyzed from different perspectives. For illustrative purposes, we will use two of the three perspectives proposed by Martin (1992)—the integrative and the differentiation perspectives. Our purpose is to illustrate, using these cultural perspectives, how the meaning and importance of demographic attributes may be moderated by the cultural manifestations of the larger organization embedding the individuals and groups.

The Integrative Perspective. Organizational culture is defined in terms of consensus and consistency in values, beliefs, and assumptions, which are widely shared and internalized by members of the organization. This single unifying organizational culture cuts across and through the organization, leading to the development of a superordinate organizational identity. From this perspective, the organization as a social category provides a positive social identity for individuals and, as an attractive psychological group, it is likely to supersede other bases of the individual's social identity, such as age, race, gender, occupation, or function.

The integrative perspective on organizational culture suggests that increasing diversity of individuals coming from outside the organization will be overridden by a unifying organizational identity once individuals enter the organization. Thus any negative impact of increasing diversity on organizational processes or outcomes would be weakened or neutralized by the presence of the superordinate organizational identity. This strong organizational identity is developed and maintained through the selection, retention, and attraction processes (Schneider, 1987) and through strong socialization (O'Reilly, 1989). Individuals may be initially attracted to an organization that will enhance their self-esteem. Once they join the organization, the socialization process reinforces the organization as an important source of their social identity. Individuals who do not fit will select themselves out or, if they remain, will be "denied," "separated," or "closed off" (Martin, 1992, p. 57).

In contrast, organizational members who are retained may adopt superordinate organizational identities, as evidenced by the following story told by the president of a company:

We have a young woman who is extraordinarily important to the launching of a major new [product]. We will be talking about it next Tuesday in its first worldwide introduction. She arranged to have her [baby born by a] Cesarean [operation] yesterday in order to be prepared for this event, so you—we have insisted that she stay home and this is going to be televised in a closed circuit television, so we're having this done by TV for her. (Jim, president, public panel discussion; Martin, 1992, p. 35)

Based on the integrative perspective, one possible interpretation of this story is that the organization is a more important social category for this woman's self-identity than her gender or her new motherhood.

In summary, when the cultural manifestations (i.e., formal and informal practices, stories, rituals, jargon, physical arrangements, and content themes) suggest that the integrative perspective is most descriptive of the organization as a cultural entity, there would be less negative impact on communication, cohesion, conflict, or performance due to demographic diversity.

The Differentiation Perspective. From the differentiation perspective, organizational culture is unifying and consistent within subcultures of the organization rather than throughout the entire organization. Stability is found within each subculture; however, particular subcultures may be quite different than one another. Here, organizational identity is subsumed under the identity associated with a particular subculture. Increasing demographic heterogeneity may be linked to specific changes in organizational processes and outcomes, depending upon the strength and pervasiveness of distinct organizational subcultures.

The importance of a particular demographic attribute to the individual will depend upon subcultural differentiation. Subcultures could be differentiated based upon functional specialty, occupation, race, or gender. Differentiation implies that there is no consistent interpretation of the same cultural manifestation at the organizational level. Employees from different subcultures may offer different interpretations of certain company practices. For example, some may interpret

the distribution of "perks" according to a manager's "pull" and surplus budget, rather than an employee's task-based need; . . . [Management by Walking Around] as a means of maintaining control over subordinate behavior, rather than making management more accessible to lower level employees; "consensus" decision-making as being controlled, in an inegalitarian manner, by upper levels of the hierarchy and certain functional areas, and so on. (Martin, 1992, p. 86)

These are examples derived from conflicts of interest between those in the organization who have power and those who do not. Conflicts of interest may also exist among subcultures defined along functional lines, occupational groups, or race and gender distinctions. Increasing demographic heterogeneity increases the likelihood of subcultures forming in the organization based on demographic attributes. This differentiation, in turn, increases the likelihood of within-group social cohesion and communication—while decreasing cohesion and communication between subcultures.

Factors bearing upon the relative positive or negative impact of subgroup identification on performance include (a) the extent to which the goals of the subgroups are congruent with one another and with the overall organizational goals and (b) the extent to which potential process issues are explicitly acknowledged and "managed" within the organization. As noted earlier, research suggests that, although heterogeneous groups may be initially less productive due to process impairment, over time these groups may be more productive (Watson et al., 1993). This enhanced productivity may be due to increased creativity and complex decision-making capacity as a result of group heterogeneity. It also could be due to the enhanced identification of the heterogeneous members with the task group over time. In other words, the task group may become a new salient category for members' social identity, superseding the members' initial categories, such as function, race, gender, or occupation. Recent laboratory studies have produced encouraging evidence on the usefulness of having role assignments crosscut category memberships (e.g., Marcus-Newhall, Miller, Holtz, & Brewer, 1993). Teams with membership that cuts across initial categories tend to express less intergroup bias than teams whose membership converges with initial categories, especially when the group task requires cooperation among team members.

Conclusions

Research on organizational demography is still in its nascent stage, and our knowledge of the results of diversity in organizations is quite limited. For example, from research to date, it appears that age and tenure heterogeneity are positively related to turnover and perhaps to creativity, but negatively related to communication and cohesion. However, our review of demography research suggests that much more work is needed in understanding and interpreting the effect of demographic diversity on performance outcomes at all levels of analysis: dyads, work teams, and the entire organization. In addition, some demographic attributes may convey task-related or relation-oriented information, or both. To better understand the significance of any demographic characteristic, future conceptual work is needed on the meaning of any particular demographic variable to different individuals. Longitudinal and cross-level studies of the differential impact of different demographic dimensions and multidimensional demographic patterns are important topics for future research.

Clearly, organizational demography is much more than the simple attributes of individuals. It is not only a group-level variable, focusing on the composition of the unit studied, in terms of sex, tenure, and so forth. It is also a relational variable. Further, its meaning and effects are modified by situational cues. Therefore theories of diversity in general or of organizational demography in particular need to take into account the effect of the organizational context that embeds individuals and groups. The organization with its associated cultural attributes is one relevant context variable that affects the meaning of demographic attributes and shapes the social identity of groups and individuals. Different manifestations of organizational culture may lead to different interpretations of demographic attributes and of their significance for individual identity, intergroup relations, and organization processes and performance. Demography in essence is both a dynamic and a context-based phenomenon. There is no one single correct interpretation of any particular demographic variable. Its meaning and its effect depend on who is interpreting the demographic variable, at what level, and in what context. Finally, research in organizational settings with organizational samples will be invaluable for providing an ecologically valid understanding of the nature and effects of demographic diversity in organizations.

Notes

1. Only empirical studies that used demography as the primary independent variable were considered as demography research in this review. Consistent with most diversity and demography

research, this chapter analyzes how the demography of organizations affects individuals and groups. We excluded working papers or papers presented in conferences but not yet published in journals or books.

2. Mittman (1992) indicated that "only a small number of studies have focused directly on the origins and determinants of demographic patterns and their trends in organizations" (p. 5). We could find only three such articles in the published literature (Baron, Mittman, & Newman, 1991; Keck & Tushman, 1988; Tolbert & Oberfield, 1991). This lack of attention to antecedents of demography is consistent with diversity research, in which demographic composition and trends are also treated as exogenous variables.

3. Following Pfeffer's definition, we excluded those studies that measured demography using either the mean (e.g., Finkelstein & Hambrick, 1990; Katz, 1982) or the proportion of a specific range in a distribution (e.g., Pfeffer & Moore, 1980). We included the study by McCain et al. (1983), which reported the size and number of gaps between cohorts. In it, the number of years between entry dates for adjacent hires was calculated, and then a distribution of such gaps was produced for each unit. This measure captures a specific distributional pattern, consistent with Pfeffer's definition.

4. The formula for the Blau index is $(1 - \text{Sum } Pi^2)$, where P is the proportion of group members in a category and i is the number of different categories represented in the group. The Shannon index (Shannon & Weaver, 1949) is of the form $1 - \text{Sum } \log(1/Pi)$, where Pi has the same meaning as the Blau index. In either case, if all members of the group are in one category, a situation of extreme homogeneity, the measure takes on a value of zero. Blau (1977, p. 67) suggests the following computational formula:

$$G = \frac{2 \text{ Sum } [S_i \, P_i \, (Pb_i - Pa_i)]}{2 \text{ Sum } S_i \, P_i}$$

where Si is the mean of the category Pi, Pi is the proportion of population in category i, Pbi is the proportion of population below Pi, and Pai is the proportion of population above Pi.

Although popular, the Gini index has problems, including an upper limit that is related to the number of categories, and a sensitivity to the underlying frequency distribution that results in an overweighing of left-skewed distributions (Allison, 1978). Because of these limitations, others (e.g., Teachman, 1980) recommend a diversity index (also referred as the heterogeneity index) based on the concept of entropy. This measure, originally developed by Shannon and Weaver (1949), has a flat sensitivity to transfers in the underlying distribution. This means that it "does not have diminishing marginal utility or where its utility of value (if any) is irrelevant" (Allison, 1978, p. 869). Thus it may be more appropriate for indexing the distribution of demographic variables. This measure is defined as

$$H = -\sum_{i=1}^{s} Pi \, (\ln \, Pi)$$

References

Abrams, D., & Hogg, M. (1990). *Social identity theory: Constructive and critical advances.* New York: Springer-Verlag.

Allison, P. D. (1978). Measures of inequality. *American Sociological Review, 43*, 865-880.

Ancona, D. G., & Caldwell, D. F. (1992). Demography and design: Predictors of new product team performance. *Organizational Science, 3*, 321-341.

Aronson, E., Blaney, N., Stephan, C., Sikes, J., & Snapp, M. B. (1978). *The jigsaw classroom.* Beverly Hills, CA: Sage.

Bantel, K. A., & Jackson, S. E. (1989). Top management and innovations in banking: Does the composition of the top team make a difference? *Strategic Management Journal, 10*, 107-124.

Baron, J. N., Mittman, B. S., & Newman, A. E. (1991). Targets of opportunity: Organizational and environmental determinants of gender integration within the California civil service, 1979-1987. *American Journal of Sociology, 96*, 1362-1401.

Blau, P. M. (1977). *Inequality and heterogeneity.* New York: Free Press.

Brewer, M. B. (1979). In-group bias in the minimal intergroup situation: A cognitive-motivational analysis. *Psychological Bulletin, 86*, 307-324.

Burt, R. S. (1982). *Toward a structural theory of action.* New York: Academic Press.

Byrne, D. (1971). *The attraction paradigm.* New York: Academic Press.

Cox, T. H. (1991). The multicultural organization. *Academy of Management Executives, 5*, 34-47.

Cox, T. H. (1993). *Cultural diversity in organizations: Theory, research, and practice.* San Francisco: Berrett-Koehler.

Cox, T. H., & Blake, S. (1991). Managing cultural diversity: Implications for organizational competitiveness. *Academy of Management Executives, 5*, 45-67.

Cox, T. H., Lobel, S. A., & McLeod, P. L. (1991). Effects of ethnic group cultural differences on cooperative and competitive behavior on a group task. *Academy of Management Journal, 34*, 827-847.

Fernandez, J. P. (1991). *Managing a diverse work force.* Lexington, MA: Lexington.

Finkelstein, S., & Hambrick, D. C. (1990). Top-management team tenure and organizational outcomes: The moderating role of managerial discretion. *Administrative Science Quarterly, 35*, 484-503.

Hoffman, E. (1985). The effect of race-ratio composition on the frequency of organizational communication. *Social Psychology Quarterly, 48*, 17-26.

Hoffman, L. R. (1979). Applying experimental research on group problem solving to organizations. *Journal of Applied Behavioral Science, 15*, 375-391.

Jackson, S. E. (1992a). Consequences of group composition for the interpersonal dynamics of strategic issue processing. In P. Shrivastava, A. Huff, & J. Dutton (Eds.), *Advances in strategic management* (Vol. 8, pp. 345-382). Greenwich, CT: JAI Press.

Jackson, S. E. (1992b). Team composition in organizational settings: Issues in managing an increasingly diverse work force. In S. Worchel, W. Wood, & J. A. Simpson (Eds.), *Group process and productivity* (pp. 138-173). Newbury Park, CA: Sage.

Jackson, S. E., Brett, J. F., Sessa, V. I., Cooper, D. M., Julin, J. A., & Peyronnin, K. (1991). Some differences make a difference: Individual dissimilarity and group heterogeneity as correlates of recruitment, promotions, and turnover. *Journal of Applied Psychology, 76*, 675-689.

Jackson, S. E., May, K. E., & Whitney, K. (1993). Understanding the dynamics of diversity in decision making teams. In R. A. Guzzo & E. Salas (Eds.), *Team decision making effectiveness in organizations.* San Francisco: Jossey-Bass.

Jackson, S. E., Stone, V. K., & Alvarez, E. B. (1993). Socialization amidst diversity: Impact of demographics on work team oldtimers and newcomers. In L. L. Cummings & B. M. Staw (Eds.), *Research in organizational behavior* (Vol. 15, pp. 45-109). Greenwich, CT: JAI Press.

Jackson, S. E., & Associates. (Eds.). (1992). *Diversity in the workplace: Human resource initiatives.* New York: Guilford.

Jameison, D., & O'Mara, J. (1991). *Managing work force 2000: Gaining the diversity advantage.* San Francisco: Jossey-Bass.

Johnston, W. B., & Packer, A. H. (1987). *Workforce 2000: Work and workers for the 21st century.* Indianapolis: Hudson Institute.

Judge, T. A., & Ferris, G. R. (1993). Social context of performance evaluation decisions. *Academy of Management Journal, 36,* 80-105.

Kanter, R. M. (1977). Some effects of proportions on group life: Skewed sex ratios and responses to token women. *American Journal of Sociology, 82,* 965-990.

Katz, R. (1982). The effects of group longevity on project communication and performance. *Administrative Science Quarterly, 27,* 81-104.

Keck, S., & Tushman, M. (1988). A longitudinal study of the change in group demographies. *Academy of Management Proceedings,* pp. 175-179.

Konrad, A. M., Winter, S., & Gutek, B. A. (1992). Diversity in work group sex composition: Implications for majority and minority members. In P. Tolbert & S. B. Bacharach (Eds.), *Research in the sociology of organizations* (Vol. 10, pp. 115-140). Greenwich, CT: JAI Press.

Kramer, R. M. (1991). Intergroup relations and organizational dilemmas: The role of categorization process. In B. M. Staw & L. L. Cummings (Eds.), *Research in organizational behavior* (Vol. 13, pp. 191-228). Greenwich, CT: JAI Press.

Lawler, E. E., III, Mohrman, S. A., & Ledford, G. E., Jr. (1992). *Employee involvement and total quality management: Practices and results in Fortune 1000 companies.* San Francisco: Jossey-Bass.

Loden, M., & Rosener, J. (1991). *Work force America! Managing employee diversity as a vital resource.* Homewood, IL: Irwin.

Marcus-Newhall, A., Miller, N., Holtz, R., & Brewer, M. B. (1993). Cross-cutting category membership with role assignment: A means of reducing intergroup bias. *British Journal of Social Psychology, 32,* 125-146.

Martin, J. (1992). *Cultures in organizations.* New York: Oxford University Press.

McCain, B. E., O'Reilly, C. A., III, & Pfeffer, J. (1983). The effects of departmental demography on turnover: The case of a university. *Academy of Management Journal, 26,* 626-641.

McGrath, J. E. (1984). *Groups: Interaction and performance.* Englewood Cliffs, NJ: Prentice-Hall.

Meyer, A. D., Tsui, A. S., & Hinings, C. R. (1993). Configuration approaches to organizational analysis. *Academy of Management Journal, 36,* 1175-1195.

Michel, J. G., & Hambrick, D. C. (1992). Diversification posture and top management team characteristics. *Academy of Management Journal, 35,* 9-37.

Mittman, B. S. (1992). Theoretical and methodological issues in the study of organizational demography and demographic change. In P. Tolbert & S. B. Bacharach (Eds.), *Research in the sociology of organizations* (Vol. 10, pp. 3-54). Greenwich, CT: JAI Press.

Morgan, G. (1986). *Images of organizations.* Beverly Hills, CA: Sage.

Murray, A. I. (1989). Top management group heterogeneity and firm performance. *Strategic Management Journal, 10,* 125-142.

Nkomo, S. M. (1992). The emperor has no clothes: Rewriting race in organizations. *Academy of Management Review, 17,* 487-513.

O'Reilly, C. A. (1989, Summer). Corporations, culture, and commitment: Motivation and social control in organizations. *California Management Review,* pp. 9-25.

O'Reilly, C. A., III, Caldwell, D. F., & Barnett, W. P. (1989). Work group demography, social integration, and turnover. *Administrative Science Quarterly, 34,* 21-37.

Pfeffer, J. (1983). Organizational demography. In L. L. Cummings & B. M. Staw (Eds.), *Research in organizational behavior* (Vol. 5, pp. 299-357). Greenwich, CT: JAI Press.

Pfeffer, J., & Moore, W. L. (1980). Average tenure of academic department heads: The effects of paradigm, size, and departmental demography. *Administrative Science Quarterly, 25,* 387-406.

Pfeffer, J., & O'Reilly, C. A., III. (1987). Hospital demography and turnover among nurses. *Industrial Relations, 26,* 158-173.

Presthus, R. (1978). *The organizational society.* New York: St. Martin's.

Schneider, B. (1987). The people make the place. *Personnel Psychology, 40,* 437-453.

Shannon, C. E., & Weaver, W. (1949). *The mathematical theory of communication.* Urbana: University of Illinois Press.

Shaw, M. E. (1981). *Group dynamics: The psychology of small group behavior* (3rd ed.). New York: McGraw-Hill.

Tajfel, H. (1982). *Social identity and intergroup relations.* Cambridge: Cambridge University Press.

Tajfel, H., & Turner, J. C. (1986). The social identity theory of intergroup behavior. In S. Worchel & W. G. Austin (Eds.), *Psychology of intergroup relations* (pp. 7-24). Chicago: Nelson-Hall.

Teachman, J. D. (1980). Analysis of population diversity. *Sociological Methods and Research, 8,* 341-362.

Thomas, R. R. (1991). *Beyond race and gender: Unleashing the power of your total work force by managing diversity.* New York: Amacom.

Tolbert, P., & Bacharach, S. B. (Eds.). (1992). *Research in the sociology of organizations* (Vol. 10). Greenwich, CT: JAI Press.

Tolbert, P. S., & Oberfield, A. A. (1991). Sources of organizational demography: Faculty sex ratios in colleges and universities. *Sociology of Education, 64,* 305-315.

Tsui, A. S., Egan, T. D., & O'Reilly, C. A., III. (1992). Being different: Relational demography and organizational attachment. *Administrative Science Quarterly, 37,* 549-579.

Tsui, A. S., & O'Reilly, C. A., III. (1989). Beyond simple demographic effects: The importance of relational demography in superior-subordinate dyads. *Academy of Management Journal, 32,* 402-423.

Turner, J. C. (1985). Social categorization and the self-concept: A self-cognitive theory of group behavior. In E. J. Lawler (Ed.), *Advances in group processes: Theory and research* (Vol. 2, pp. 77-121). Greenwich, CT: JAI Press.

Turner, J. C. (1987). *Rediscovering the social group: A self-categorization theory.* Oxford: Blackwell.

Wagner, W. G., Pfeffer, J., & O'Reilly, C. A., III. (1984). Organizational demography and turnover in top-management groups. *Administrative Science Quarterly, 29,* 74-92.

Watson, W. E., Kumar, K., & Michaelsen, L. K. (1993). Cultural diversity's impact on interaction process and performance: Comparing homogeneous and diverse task groups. *Academy of Management Journal, 36,* 590-602.

Wharton, A. S., & Baron, J. N. (1987). So happy together? The impact of gender segregation on men at work. *American Sociological Review, 52,* 574-587.

Wiersema, M. F., & Bantel, K. A. (1992). Top management team demography and corporate strategic change. *Academy of Management Journal, 35,* 91-121.

Zenger, T. R., & Lawrence, B. S. (1989). Organizational demography: The differential effects of age and tenure distributions on technical communication. *Academy of Management Journal, 32,* 353-376.

8

Organizational Implications of Diversity in Higher Education

DARYL G. SMITH

The issue of diversity in our society is one of the most widely discussed topics today. The amount of attention to it is related to a number of factors, including the changing demographic characteristics of the society, in which 85% of the new entrants to the domestic workforce will be minorities, women, and immigrants; insufficient progress in responding to these changes; and the growing occurrence of incidents of intolerance (Fernandez, 1991; Smith, 1989). All of these reasons suggest the need for change in organizational practices. How fundamental the change needs to be and what it suggests for society in general are the topic of much analysis and debate (Copeland, 1988; Fernandez, 1991; Loden & Rosener, 1991; Schlesinger, 1992; Thomas, 1990, 1991). This chapter aims to bring the broader topic of diversity in organizations "home" to higher education, and to discuss an evolving concept of diversity and its implications for institutional practice and research.

Because those who study and work with organizations are often, at the same time, academics situated on a college or university campus where the topic of diversity may be highly charged and visible, the chapter will take a binocular view of contemporary issues of diversity in higher education. One lens will focus on higher education and on a conceptual framework for diversity. The second will look at psychological research on diversity, and I will suggest that such research needs to be reframed and reconstituted if it is to play a role in informing the changes underway in organizations in general and in higher education in particular. Such a binocular view is particularly appropriate because the sphere of higher education and its role in producing knowledge intersect strongly with the applied context of organizational behavior. Much of the research in psychology has been campus-based, on college students, and some of what we know about human behavior and organizations has emerged from organizational studies of higher education (e.g., Pfeffer, 1983; Weick, 1976).

Diversity Is an Evolving Concept

It has been said that the way a question is framed shapes the research we do, the methodology employed, and the range of solutions explored (Edelman, 1977; Willie & Edmonds, 1978). Similarly, the way diversity issues are framed is critical to organizational approaches to the topic. Like everything else related to diversity in higher education, the definition of diversity continues to evolve, and the questions being asked about it are shifting. More and more scholars and practitioners have moved from focusing solely on affirmative action to inclusion of other, broader perspectives (Ferdman, 1992; Morrison, 1992; Pettigrew & Martin, 1987; Thomas, 1990). However, the literature often fails to reflect these changes explicitly in ways that illuminate how relevant theory and practice are developing.

Judging from the evolution of diversity issues in higher education, it seems useful in this chapter to describe some of the conceptual developments involved in organizational issues concerning diversity. Readers should be aware that this is a contemporary perspective of a participant observer in the process, and that the process being described is not yet complete. Thus full understanding of the issues may not be possible. Yet, in keeping with higher education's several roles as educator, social institution, and producer of knowledge, reflection on these diversity issues is crucial.

Dimensions of Diversity

Defining diversity has been quite problematic. Increasingly, however, applied researchers and practitioners have called for more careful definitions, on the assumption that the way diversity is defined affects all aspects of the topic (Levine, 1991; Thomas, 1990). For example, does diversity refer only to underrepresented groups such as African Americans and Latinos, or does it also include women? How inclusive should a study of campus climate be? Should it include attention to the climate for gays and lesbians and/or Asian Americans? Conceptually, is curriculum transformation an inevitable result of changing campus and societal demographic factors, or is it more than that? Because of the inherent complexity of the topic and the significance of the outcomes, discussions about definitions of diversity have the potential to delay action and to become divisive. Particularly in academic contexts, discussions about definitions, much like discussions of institutional mission, can be a ready substitute for problem solving and institutional change. Thus a focus on defining diversity precisely may not be strategic (Weick, 1979).

Nevertheless, framing discussions in terms of the evolution of our understanding of the concept, rather than presenting a concrete definition, can potentially illuminate what diversity has come to mean while still allowing for the continuing evolution of the term. Weick (1979) has suggested that reflecting upon institutional actions can clarify conceptual issues and institutional values in a way that abstract discussion does not. Thus discussing the evolution of the concept of diversity over the last decades in higher education provides a way to illustrate changes in the framing of questions about diversity and to shed light on today's picture, in both research and institutional practice. This approach also highlights the multidimensional nature of diversity.

The following sections outline four dimensions of diversity that represent phases of its evolution over time in higher education and in society. The outline is not meant to reflect a precise historical sequence but to highlight the broadening perspective of diversity, which is also illustrated in Figure 8.1.

Dimension I: Representation.   The first dimension of diversity has focused on representation of previously unincluded groups. This is the most commonly understood element, and it has emerged from a concern for those who had been underrepresented in organizations and in higher education (Olivas, 1992). Thirty years ago, higher education greatly augmented its efforts to create opportunities for access and to lower barriers for groups that had formerly been precluded from attending many colleges and universities. The focus then was on students of color from "historically underrepresented groups," and in some fields on Euro-American women. Affirmative action programs became a legal mandate to *redress past discrimination* for such groups and

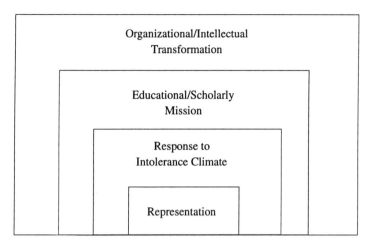

Figure 8.1. Dimensions of Diversity

required that positive actions be taken in recruitment and hiring. Other steps to contribute to greater access included targeted financial aid, desegregation, the building of community colleges, and men's colleges becoming coeducational. These efforts were conceptualized primarily in terms of social justice and equity, and they created a spurt of activity, which later in the 1970s began to die out, as many social justice efforts did (Olivas, 1984; Thomas, 1989). Nevertheless, affirmative action and a focus on representation and numbers became and have remained a fundamental core of the topic of diversity.

The student population of higher education today is quite different than it was just 30 years ago. Of 12,500,000 current college and university students, 53% are women, 42% are over age 25, 43% attend part-time, and 20% are persons of color (National Center for Educational Statistics, 1994). In California, the statistics reflect even greater diversity. While higher education is more diverse racially and ethnically, the changes in the student body are not nearly commensurate with the overall population figures or with high school graduation rates, and little change has occurred at faculty and administration levels. Students of color are still largely located in the community colleges, and some sectors and fields of higher education are still far from reflecting the aggregate gender distribution (Mingle, 1987; Smith, 1989). Many campuses are still confronting the implications of having populations of students, faculty, or staff that do not reflect the changing demographic characteristics of the society. Nevertheless, patterns of increasing diversity of student background are beginning to touch even the small, traditional liberal arts institutions and the major research institutions. For example, Stanford's entering freshman class for 1993-1994 was 50% women, 45% students of color, and 5% international, reflecting the greater diversity of California and the applicant pool.

Affirmative action programs and other efforts to increase diversity of representation have been maintained in part because of pressure from external constituencies, in part due to increasing student activism, in part from enrollment pressures, and in part from a recognition that the social fabric of our society will depend on its ability to actively involve a diverse cross section of the population. As the population becomes increasingly diverse in terms of racial and ethnic background, colleges and universities are also expected to become increasingly diverse. Thus representational issues remain in the 1990s a central and essential element of institutional concern.

Dimension II: Climate and Responses to Intolerance. While the changes in student demographic characteristics, in particular, mark some progress in terms of access, many issues remain. There is not only a continuing concern about access, but also urgent issues concerning student retention, graduation rates, alienation, harassment, and isolation. Campuses have had to address incidents of racism, anti-Semitism, and gay-bashing, as well as charges that access and support are lacking for students with physical and learning challenges (Hurtado, 1992; Smith, 1989). Thus discussions of diversity inevitably include, in addition to issues of social justice and representation, problems concerning retention, academic success, the quality of campus life including its climate and intergroup relations, and continuing stories of groups feeling excluded even as the rhetoric of inclusion grows (Madrid, 1990; Sandler & Hall, 1986; Smith, 1989).

These concerns have resulted in the development of programs (a) to support the educational goals of groups and individual students from underrepresented groups and (b) to support students from groups that, though not underrepresented, experience hostility, harassment, and alienation, including gay, lesbian, and Jewish students. As campuses have broadened their diversity concerns from representation to the quality of students' experience, an important shift has occurred. The quality dimension requires addressing institutional behavior and practices that affect the psychosocial environment and making explicit the impact of the environment on academic success. Within this dimension, the groups that are included broaden, and the focus is more squarely on institutional ethos, practice, climate, and responses to intolerance. Institutional responses in this area have typically included programs that stress valuing of differences, sensitivity training, and provision of support groups (Bowser, Auletta, & Jones, 1993; Rowe, 1990; Thomas, 1990). While quite prevalent on campuses throughout the country, these activities, as a primary approach, have been criticized by those who have pointed to the limits of human relations training that neglects structural and social inequities (Mohanty, 1993).

Dimension III: Educational/Scholarly Mission. From the beginning, part of the dialogue about diversity has focused on the curriculum. Early literature focused on the significance of an inclusive curriculum for the "new students" who were coming to the institution (e.g., Blassingame, 1973; Mohanty, 1993). Perceiving that the curriculum was connected to self-esteem and that it provided role models, and recognizing that much had been omitted from traditional academic fields, many early programs focused on an educational dimension of diversity. The development of ethnic studies and women's studies fields provided the scholarly and intellectual base for these efforts. These new fields developed important areas of scholarly inquiry while also raising questions about traditional practices in the academic disciplines that had excluded certain groups and topics. By their nature, these new fields tended to be interdisciplinary and to bridge theory and practice.

As many institutions have encountered and tried to grapple with incidents of intolerance, as institutions throughout the society have been affected by the changing demographic characteristics of the country, and as international boundaries have become increasingly porous, many campuses have begun to see that educating *all* students for a diverse society and world is part of an emerging institutional mission—one from which all students might benefit and, indeed, one to which students who come from diverse backgrounds bring important new perspectives. The result has been an emerging effort to reconsider those areas of the curriculum and of knowledge that have been underrepresented from an academic point of view. These current efforts to make the curriculum more diverse are not promoted merely so that some groups of students will see themselves reflected there. While that will certainly happen, higher education, for better or worse, has never defined its disciplines and curricula for that purpose. Rather, the focus in this effort is on educating students—all students—to live in a multicultural society and world.

This movement is very similar to earlier discussions about computers and technology that led to profound changes in academic curricula and resources

(Carnegie Council, 1981). As campuses began to observe the increasing centrality of technology, profound changes were introduced into institutional practices and goals. Computers were introduced throughout the campus. Courses were developed to educate broad cross sections of students about changing technologies, and faculty were hired for departments and programs that had not previously existed except in highly specialized sectors of the institution. Relevant to our discussion of diversity, it is important to note that campuses moved forward on issues related to computers even with unclear and sometimes controversial definitions of "computer literacy" and "educating for technology." Faculty and administrators understood that they had to take part in broadening the definition of education to include technology.

Similarly, the curricular discussions of diversity that stem from an evaluation of the educational mission have provided powerful contexts for change on many campuses. Just as colleges and universities embraced the notion of educating for computer and technological literacy, many campuses are increasingly emphasizing that all students must be educated to live and work in a diverse society and world (although this change is occurring with much greater reluctance and controversy). Today about 20% of campuses require students to take at least one course dealing with race and gender, and about 46% require a course concerned with world civilizations (Levine & Cureton, 1992). These requirements reflect a belief that, through education, students will be able to participate more fully in a diverse world and will be able not only to appreciate cultures other than their own but also to understand how constructs such as race and gender are implicated in continuing concerns about societal discrimination and injustice (Mohanty, 1993).

To a greater or lesser degree, virtually all fields are having to reconsider issues of whose story has been told, which questions have been asked, and which methodologies have been used. Even more fundamentally, such issues challenge existing paradigms and theories. In these dialogues, there is increasing attention to scholarship and scholars in ethnic studies and feminist thought.

In this area, higher education is rather unique among types of organizations. The first two dimensions of diversity, representation and climate, are clearly relevant to any organization. However, with regard to mission, the primary purpose of most organizations is not directly related to diversity even if the organizations are affected by diversity issues. Thus contemporary studies of workforce diversity focus on how businesses need to consider the changing demographic characteristics of society and how their own work-force can function effectively in such an environment (Thomas, 1990).

In contrast, higher education's contemporary mission can be seen as centrally related to diversity. Educating students for positions in society, in both a narrow vocational sense and a larger civic sense, is at the heart of the educational enterprise. If students are not prepared to function in a pluralistic society and world, educational programs could be as anachronistic as business programs that focus mainly on typewriters and adding machines. Thus, in viewing diversity not only as an issue of social justice for those who have been excluded, and not only as an issue of creating a supportive climate for increasing numbers of students, but also as an issue of educational purpose for all students, the discussions about diversity go to the heart of education. Emerging scholarship on issues of cultural democracy, and on higher education's role as a model of civic community in a diverse society, are significant elements of education today (Cortes, 1994; Darder, 1991; Mohanty, 1993; Murchland, 1991; Ramirez & Castaneda, 1991). Thus the third dimension, "educational mission," can and must play a central role in engaging diversity on campus, and it has the potential to involve broad cross sections of faculty and staff who understand that the intellectual and educational dimensions of diversity are critical.

Dimension IV: Transformation. With the addition of new perspectives, from students and particularly from faculty, scholarship in higher education has been profoundly altered. New fields have emerged, interdisciplinary study has increased, and fundamental critiques of traditional scholarship have been presented. Many of the approaches that focus on incorporating multiple perspectives have also helped to break down traditional barriers between the researcher and those under study, encouraged links with communities outside of academe, and required new and more qualitative methodologies. The important point here is that, though these changes have been spurred in part by the changing demographic characteristics of students and faculty, they have brought new perspectives to traditional theory and practice in virtually all academic fields (Harding, 1986; Lincoln, 1989; McIntosh, 1983, 1990; Minnich, 1990).

. In addition to fundamental changes in scholarship, many institutional practices have been subjected to scrutiny, and new efforts and approaches are being developed in virtually all segments of institutional life. Higher education is having to reconsider many concepts and practices—the ways in which excellence is measured, concepts of leadership, teaching and learning practices such as grading on the curve, and decision-making processes, to name just a few. Many more colleges and universities are starting to ask this fundamental question: What would our institution look like and be like if we were truly educating a diverse student body to live and work in a pluralistic society? The answer to this question goes far beyond addressing the background characteristics of members of the campus community; it involves new understandings about education, teaching and learning, and, indeed, institutional practice. The procedures of standardized testing, pitting students against one another through competitive grading practices, and traditional hierarchical forms of leadership have all been criticized as being counterproductive to learning and decision making. Moreover, campuses are having to confront their own capacity to model civic communities. Significantly, many of the emerging transformations in higher education are consistent with other conceptual shifts occurring in organizational theory and other disciplines. These changes have been described by some as no less than a paradigm shift—one that encourages multiple perspectives, holistic thinking, and complex rather than dichotomous understanding of issues (Berquist, 1993; Ferdman, 1992; Lincoln, 1989).

Negotiating Changes on
the Four Dimensions at Once

The four dimensions of diversity, on most campuses, are being engaged to greater or lesser degrees, and these strands are often occurring simultaneously. Thus institutional conversations about diversity are generally complex because each dimension focuses on different groups and has different, though related, implications for action (Kanter, 1976; Konrad & Gutek, 1987; Tajfel, 1982). The continuing concerns about representation affect groups that have been historically underrepresented, while the issue of a hostile climate for diversity also strikes at other groups even if they are not underrepresented. The research evidence is growing that shifting demographic factors do have an impact on social relations (Kanter, 1976; Konrad & Gutek, 1987; Tajfel, 1982).

Educating for diversity should engage everyone because it involves educating students for the world in which they live. This is a serious challenge because most students come from highly segregated backgrounds with limited exposure to students from different backgrounds. At the same time, scholarly knowledge about intergroup relations is being created, and our institutions are being pushed to change. In most cases, the leaders responsible for implementing these changes have little experience or expertise in the area. And those who have had some engagement with these issues over the last years find themselves spread too thin and placed in exposed positions (Davis, 1993). Nevertheless, each of these dimensions of diversity can reinforce the others and create a potential synergy toward revising education and scholarship.

For those who have been engaged in the diversity area for some time, there is no disjunction in talking about recruitment, affirmative action, campus climate, and curricular transformation under a single agenda of diversity. For those less familiar with the issue, or those who are particularly concerned about one dimension or another, an undifferentiated discussion may create tension and controversy.

Perhaps one of the most striking observations about the growing scope and depth of diversity issues is that the work of diversity has only begun when there is sufficient diversity of representation in the institution to engage the other three dimensions. The task is challenging because so few leaders have had experience working with the complexities of diversity in building and developing organizations. Effective decision making in such a context will require that there be sufficient diversity among participants so that multiple perspectives and implications can be considered. Thus, while student demographic factors may reflect remarkable diversity, the lack of significant diversity in faculty, administration, and trustee ranks will place institutional decision making at risk. This issue is being worked through again and again on campuses throughout the country. The imperative for diversification thus goes far beyond the need for role models for particular groups of students. It requires us to model the diverse community needed for the future and for effective decision making.

Research Practice and Phases in the Study of Higher Education

Particularly since the 1960s, applied researchers have been studying diversity and have been central in framing the questions about diversity. As many critics have pointed out, however, the research in many ways reflected the prevailing assumptions and paradigms of the context in which it was developed. We must realize that research, particularly concerning human and organizational behavior, is not "neutral" and "objective" in the ways that the traditional social sciences had hoped. Indeed, research in psychology has often reflected currently prevailing biases (Gilligan, 1982; Harding, 1986; Keller, 1982; Spence, 1993; Thomas, 1989; West, 1991). From an insider's perspective, it is difficult to see the limitations of existing knowledge or research. It is no coincidence that many compelling critiques of the social sciences, of research in general, and of the curriculum have been offered by those who have been marginalized in the field and who thus bring an alternative perspective to research and to scholarship. For example, feminist scholarship, developed by women who could see the problems with existing models of gender; Black studies researchers, who could see the bias in research on issues of race; and African American women, who saw the intersection of these two fields, have been among the most astute critics of traditional social scientific methods (Butler & Walter, 1991; Foucault, 1977; Giroux, 1990; Hull, Scott, & Smith, 1982; Takaki, 1989).

There seem to be some emerging patterns of new frames of reference regarding educational institutions and the nature of our knowledge concerning human behavior, organizations, and intergroup relations. These changes are fundamental and important in our efforts to improve education for all students. However, they raise issues that are not easily introduced in academic contexts because they challenge deeply held assumptions about the objectivity and neutrality of scholarly work and because they introduce emotionally loaded constructs such as power and privilege. In contrast to discussions about computers, discussions about diversity are more often threatening (Sherif, 1987; Thompson & Tyagi, 1994).

In examining various ways in which psychological research in such areas as organizational behavior, intergroup relations, and student success has been framed, a useful model is one originally proposed by McIntosh (1983, 1990) to describe stages of curriculum transformation. I have adapted it here to a more generic form. This model has been widely used to indicate whether and how issues of diversity are engaged. Even though it looks like a stage theory, it should not be viewed as such; the phases can be cyclical but they can also coexist. Each phase has different ways of framing questions, which lead to very different results. The model is a heuristic device, providing a way of thinking about research, psychology, organizations, and the development of knowledge. The model describes five phases of change or transformation.

(1) Absence of Diversity. In this phase, diversity is not engaged. While this is often described as the White male Eurocentric perspective, it is more accurately a reflection of periods where science and research were seen as objective and where the perspective of the researcher was not acknowledged as an influence on what questions were asked, how studies were done, and what conclusions were drawn (Bevan & Kessel, 1994; Sampson, 1993). The goal of developing universal theories about human behavior in the social sciences has been an important pressure to eliminate variation. The significance of scientific research has been measured, in part, in terms of its universal applicability. When norms of human behavior were based on such theories, which were often grounded in rather homogeneous data, all those who didn't fit were typically seen as irrelevant or deficient. For example, in psychology, the theory of achievement motivation was developed solely on men because women's data didn't fit the theory (McClelland, 1961). Key psychological theories about identity were based on White males as models even when sex differences were observed (Erikson, 1968). Notions of power and leadership emerged from studies of traditional men in organizations or men in society (Chafe, 1991; Lipman-Blumen, 1989). Women's deficiency in achievement motivation and identity, and the lower native intelligence of African Americans, were all "scientifically" justified through research (Fausto-Sterling, 1981).

In higher education, early research on students simply described students in general. Group differences were either ignored or controlled by eliminating subgroups who were different. Differences that were acknowledged, such as lower IQ scores or SAT scores, were often attributed to individual or group limitations in intelligence and aptitude rather than seen as functions of test biases, of generic norms about human development based only on a homogeneous group, or of environmental factors. Thus the absence of diversity in a setting was viewed as reflecting a flaw in the absent groups. The absence of "great" women mathematicians was attributed to women's lack of ability in math. The absence of great leaders from a given background was described as a sad commentary about the state of that group.

(2) Notable Exceptions. This phase begins to identify the notable exceptions among underrepresented groups and can be viewed as the beginning of a representational approach. An academic subject is taught as before, but with

the addition of notable exceptions—notable women or persons of color who fit the traditional criteria for inclusion. For example, in history, Joan of Arc is added to the study of war. Studies of the notable exceptions may take the form of biographies of famous mathematicians or psychologists, who can serve as heroes or role models. Faculty and scholars have often found this approach uncomfortable because it seems like an inappropriate stretch. Nevertheless, calls for inclusivity and sensitivity to neglected groups have often resulted in consideration of notable exceptions while leaving the field itself relatively unexamined.

(3) The Group as Problem. The third phase asks why groups have been absent and is often framed in terms of "the group as problem." In the early years of feminist scholarship, there were many studies on women and depression, why women can't lead, and women's lack of assertiveness. Matina Horner's (1972) work on fear of success is a classic example of this. Research on why women were not in math and science, or why students of color were not admitted to higher education or did not succeed, was conducted by examining such explanatory characteristics as performance on the SAT, courses in high school, aptitude, family values toward education, hormones, brain function, and so on. In such a research design, the locus of causation is rooted in the individual and in characteristics such as race, gender, and age or in indicators such as SAT scores, which are strongly related to race and gender. The ways in which the institution responds to such students or the ways in which other variables play a significant role are not the focus of attention. Thus we have had generations of research focusing on cultural values of students who fail, their parents' attitudes, their poor preparation, and so on. This approach assumes that the answers to "the problem" are in characteristics of the target group. It ignores the environment (e.g., the educational institution) as a locus of the problem and leaves unexamined the ways in which the status quo is served by pointing at nontraditional students as the cause of problems.

This approach has been called a deficit model because it focuses on assumed deficits to explain causes of failure or absence (Boocock, 1980; Ladner, 1987). Such research continues to be common today, and it fails to consider that characteristics such as race and gender can be viewed as social constructs, which are responded to by observers (Hare-Musten & Marecek, 1988). Thus gender and race, rather than being treated as background variables, might well be treated as stimulus variables to which institutions and environments respond. For instance, women may drop out of science courses in part because of the response of faculties to women in science or the climate for women in science, not because of gender characteristics (Sandler & Hall, 1986). Moreover, though it is certainly relevant to study the interaction between institutional characteristics and student characteristics, that aim is often difficult to achieve pragmatically. Thousands of research studies take place on single campuses or from the perspective of a single organization. A research tradition that asks which background characteristics predict success or excellence within a single setting can *only* lead to explanations based on those background characteristics. The very framing of this common research question inevitably leads to explanations in terms of personal characteristics (whether they are brain size, family values, or SAT scores), ignoring the impact of the environment or organization on individuals or groups.

(4) The Group in Its Own Right. The phase of focusing on the group in its own right is important because it begins to ask questions from other perspectives. This phase involves study of the group on its own terms—not as having a deficit or being marginal to the traditional norm. In the case of traditionally marginalized groups, these studies often provide cultural critiques of social and institutional factors that affect race, class, gender, and the interrelationships among them. Among studies following this approach, ethnic studies and women's studies, women's education, and African American family life are examples of important research topics (Anzaldua, 1990; Denmark, 1993; Giddings, 1984; Hull et al., 1982; McAdoo, 1992). Research from this standpoint not only sheds light on the group itself but also begins to add a new perspective about general themes and approaches in more traditional fields. Methodologies may change, different questions may be asked, and notions of excellence may even get reconsidered. It is here that critiques of the social sciences are made, and efforts to develop universal theories to predict human behavior come under fire.

Fortunately, for over 30 years there have been scholars in ethnic studies and women's studies, in particular, who have been studying groups, organizations, and communities from this perspective. Their work has made some of the new scholarship of today possible. Of interest, the newly emerging field of men's studies and research on men's lives fits here. As long as research was generic and universalized, as in Phase 1, and even though the subjects were almost always men, it was impossible to seriously study men's lives in their capacity as men. They were being studied as generic human beings.

There is now an extensive literature on the student experience in higher education, which suggests that for many students who come from nontraditional groups, the experience is likely to be one of alienation, not involvement (Smith, 1989). This research shifts the focus from students as the problem to student perspectives on the institution. There are also many studies of faculty and staff members, suggesting that adverse reactions to academic social climates are also experienced by faculty and staff (e.g., Mitchell, 1982). Another example is provided by a recently released report on women faculty at Stanford, which represents a second stage of an earlier extensive report on racial and ethnic diversity (University Committee, 1989). These studies focus on the institution and the experience of marginalized groups in the institution.

As studies have begun to identify alienation and other undesirable effects of campus climates, it has become clear that, regardless of a person's background, the institution's climate and expectations become central influences. Consequently, educational change has become essential. Campuses have had to start, however reluctantly, to address institutionalized as well as individual acts of bias (de la Reyes & Halcon, 1988). For instance, hiring practices, criteria for selection, and the content of curricula have all been subjected to critical review.

The way that research questions are framed is not simply a semantic issue. How a research question is framed guides our understanding of the problem and, in applied research, the focus of solutions. As the frame of research shifts, topics of discussion shift as well—to research methodologies, teaching, curriculum, campus climate, and the role of faculty and staff as important factors in educational success.

Research is now growing on what I have called "special purpose institutions"—institutions, such as women's colleges and historically Black institutions, that have been extraordinarily successful in serving particular populations. A number of scholars have been investigating how these colleges and universities, many of which are not resource-rich, have the impact they do. Among the themes emerging are their high expectations, belief in a student's capacity to learn, the significance of failure to the community, supportive climate, sufficient and divergent role models, and being places where individuals are more free to focus on education rather than on racism and sexism (Carnegie Foundation, 1989; Morris, 1979; Riordan, 1992; Smith, 1989; Tidball, 1980; Willie, 1978).

This approach to research has prompted some criticism. The study of groups in their own right raises concerns about the increasing fragmentation of society and about increasing fragmentation of the study of human behavior to a point where no general principles can be developed. There is a concern that psychology as we know it cannot sustain all these complexities and variations. In contrast, however, if these studies are viewed as phases in the evolution of knowledge about human behavior and organizations, they serve the important function of informing us about the particulars of individuals and of groups. At face value, such research can be viewed as important, interesting, and culturally enriching. However, its more crucial role is to shed light on the ways in which prevailing theories and research need to be altered and reconstructed. How, and whether, universal theories will emerge in this process is still not clear, though it appears that knowledge in context will yield richer approaches to theory than that which is decontextualized (Dill, 1987).

The resistance to such change—that is, the resistance to using new methodologies to address complex new issues like institutional climate—makes the movement of new topics and approaches from the margin of research to the center of research difficult. Indeed, those who do research in these areas are often cautioned about the risks of doing research in "marginalized" areas (Aiken, Anderson, Donnerstein, Lensink, & MacCorquodale, 1987; Padilla, 1994; Sampson, 1993). Yet, as long as women's leadership or African American education is seen as marginal, the study of leadership and the study of education will remain partially uninformed. The titles of articles in academic journals today still reflect this issue of marginality. How is it that a study of leadership involving only men, for example, can be called "today's leaders," whereas a study of women's leadership must be labeled "women's leadership" if it is to be published? The same point applies to the literature on minority women, which requires that research on Latinas or African American women be labeled as such, while research on Euro-American women is called simply a study of women.

Many fields are now producing the knowledge base that is necessary for the further development of inclusive theory and research. The resistance to recognizing these areas as central rather than marginal, however, shows that change in scholarship does not come easily (Bevan & Kessel, 1994; Butler & Walter, 1991; de la Reyes & Halcon, 1988). While this phase of change may be the most threatening to traditional areas of education, the long-term danger to our society as a whole will come not from these areas of scholarship but from institutional responses. Will institutions learn from or ignore the important lessons in this phase?

(5) Inclusive Scholarship. The last phase, often called inclusive scholarship, consists of development of the disciplines, theories, methodologies, questions, perspectives, and pedagogies that will build on the work that has come before. Concepts and theories about such central constructs in psychology as identity, leadership, intergroup relations, and organizational theory, along with the growing use of both qualitative and quantitative methods, are currently altering what we study and how it is studied.

In some institutions and in some disciplines, one sees this transformation beginning. In other fields, often in the social sciences, there is greater resistance to shifting paradigms and to seeing how diversity influences the development of knowledge. As Sampson (1993) reflected: "Most of us have been trained not to encounter others' unique specificity but to reduce them to one of our discipline's categories. . . . [W]e will need to reconsider a separation that sustains the privilege of some at the expense of many" (p. 1228).

The lasting hold of the scientific paradigm may make it more difficult to conceptualize social science fields in new ways. Part of the intensity of the current discussions about diversity reflects the "contested terrain" of who gets to define and who gets to name the questions and the methods of our research. Such struggles are not new; they have happened historically each time fundamentally new changes have been introduced in the academy (Darder, 1991; Foucault, 1977; Giroux, 1990; Twombly & Moore, 1991). Despite the resistance, there are many authorities who suggest that these transformations in the field are essential to the continuing development of new knowledge and scholarship. For instance, Bevan and Kessel (1994) urge that

> psychology . . . seek to understand better the processes of scholarly inquiry as a human social enterprise. . . . All of this implies a recognition that psychological methods and methodologies must be less rigid and our discipline's view of what is scientifically acceptable must be far more pragmatic than has been the case for many decades. (pp. 506-507)

References to a new paradigm increasingly call for multiple perspectives, less focus on cause-and-effect relationships, more holistic ways of describing and understanding observations, and more tolerance for looking at a phenomenon or organization by studying its margins (Berquist, 1993; Gergen, 1991; Gioia & Pitre, 1990; hooks, 1990; Minnich; 1990).

Implications

The two models introduced in this chapter, concerning the dimensions of diversity and the phases of transformation of knowledge, can be used to examine some pressing issues in higher education today. While space does not permit an in-depth analysis of each, a quick overview will highlight several issues from the perspectives of the two models.

The first issue is the nature of quality and excellence. On some of the traditional indicators of excellence, many of those who have been marginalized in higher education come up short—hence, in part, the presumed conflict between excellence and diversity. Indicators such as SAT scores, or publication in certain journals, or research on mainstream topics in scholarly areas, or use of certain "acceptable" methodologies—all of these are now under scrutiny. The standardized approach to testing, so long a mainstay of psychology, is now the subject of vigorous study and debate (Darling-Hammond, 1994; Duran, 1986; Madaus, 1994; Rosser, 1992).

Recently, the New York Supreme Court rejected the SAT as the sole criterion for awarding New York State scholarships. The court ruled that there was clear evidence of gender bias in the SAT's predictive validity (Rosser, 1992). Today the national merit exam continues to be based on the PSAT and, as would be expected, two-thirds of the awards go to men, even though high school grades, percentage of valedictorians, and college grades are higher for women. In particular, the SAT is not a good predictor for many of the groups we now consider "nontraditional" in higher education (Rosser, 1992; Smith, 1989; Wainer & Steinberg, 1992), yet it continues to be used as an important indicator of student aptitude and of institutional prestige—a fact that can only continue to limit institutional success and change.

Embedded in these tests and in our system of education is the construct of aptitude, which is considered to be related to innate ability and is evaluated through testing. The concept of aptitude is also being subjected to scrutiny as a construct that does little more than maintain the status quo with respect to access to education and success. In contrast, many current approaches (e.g., Jackson, 1989; Treismann, 1985), and the experience of women's colleges and historically Black colleges, indicate that high expectations and effective educational interventions yield high results. While potential and talent will continue to be interesting and relevant concepts, the concept of aptitude as a critical component of success must be challenged, along with the assumption that all talent and achievement can be measured by a test. Indeed, ETS has now changed the name of the SAT from the Scholastic *Aptitude* Test to the Scholastic *Assessment* Test. Rethinking "aptitude" will also require us to challenge such long-standing educational practices as grading on the curve—a procedure built on the notion that the normal distribution of ability should result in a normal distribution of learning, an assumption that gives little scope to the role of education, learning, and effort.

A second issue today is the notion of community. One reason for the new stress on community is a fear that somehow diversity will produce balkanization of our society (Greene, 1993; Schlesinger, 1992; Smith, 1994). True to form, many discussions of this issue imply that the problem is with the new and diverse student populations, who have caused the breakup of community (the implication being that in the "old days" campuses were one happy family). The visible presence of students and faculty of color, the visible existence of ethnic centers and of a wide variety of support groups, are all used as evidence for this concern about balkanization. Again, the focus in these jeremiads is on those at the margin rather than on the characteristics of our institutions. Too often forgotten are the past and present segregationist policies of fraternities and sororities with respect to race, gender, and religion. Overlooked as well are the awkward facts that the football team typically ate together and that people assemble in many different groups of choice all the time.

In considering the issue of community, we are challenged to reenvision what a healthy community in a pluralistic society might look like. Instead of polarizing the issue as if community is at one end and diversity at the other, we might study more closely healthy communities, which often build on multiple memberships and crossover memberships. Communities are not built solely at large all-community events like graduations and football games, and they are certainly not built when individuals and groups stay isolated from one another. They are built by people continually crossing boundaries, with the recognition that each person brings multiple identities and loyalties into organizations—identities that, instead of being characterized as problems, might be considered as assets on which to build strengths. Here, talking about *identity* as a monodimensional term limits conceptualizations of organizations, communities, and individuals. Moreover, viewing community and diversity as dichotomous characteristics serves only to limit alternative conceptualizations of both. This issue requires rethinking the concept of community and the concept of identity and group membership (Gergen, 1991; Smith, 1994).

A third issue is the call for diversification of faculty and administration. Here too, many institutions and people are still focusing on the representational level of diversity without acknowledging the very powerful needs for diversity so as to achieve progress in scholarly areas, decision making, and curriculum development. As a result, the issue often continues to be framed in terms of the "emptiness of the pipeline." To the degree that the conceptualization of diversity stops with the dimension of representation, higher education will make little headway, because standards, job descriptions, and images will not have changed to reflect a more complex understanding of what institutions today require.

Traditional indicators of excellence for search committees, such as where candidates went to school, or traditional areas of research, or specific methodologies, will militate against diversifying the faculty in substantive areas unless more sensitive indicators are developed. Search committees today are often fairly homogeneous and are likely to be unprepared to depart from long-assumed expectations about new colleagues or new areas of scholarship (de la Reyes & Halcon, 1988). Instead of pointing to perceptions of unavailability in the pipeline, institutions need to be aware of the ways in which doors are not yet open for those in the pipeline. The presence of a "glass ceiling," bias on search committees, and preferences for traditional specialization areas, rather than familiarity with new approaches and new knowledge, all contribute to the problem. While faculty and administrators of color have been studying this problem and writing about it for years, institutions have been much less willing to acknowledge the subtle and not-so-subtle forms of bias that are introduced at every level.

No one disputes the need for quality in staffing—but there is a great need to discuss what the indicators of quality are, who defines them, and how one develops the skill to evaluate them.

Lessons for Research and Practice

A number of lessons emerge from this analysis.

1. Conversations about diversity, in all its dimensions, bring a strong impetus for reconsideration of research and practice—and with that, an exciting

opportunity to rethink education and scholarship at all levels. These changes have been described by some as no less than a paradigm shift. If higher education is in the process of such a shift, then the resistance and controversy surrounding the change are to be expected. At the same time, there is a potential for exciting new perspectives that inform and advance institutional life at every level.

2. The changes underway will require sustained dialogue, time, and a process that incorporates multiple perspectives. Changing the framing of issues will help, but implementing the cognitive lessons will be extraordinarily difficult. On campuses across the country, people may hear the change in language, but often they don't see changes in behavior. There are also signs of fatigue and backing away from the hard choices. However, with the changing demographic characteristics of students, the issue of increasing other aspects of diversity will likely stay in the foreground on most campuses. Reframing the issue in terms of the essential mission of higher education and of maintaining the integrity of academic disciplines will help ensure continued initiatives for transformation. The future of institutions and research will rely in part on leaders who have the capacity to engage multiple perspectives and to respond to complex changes, and on institutions that have diversity on every dimension and at every level.

3. Whether the focus is on involving multiple perspectives at every level of decision making, or on reconceptualizing previously static and homogeneous concepts such as identity in multiple ways, the notion of multiplicity is emerging as central. This applies both to discussions about diversity and to discussions about new directions in scholarship. The task of engaging these questions is a challenging one, but one that is certainly intrinsic in the mission of higher education.

4. It is becoming clear that both institutional issues and scholarly questions are in the midst of a major change process. To study current initiatives about diversity as if they are the final point in the process is a mistake. Rather, these issues should be seen as part of an evolutionary process, the end point of which is not yet clear.

5. Psychology has an important and central role to play in the way these issues are framed and how the results are used. By the same token, psychology could become increasingly irrelevant or counterproductive unless it continues to reflect on its questions, its methods, and its conclusions.

For many years we talked about the "problem of diversity" and the "challenge of diversity" as if the problem was with diversity itself. It now appears that it is really through our engagement of diversity in all its dimensions that psychology, research, and educational institutions will be transformed and positioned for the future. That process has begun—but there is a long way to go.

References

Aiken, S. H., Anderson, K., Donnerstein, M., Lensink, J., & MacCorquodale, J. (1987). Trying transformations: Curriculum integration and the problem of resistance. *Signs, 12,* 2.

Anzaldua, G. (Ed.). (1990). *Making face, making soul.* San Francisco: Aunt Lute Foundation.

Berquist, W. (1993). *The postmodern organization.* San Francisco: Jossey-Bass.

Bevan, W., & Kessel, F. (1994). Plain truths and home cooking: Thoughts on the making and remaking of psychology. *American Psychologist, 49,* 505-509.

Blassingame, J. W. (Ed.). (1973). *New perspectives on Black studies.* Urbana: University of Illinois Press.

Boocock, S. S. (1980). *Sociology of education: An introduction.* Boston: Houghton Mifflin.

Bowser, B. P., Auletta, G. S., & Jones, T. (1993). *Confronting diversity issues on campus.* Newbury Park, CA: Sage.

Butler, J., & Walter, J. (1991). *Transforming the curriculum.* Albany: State University of New York Press.

Carnegie Council on Policy Studies in Higher Education. (1981). *Three thousand futures.* San Francisco: Jossey-Bass.

Carnegie Foundation for the Advancement of Teaching. (1989). *Tribal colleges: Shaping the future of Native America.* Princeton, NJ: Princeton University Press.

Chafe, W. (1991). *The paradox of change: American women in the 20th century.* London: Oxford University Press.

Copeland, L. (1988, June). Making the most of cultural differences at the workplace. *Personnel,* pp. 52-60.

Cortes, C. (1994). Backing into the future: Columbus, Cleopatra, Custer, and the diversity revolution. In *Higher education exchange* (pp. 6-14). Dayton, OH: Kettering Foundation.

Darder, A. (1991). *Culture and power in the classroom.* New York: Bergen & Garvey.

Darling-Hammond, L. (1994). Performance-based assessment and educational equity. *Harvard Educational Review, 64,* 76-95.

Davis, J. D. (Ed.). (1993). *Coloring the halls of ivy: Leadership and diversity in the academy.* Boston: Anker.

de la Reyes, M., & Halcon, J. J. (1988). Racism in academia: The old wolf revisited. *Harvard Educational Review, 58,* 299-314.

Denmark, F. (1993). Women, leadership, and empowerment. *Psychology of Women Quarterly, 17,* 343-356.

Dill, B. T. (1987). The dialectics of Black womanhood. In S. Harding (Ed.), *Feminism and methodology* (pp. 97-108). Bloomington: Indiana University Press.

Duran, R. (1986). Prediction of Hispanics' college achievements. In M. Olivas (Ed.), *Latino college students* (pp. 221-245). New York: Columbus University Press.

Edelman, J. M. (1977). *Political language: Words that succeed and policies that fail.* New York: Academic Press.

Erikson, E. (1968). *Identity: Youth and crisis.* New York: Norton.

Fausto-Sterling, A. (1981). The myth of neutrality: Race, sex and class in science. *Radical Teacher, 19,* 21-24.

Ferdman, B. M. (1992). The dynamics of ethnic diversity in organizations: Toward integrative models. In K. Kelly (Ed.), *Issues, theory and research in industrial/organizational psychology* (pp. 339-384). Amsterdam: Elsevier.

Fernandez, J. (1991). *Managing a diverse workforce.* Lexington, MA: Lexington.

Foucault, M. (1977). *Power/knowledge.* New York: Pantheon.

Gergen, K. (1991). *The saturated self: Dilemmas of identity in contemporary life.* New York: Basic Books.

Giddings, P. (1984). *When and where I enter.* New York: Morrow.

Gilligan, C. (1982). *In a different voice.* Cambridge, MA: Harvard University Press.

Gioia, D. A., & Pitre, E. (1990). Multiparadigm perspectives on theory building. *Academy of Management Review, 15,* 584-602.

Giroux, H. (1990). The politics of postmodernism: Rethinking the boundaries of race and ethnicity. *Journal of Urban and Cultural Studies, 1,* 5-38.

Greene, M. (1993). The passions of pluralism: Multiculturalism and the expanding of community. *Educational Researcher, 22*(1), 13-18.

Harding, S. (1986). *The science question in feminism.* Ithaca, NY: Cornell University Press.

Hare-Musten, R. T., & Marecek, J. (1988). The meaning of difference: Gender theory, postmodernism, and psychology. *American Psychologist, 43,* 455-464.

hooks, b. (1990). Marginality as site of resistance. In R. Ferguson et al. (Eds.), *Marginalization and contemporary culture* (pp. 341-344). New York: New Museum of Contemporary Art.

Horner, M. (1972). Toward an understanding of achievement related conflicts in women. *Journal of Social Issues, 28*(2), 157-174.

Hull, G. T., Scott, P. B., & Smith, B. (Eds.). (1982). *All the women are White, all the Blacks are men, but some of us are brave. Black women's studies.* New York: Feminist Press.

Hurtado, S. (1992). The campus racial climate. *Journal of Higher Education, 63,* 539-569.

Jackson, A. (1989, Spring). Minorities in mathematics: A focus on excellence, not remediation. *American Educator,* pp. 22-27.

Kanter, R. (1976). *Men and women of the corporation.* New York: Basic Books.

Keller, E. F. (1982). Feminism and science. *Signs, 7,* 589-602.

Konrad, A., & Gutek, B. (1987). Theory and research on group composition: Applications to the status of women and ethnic minorities. In S. Oskamp & S. Spacapan (Eds.), *Interpersonal processes* (pp. 85-121). Newbury Park, CA: Sage.

Ladner, J. A. (1987). Introduction to tomorrow's tomorrow: The Black woman. In S. Harding (Ed.), *Feminism and methodology* (pp. 74-83). Bloomington: Indiana University Press.

Levine, A. (1991, September/October). The meaning of diversity. *Change,* pp. 4-5.

Levine, A., & Cureton, J. (1992). The quiet revolution: Eleven facts about multiculturalism and the curriculum. *Change, 24*(1), 25-29.

Lincoln, Y. (1989). Trouble in the land: The paradigm revolution in the academic disciplines. In E. Pascarella & J. Smart (Eds.), *Higher education: Handbook of theory and research* (Vol. 5, pp. 52-133). New York: Agathon.

Lipman-Blumen, J. (1989). Female leadership in formal organizations: Must the female leader go formal. In H. J. Leavitt, L. R. Pondy, & D. M. Boji (Eds.), *Readings on managerial psychology* (pp. 325-344). Chicago: University of Chicago.

Loden, M., & Rosener, R. (1991). *Workforce America.* Homewood, IL: Business One Irwin.

Madaus, G. (1994). A technological and historical consideration of equity issues associated with proposals to change the nation's testing policy. *Harvard Educational Review, 64*(1), 76-95.

Madrid, A. (1990). Diversity and its discontents. *Academe, 76*(6), 15-19.

McAdoo, H. P. (1992). Upward mobility and parenting in middle-income Black families. In A. K. H. Burlew, W. C. Banks, H. P. McAdoo, & D. A. Azibo (Eds.), *African American psychology* (pp. 63-86). Newbury Park, CA: Sage.

McClelland, D. C. (1961). *The achieving society.* New York: Free Press.

McIntosh, P. (1983). *Interactive phases of curriculum revision: A feminist perspective* (Working paper No. 124). Wellesley, MA: Wellesley College, Center for Research on Women.

McIntosh, P. (1990). *Interactive phases of curricular and personal re-vision with regard to race* (Working paper No. 219). Wellesley, MA: Wellesley College, Center for Research on Women.

Mingle, J. R. (1987). *Forces in minorities: Trends in higher education participation and success.* Denver, CO: Education Commission of the States/SHEEO.

Minnich, E. K. (1990). *Transforming knowledge.* Philadelphia: Temple University Press.

Mitchell, J. (1982). Reflections of a Black social scientist. *Harvard Educational Review, 52*(1), 27-44.

Mohanty, C. T. (1993). On race and voice: Challenges for liberal education. In B. W. Thompson & S. Tyagi (Eds.), *Beyond a dream deferred: Multicultural education and the politics of excellence* (pp. 41-65). Minneapolis: University of Minnesota Press.

Morris, L. (1979). *Elusive equality.* Washington, DC: Howard University Press.

Morrison, A. (1992). *The new leaders.* San Francisco: Jossey-Bass.

Murchland, B. (Ed.). (1991). *Higher education and the practice of democratic politics.* Dayton, OH: Kettering Foundation.

National Center for Educational Statistics. (1994). *Trends in enrollment in higher education by racial/ethnic category.* Washington, DC: U.S. Department of Education.

Olivas, M. A. (1984). New populations, new arrangements. In S. Adolphus (Ed.), *Equality postponed* (pp. 85-94). New York: College Entrance Examination Board.

Olivas, M. A. (1992). Legal norms in law school admissions: An essay on parallel universes. *Journal of Legal Education, 42*(1), 103-117.

Padilla, A. M. (1994). Ethnic minority scholars, research, and mentoring: Current and future issues. *Educational Researcher, 23*(4), 24-27.

Pettigrew, T. F., & Martin, J. (1987). Shaping the organizational context for Black American inclusion. *Journal of Social Issues, 43*(1), 41-78.

Pfeffer, J. (1983). Organizational demography. *Research in Organizational Behavior, 5,* 299-357.

Ramirez, M., & Castaneda, A. (1991). Toward a cultural democracy. In B. Murchland (Ed.), *Higher education and the practice of democratic politics* (pp. 115-121). Dayton, OH: Kettering Foundation.

Riordan, C. (1992). Single and mixed-gender colleges for women: Educational, attitudinal, and occupational outcomes. *Review of Higher Education, 15*(3), 327-346.

Rosser, P. (1992). *Sex bias in college admissions tests: Why women lose out.* Cambridge, MA: Fair Test.

Rowe, M. P. (1990). Barriers to equality: The power of subtle discrimination to maintain unequal opportunity. *Employee Responsibilities and Rights Journal, 3*(2), 153-163.

Sampson, E. E. (1993). Identity politics: Challenges to psychology's understanding. *American Psychologist, 48*(12), 1219-1230.

Sandler, B. R., & Hall, R. M. (1986). *The campus climate revisited: Chilly for women faculty, administrators, and students.* Washington, DC: AAC.

Schlesinger, A. M., Jr. (1992). *The disuniting of America: Reflections on a multicultural society.* New York: Norton.

Sherif, C. W. (1987). Bias in psychology. In S. Harding (Ed.), *Feminism and methodology* (pp. 37-56). Bloomington: Indiana University Press.

Smith, D. G. (1989). *The challenge of diversity: Involvement or alienation in the academy?* (Report No. 5). Washington, DC: George Washington University.

Smith, D. G. (1994). Community and group identity: Fostering mattering. In *Higher education exchange* (pp. 29-35). Dayton, OH: Kettering Foundation.

Spence, J. T. (1993). Women, men, and society: Plus ça change, plus c'est la même chose. In S. Oskamp & M. Costanzo (Eds.), *Gender issues in contemporary psychology* (pp. 3-17). Newbury Park, CA: Sage.

Tajfel, H. (1982). Social psychology of intergroup relations. In M. R. Rosenzweig & L. W. Porter (Eds.), *Annual Review of Psychology, 33,* 1-39.

Takaki, R. (1989). *Strangers from a different shore: A history of Asian Americans.* New York: Penguin.

Thomas, G. E. (1989). *Theories of race and ethnic relations challenges for social scientists.* Tulsa: University of Oklahoma, Center for Research on Minority Education.

Thomas, R. R., Jr. (1990). From affirmative action to affirming diversity. *Harvard Business Review, 68*(2), 107-117.

Thomas, R. R., Jr. (1991). *Beyond race and gender.* New York: Amacom.

Thompson, B. W., & Tyagi, S. (Eds.). (1994). *Beyond a dream deferred: Multicultural education and the politics of excellence.* Minneapolis: University of Minnesota Press.

Tidball, E. (1980). Women's colleges and women achievers revisited. *Signs, 5,* 504-517.

Treismann, U. (1985). *A study of the mathematics performance of Black students at the University of California—Berkeley.* Unpublished doctoral dissertation.

Twombly, S. B., & Moore, K. M. (1991). Social origins of higher education administrators. *Review of Higher Education, 14*(4), 485-510.

University Committee on Minority Issues. (1989). *Building a multiracial, multicultural university community* (Final report of the committee). Stanford, CA: Stanford University.

Wainer, H., & Steinberg, L. S. (1992). Sex differences on the mathematics section of the Scholastic Aptitude Test: A bidirectional validity study. *Harvard Educational Review, 62*(3), 323-336.

Weick, K. (1976). Educational organizations as loosely coupled systems. *Administrative Science Quarterly, 21*(1), 1-18.

Weick, K. (1979). *The social psychology of organizing.* New York: Random House.

West, C. (1991). The new cultural politics of difference. In B. Murchland (Ed.), *Higher education and the practice of democratic politics* (pp. 136-156). Dayton, OH: Kettering Foundation.

Willie, C. V. (1978). Racism, Black education and the sociology of knowledge. In C. V. Willie & R. R. Edmonds (Eds.), *Black colleges in America* (pp. 3-13). New York: Teachers College Press.

Willie, C. V., & Edmonds, R. R. (1978). *Black colleges in America.* New York: Teachers College Press.

9

A Diversity Framework

R. ROOSEVELT THOMAS, JR.

For the past few years, much discussion has taken place around the topics of *diversity* and related subjects such as affirmative action, understanding differences, valuing differences, understanding diversity, valuing diversity, pluralism, multiculturalism, and inclusion. All of these subjects and others are often considered under the umbrella of *diversity*. Unfortunately, because little time has been devoted to understanding diversity per se (independent of workforce issues), the ongoing discussions have positioned diversity as akin to affirmative action and have caused a substantial amount of confusion.[1]

I believe that waiting to be teased out on its own merits—rather than on the premise of being the next generation of affirmative action—is a diversity framework that can strengthen managerial and organizational approaches to a variety of issues (functional conflicts, acquisitions/mergers, multiple lines of business, managing change, teaming, work/family issues, globalism, total quality, and workforce demographic characteristics—just to name a few obvious possibilities). As such, the diversity framework most importantly will provide a way of thinking, a way of approaching and framing a set of issues.

My purpose in this brief chapter is to contribute to the evolution of this framework. Accordingly, unlike much of what I have said and written in previous settings, the focus is not on managing diversity or understanding differences or affirmative action but on *diversity* itself. What follows is only the beginning of what promises to be a long evolutionary process, given that we have just started to acknowledge and recognize something called diversity.

A Definition

Diversity refers to any mixture of items characterized by differences *and* similarities. Several thoughts flow from this definition.

(1) Diversity is not synonymous with differences but encompasses differences and similarities. The manager addressing diversity does not have the option of dealing only with differences or similarities; instead, he or she must deal with both simultaneously.

(2) A discussion of diversity must specify the dimensions in question (race, gender, sexual orientation, product line, age, functional specialization). A failure to specify can lead to a discussion of apples and oranges. Stated differently, in a very fundamental sense, diversity does not automatically mean "with respect to race and gender." When someone says, "I'm working on diversity issues," I do not know what he or she means unless I inquire about dimensions.

(3) Diversity refers to the collective (all-inclusive) mixture of differences and similarities along a given dimension. The manager dealing with diversity, then, is focusing on the collective mixture. For example, the manager coping with racial diversity is not dealing with Blacks, Whites, Hispanics, or Asian Americans but with the collective mixture.

To highlight this notion of mixture, consider a jar of red jelly beans and assume that you will add some green and purple jelly beans. Many would believe that the green and purple jelly beans represent diversity. I suggest that diversity instead is represented by the resultant mixture of red, green, and purple jelly beans.

When faced with a collection of diverse jelly beans, most managers have not been addressing diversity but, instead, have been addressing how to handle the last jelly beans added to the mixture. What this means is that we have not failed to deal with diversity, but many of us are just now putting the mixture on our managerial agenda. Even today, with all the talk about diversity, most people are concerned with their pet aspect of a dimension. Blacks often are concerned with Black issues, senior citizens with issues of age, women with gender issues, and people with different physical abilities only with disability issues.

The true meaning of diversity suggests that if you are concerned about racism, you include all races; if you're concerned about gender, you include both genders; or if you're concerned about age issues, you include all age groups. In other words, the mixture is all inclusive.

Why Now?

Why develop and use the diversity framework now? What places it on our agenda? A prime rationale offered by many managers is the changing composition of the workforce. *Workforce 2000* (William & Packer, 1987) documented and popularized projected demographic shifts for the 1980s and the 1990s. These projections of more minorities, women, and immigrants in the workforce have moved many executives to initiate "diversity" efforts.

While I acknowledge the importance of *Workforce 2000*, I am not convinced that it is the driving force behind the reality of diversity or the increasingly urgent managerial need to address its challenges and opportunities. For me, a more fundamental causal factor has been a changing attitude toward being different. Being different historically has implied being "not as good as" or inadequate in some way. People who were different wanted to be "mainstreamed" as quickly as possible. Today, a growing number of individuals who see themselves as "different" are much more comfortable with being different. They see being different not as "less than" or as "more than" but, instead, as simply different. Some are even inclined to celebrate being different.

I offer a couple of examples of people with different attitudes about being different. Individuals with work/family parameters other than those *assumed* by corporations are now much more vocal about these differences. This is because they are comfortable in being different. Child-care and elder-care challenges have always existed, but they were viewed as the individuals' personal problems. Accordingly, employees were to take care of these matters before or after work or make a quick monitoring telephone call at lunch. Now, individuals are comfortable in raising these issues for consideration as workplaces are modified to enhance productivity.

The second example was related by a woman of Italian ancestry. She said that when she was growing up, her father and grandfather would under no circumstances allow anything but English to be spoken in their home. The emphasis was on assimilation and minimizing differences. She indicated that she now tells her daughter: "In addition to speaking English and whatever other language, you will speak Italian as well. You will know your heritage and you will be no less an American." For her, the emphasis is on knowing who you are and how you are different while simultaneously being part of the whole as an American. As I have talked to numerous executives, managers, and employees, I have found immigrants more comfortable in being different and Americans at the same time.

Organizational participants with these new attitudes resist fitting in, or assimilating. They understand and accept the need for assimilation but want to do so only around true requirements—not preferences, conveniences, or traditions. Under these circumstances, the *mixture* of red, purple, and green jelly beans is likely to be much more unassimilated than is the case when the individual beans are uncomfortable with being different. In the past, there might have been a similar mixture of red, green, and purple beans, but they would have been much more assimilated. For example, if the dominant group were red, the green and purple beans would be inclined to act as if they were red, despite the extent to which they might differ on the surface.

The notion of "true requirement" is critical here. Most managers have not moved to differentiate requirements from traditions, preferences, and conveniences. In one accounting department, concern is surfacing about the requirement of a master's degree to secure upward mobility into the managerial ranks. Recently, the manager appointed a task force to determine why employees without a master's degree were increasingly unhappy. Their findings revealed that those without the degree believed that after they trained employees with the degree, these individuals experienced upward mobility but really did not exhibit any competencies that had not been taught by employees without graduate training. As a consequence, the nonmaster's employees were beginning to doubt that the graduate degree was a requirement.

If not a requirement, what was the degree? It was not tradition—something that had been in place through the years, as it was a recent "requirement." For some senior managers, the degree "requirement" was a preference. They preferred people with graduate training, because they brought a "certain kind of thinking with them." For others in leadership, the "requirement" was an "insurance policy" that gave them the convenience of being able to assume minimum competency. With this insurance in recruiting and selecting candidates, managers benefited from the convenience of not having to screen for competency but focusing on other variables to determine the candidate's "fit" with the organization. No person—managerial or otherwise—contended that the graduate degree was essential to do department work at any level. Stated differently, no one said that the degree was a "true requirement" in the sense of being a necessary condition for competence—the job at all levels could be done without a master's but the degree had met some managers' desires around preferences and conveniences.

The Dynamics of Diversity

How do managers respond to diversity? Essentially, there are eight basic responses.

(1) Exclude. Here, we aim to minimize diversity by keeping diverse elements out or by expelling them once they have been included. An example would be the selection criteria used by a corporation in screening candidates for employment. While these criteria can be used to identify candidates with high potential for success, they in effect also control the amount of diversity within a corporation. Recruiting only electrical engineers produces much less diversity than simply requiring an engineering degree.

(2) Deny. This option enables individuals to ignore diversity dimensions. They look at a green jelly bean and see only a jelly bean. Examples would be managerial aspirations to be color-blind, gender-blind, or school-blind.

It should be noted that denial is viable only if the object of your denial permits the practice. Entities that celebrate being different are reluctant to allow denial. For example, today, many Black males do not react positively toward managerial protestations of race blindness or gender blindness such as, "We assure you that we will not see you as a Black male." Twenty-five years ago, my fellow Morehouse students and I saw such a statement as an indication that our talent and performance—not race and gender—ultimately would determine our success. Students today see such statements as insults and react by saying, "I will not allow you to deny my blackness, my maleness. I will not grant you the option of denial."

(3) Suppress. Managers here encourage entities that are different to suppress their differences. For example, holders of nonmainstream political or religious views may be encouraged not to express their philosophies for the sake of maintaining good team spirit or minimizing conflict.

Another suppression example is the treatment old-timers often give inquisitive newcomers who inquire, "Why do we do things this way?" A frequent response from old-timers is, "How long have you been here?" What they mean is, "Suppress your questions until you've been here long enough to understand how things work. At that point, if you still have questions, then you can raise them." Of interest, in some organizations, newcomers never can accumulate enough years to give them the right to question.

(4) Segregate. Here, I am referring not only to back-of-the-bus segregation but also to other practices such as clustering members of racial or ethnic groups in certain departments (sometimes called ghettos), isolating or piloting a change in a corner of the corporation, or isolating an acquisition as a subsidiary.

I do not mean to imply that these segregational practices are wrong or should be discontinued but simply that each represents a form of segregation comparable to the prototypical back-of-the-bus racial segregation.

(5) Assimilate. Here, managers attempt to transform the element with differences into clones of the dominant group. For example, when a corporation makes an acquisition, its managers often move to make the acquired company like the parent company, thereby minimizing differences between the two entities.

(6) Tolerate. Here, the diverse elements adopt a "we don't bother them, they don't bother us" attitude. Each acknowledges the right of the other to exist or to be included, but takes steps to minimize interaction. Examples are the relationships between functions that are not required to interact or between subsidiaries that have little to do with each other.

(7) Build relationships. The assumption is that a good relationship can overcome differences. While this approach has the potential to foster acceptance and understanding of differences, often it is used to minimize differences. This happens when the governing principle is as follows: "If we just can talk and learn more about each other, despite our differences, I think we'll find many similarities that can be grounds for a mutually beneficial relationship." In other words, by focusing on *similarities*, the hope is to avoid challenges associated with differences.

(8) Foster mutual adaptation. Under this option, the parties involved accept and understand differences and diversity, recognizing full well that those realities may call for adaptation on the part of all components of the whole. As an illustration, a corporation's managers may hire people who are different while knowing and expecting that they (the managers) must explore possibilities of system and culture changes to assure that an environment works for everyone.

Three points regarding these dynamics merit our attention. First, only one of the eight options unequivocally endorses diversity. The other seven seek to ignore, minimize, or eliminate diversity. This suggests that we have difficulty accepting the reality of diversity. Only the "foster adaptation" approach unequivocally accepts the reality of diversity and seeks to build on the mixture. In practice, the option of mutual adaptation only recently has been placed on the managerial agenda.

Second, there is no inherent positive or negative value associated with the options. Whether an option is appropriate depends on the circumstances. As an illustration, consider the case of a company buying a healthy enterprise that is substantially different. Segregation of the acquired company as a subsidiary would be appropriate, as opposed to assimilating the entity and risking compromising the success of the purchased enterprise.

Another example is provided by a White Protestant church that experienced a surge of Hispanic members. The reaction was to recruit a Hispanic minister and to encourage the new parishioners to worship at 3:00 p.m. with their newly hired leader. Obviously, this is a segregated service.

On the other hand, whether this is good or bad depends on the context. A conversation with the church's senior pastor might produce at least one of two scenarios that differ greatly. The minister might indicate, "We feel a moral responsibility to assist these people in being able to worship, but we have little desire or need to interact with them. We worship at 11:00 a.m. and leave by 2:00 p.m., while they begin arriving at 2:15 or so. We don't have to interact."

Another scenario could be: "We know we will have to change the 11:00 a.m. service eventually, but we do not know how. By allowing the new members to worship at 3:00 p.m., we are setting up a transition arrangement where their worship needs can be met until we determine how to modify the main service. In the meantime, the two groups can visit with each other in preparation for identifying the parameters of the new unified service." How one views each scenario would influence the evaluation of the segregated arrangements as good or bad.

Third, each of these response options can be used with *any* collective mixture of differences and similarities. While we are most familiar with them in the context of race and gender, they can be found where there is diversity of any kind.

The three points above collectively suggest a need to redefine *Managing Diversity.* Managing Diversity is not simply mutual adaptation but is the process of responding appropriately to diversity mixtures. In this process, the manager must (a) recognize diversity mixtures when they are present, (b) ascertain whether a response is required, and (c) select the appropriate response or blend of responses. The effective manager of diversity is capable in all aspects of the process.

In the absence of a diversity paradigm, managers have had little guidance in systematically assessing situations characterized by diversity mixtures. The framework proposed in this chapter can be used for diagnostic and action-planning purposes. It defines diversity, sets forth the notion that the amount and kind of diversity tension determine whether a response is needed, and offers an initial list of response options. As such, the framework provides a point of departure for evolving a framework to guide managers in making decisions regarding diversity mixtures of all kinds.

Determinants of Responses

How does one select the appropriate option? I believe it is a function in large part of an individual's diversity inclination. This inclination, not unlike that of a person's tendency to be left-handed, is learned or developed early in life and, accordingly, is enduring. An individual's diversity inclination can be difficult to change.

Also coming into play are the individual's mind-sets (ways of thinking about an issue), which are much more current than inclinations. My inclination, based on early learnings, teachings, and experiences, may be not to trust or respect White males, but my mind-set is that *some* White males are worthy of trust and respect, given that some of my *current* best friends are White males.

Mind-sets can reinforce inclinations or stifle them. The greater the incongruence, the greater the psychological stress for the individual. Similarly, individuals are not always able to act on their inclinations and mind-sets. Here are some examples:

- My inclination and my mind-set may be to avoid Black males, but they represent a significant portion of my workforce and some of my best employees are Black males. If I refuse to relate to them, I will not be able to achieve my objectives. I cannot act on my inclination or my mind-set because of my dependence on these individuals. In this instance, I might interact with these individuals on the job but play out my inclination by refusing to socialize with them away from work. The potential for stress is enormous in this case.

- My inclination and mind-set may be to accept all individuals, regardless of their differences. However, because I am not skilled in changing systems or building cultures, I am managerially unable to build an organization reflecting my inclination and mind-set. Here, a lack of managerial and leadership skills limits the ability to act, even where inclination and mind-set might encourage action.

Another determinant is the individual's environment. As I indicated earlier, environmental factors have encouraged placing diversity on the managerial agenda. Similarly, environmental factors influence the manager's response to diversity. A manager's predispositions and mind-sets might argue against diversity while the environment dictates mutual adaptation. Or a manager might prefer to practice denial, but workers and peers might not allow that option.

In sum, an individual's response to diversity mixtures is shaped by his or her inclinations, mind-sets, and organizational environment. All three factors can be critical determinants. Depending on the individual and organizational parameters, in a given situation either factor can assume the dominant role.

Illustrative Applications
of the Diversity Framework

As a way of demonstrating the potential of this framework, I will apply it briefly to three areas where it is not normally used: functional conflicts, acquisitions/mergers, and work/family situations.

Managers, researchers, and managerial theorists have been concerned with *functional conflicts* for decades. A major breakthrough occurred with the work of Lawrence and Lorsch (1969) in the late 1960s when they introduced the concepts of functional differentiation and functional integration.

Lawrence and Lorsch argued that a major requirement for effectiveness and efficiency is to assure simultaneously that a corporation's functions (departments or units of specialization, such as marketing, research, engineering, and manufacturing) have appropriate amounts of differentiation and integration. Differentiation is the task of assuring that each function's organizational parameters (for example, policies, structure, degree of formality, and reward systems) and participant behaviors are congruent with the unit's task environment. The more diverse the task environments, the more differentiated will be the organizational parameters and participant behaviors. This differentiation enhances effectiveness and efficiency. These benefits of differentiation provide the rationale for grouping similar tasks together.

A challenge materializes when it becomes necessary for differentiated units to interact. The greater the need for cross-communication, cross-cooperation, and cross-collaboration, the greater the need for integration and integrative mechanisms to bring about the required interactions. Examples of integrative mechanisms would be structural arrangements grouping units requiring integration under a common boss who would serve as the connecting link, positions such as project managers or schedulers designed to facilitate integration, policies presenting and framing the required integrative behavior, or reward systems that encouraged appropriate linkages.

In any event, the manager's job is that of bringing about the necessary differentiation (diversity) and integration. The driving force would be task environments, individually and collectively. Where individual task environments differed greatly (for example, the research task versus the manufacturing task), department arrangements and participant behaviors would differ greatly. And if the research and manufacturing task environments were also interdependent as well as substantially different, the successful differentiation of them would make the necessary integration more difficult. This is the prototypical Managing Diversity challenge of fostering differences while simultaneously addressing the cohesiveness and integrity of the whole.

Lawrence and Lorsch were dealing with diversity in very concrete ways. They noted the reality of functional conflicts, explored how task environments contributed, and provided a framework for coping with these challenges. The diversity framework does not contradict this approach but simply contends that the functional conflicts "tree" is part of a diversity "forest" and provides a framework for enhanced understanding and problem solving.

Incidentally, Lawrence and Lorsch were dealing with diversity because they were concerned with strengthening the effectiveness of *all* functions for the benefit of the enterprise. They were concerned about the mixture, as opposed to, for example, advocating the inclusion or greater use of a single function.

With respect to *acquisitions/mergers*, a growing awareness is evolving about the importance of diversity as a determinant of success. An executive involved in planning and implementing acquisitions and mergers recently made the following observation:

> People who actually make deals will tell you that cultural differences are the principal reasons for failures of acquisitions and mergers. A number of other factors may be cited officially for failures—declining markets, inadequate earnings, disappointing cash flow—but the real reasons are the cultural differences.

Peters and Waterman (1982), in their classic *In Search of Excellence*, recommended that companies should "stick to their knitting" when considering growth:

> Our principal finding is clear and simple, organizations that do branch out (whether by acquisition or internal diversification) but stick very close to their knitting outperform the others. The most successful of all are those diversified around a single skill—the coating and bonding technology at 3M, for example. (p. 293)

Because the parent organization and the acquisition or merger partner represent a mixture of similarities and differences, they are characterized by diversity. Peters and Waterman found that when corporations stray from their core, they risk compromising or diluting what has made them successful.

I concur with their findings. However, the evolving diversity paradigm and Managing Diversity suggest that managers *can* seek growth beyond their core business, *if* they have the capability to accept and manage diversity. For a corporation with a stagnant core, this possibility is most significant and further highlights diversity and Managing Diversity as managerial priorities. Without a Managing Diversity capability, corporations desiring growth have limited opportunities.

All of this means that a critical criterion for success is the ability to deal with the diversity. A company that tries *inappropriately* to minimize this diversity by *assimilating* the acquisition or merger partner threatens the viability of the partner. If the partner's business environment dictates the differences, eliminating them could reduce the partner's viability and contribute to the failure of the acquisition/merger.

On the other hand, the inappropriate fostering of differences can minimize opportunities for synergy with the acquisition/merger partner and contribute to the failure of the acquisition/merger. So, in essence, the critical task again is to determine and bring about the *required* amounts of differentiation and integration between the acquisition/merger partners. Stated differently, managers must deal effectively with diversity.

Increasingly, managers are exploring the relationship between *work/family* issues and diversity. For example, in the spring of 1994, the Women's Legal Defense Fund and Aetna Life and Casualty co-sponsored a symposium examining this relationship.

Work/family issues are now topical because men and women with different work/family parameters than those presumed by corporations have become vocal about these differences. In essence, they argued that the variety of work/family differences and similarities among workers were much more diverse than previously thought.

Two examples deserve mention. One, men and women with different child-care and elder-care requirements have become more comfortable with bringing these issues into the workplace. These employees are more comfortable in saying "I don't fit the work/family assumptions on which this organization is grounded." This openness has transformed personal work/family issues into managerial concerns.

Two, women are becoming more comfortable in acknowledging that they are different and that being different does not imply inadequacy. This parallels what has been common throughout the diversity arena. Traditionally, given the stress on assimilation and conformity for success, people who were "different" were reluctant to admit being different. This denial helped the individual in his or her push for success and made it unnecessary for the manager to have to deal with differences.

Now that people are more comfortable in acknowledging work/family differences and women are more comfortable in admitting their differences, managers are facing a much more diverse workforce. With this increase in work/family diversity has come tension. The tension stems from realization that organizational environments are not compatible with the realities of work/family diversity and the needs of women. So managers have attempted to foster programs to meet work/family needs of men and women and also enable or empower women. Signs of this stress are the continuing debates about glass ceilings, child care, elder care, and dual-career families. Another sign is an arising backlash from single employees about the "preferential treatment" being given to those with child-care and elder-care concerns.

My point is that the diversity framework and its notions of diversity mixtures, diversity tension, and response options can help explain the rise in prominence of work/family issues on the managerial agenda.

In the discussions of functional conflicts, acquisitions/mergers, and work/family issues, I have sought to illustrate how the diversity framework can be used to examine the dynamics of differences and similarities wherever they are found, particularly in realms other than the workforce. Obviously, each of these cases could provide the basis for a much more elaborate treatment.

The implications for managers dealing with diversity mixtures are threefold. First, if you wish to learn about diversity per se and Managing Diversity in general, you are not confined to the arenas of race and gender, where deliberation and analysis are compromised by emotionally charged baggage. You have the option of looking at experiences with diversity mixtures in general, gleaning lessons, and then returning to apply them to race and gender concerns. This is an important implication, given that much of the thinking and writing about diversity have been colored by experiences with race and gender in the workplace. The framework and its recognition that diversity is more than race and gender broaden the opportunity for systematic inquiry by the practitioner and the scholar.

Second, the practitioner desiring to institutionalize Managing Diversity as a process may wish to begin in an arena other than race or gender, or at least to include areas in addition to these two traditional dimensions. Often, individuals cannot come to grips with *diversity* in the context of race and gender because of their preoccupations and emotions regarding these two issues.

Focusing on another dimension would enhance the possibility of more illuminating analysis and discussion.

Third, the manager who confines Managing Diversity to race and gender risks greatly underusing this process. Managing Diversity can be practical and beneficial *wherever* managers encounter diversity mixtures and diversity tensions.

Three Critical Questions

As I have discussed the diversity framework with others, they frequently have raised several questions.

Question 1: Within this diversity framework with its multiplicity of diversity dimensions, how will the manager know where to direct his or her attention? To determine where to focus, managers must assess diversity tension and direct their efforts to areas offering the greatest bottom-line gain from addressing tension. At a minimum, managers must assess the nature of the tension, its intensity, and its impact on the bottom line. Below are some examples of this process.

- An "engineering development" department had the task of converting engineering designs from research and development to plans appropriate for manufacturing. This was a critical task, because most of the company's business called for customization. The "engineering development" department, however, consistently angered research and development and also manufacturing. Senior management considered this conflict dysfunctional and sought to resolve it repeatedly by finding a less cantankerous department head capable of establishing good relations. Unfortunately, each newly appointed head in turn proved incapable of minimizing this conflict. As matters evolved, the company reportedly went out of business. A contributing factor no doubt was this continuing conflict.

Here, management recognized the impact on the business but did not understand the conflict or take appropriate action. They diagnosed the challenge as one of personalities and failed to realize they were dealing with a diversity mixture of research and development, manufacturing, and the "engineering development" department. These three departments differed greatly. For example, research and development valued the "science" component of their work and sought scientific excellence regardless of the implications for producing the product, while manufacturing focused on the need for effective, economical production runs and often complained that research and development sent out "unrealistic" plans in terms of production implications. The "engineering development" task became that of satisfying both of the other departments by preserving the scientific excellence of research and development while developing plans sufficiently practical for manufacturing's purposes. The reality is that the conflict was not personal but was a consequence of the diversity of the departments. Having misdiagnosed the situation, the managers were hard pressed to take effective action involving one of the eight framework responses.

- In one setting where the product was a commodity and price and customer service were key success factors, the manufacturing scheduler had the task of scheduling production runs in such a way as to minimize costs and yet allow for customer satisfaction. Customers often had urgent, emergency requests that meant production interruptions and less than optimal runs that caused price increases. This caused the scheduler's task to be characterized by great tension as well as continuing dissatisfaction on the part of either manufacturing or sales. In essence, every time the company had to choose between satisfying a customer and minimizing costs with economic production runs, the scheduler facilitated an ongoing "mutual adaptation" process. Both sides had to adapt to the reality that, for the good of the company, neither side could have its needs met all the time. Depending on the specifics of the given situation, one or the other unit would have to adapt.

   Because of the enormous tension generated by these circumstances, management reviewed the situation to see if steps could be implemented to ease the conflict. With the help of a consultant, they concluded that the tension was built into the realities of the company and that, to be successful, the company had to balance, on a case-by-case basis, minimization of costs versus customer service. Depending on such variables as the identity of the customer and the current status of production costs, the scheduler's job was to facilitate the necessary case-by-case mutual adaptation.

This situation demonstrates that "mutual adaptation" in the context of an organization's goals does not always mean the elimination of diversity tension. Here, the prescription was to assist all parties in understanding the tension and the "mutual adaptation" (case-by-case problem-solving) approach. In particular, participants were encouraged to understand that the tension was not personal.

- I remember a small group that used "exclusion" to deal with diversity tension. This group had met several times, and at each session one member had taken a substantial amount of time to press a point of view not understood by his colleagues. Finally, one group member told the persistent presenter that he was tired of hearing and attempting to understand the point of view being presented. Another member commented, "We are trying to decide how much time we should devote to understanding your perspective, and whether we should insist that you assimilate or leave." As they listened to themselves, it became clear that they were experiencing diversity tension, although they shared a strong common interest in the topic under discussion and were alike in other significant ways.

The group decided that their goal of productive discussion could not be met by continuing to include this individual; thus they elected to exclude him.

In the context of the diversity framework, the process of assessing diversity tension and determining what, if any, action is necessary requires addressing the following questions:

1. What are the requirements for the success of the enterprise?
2. What is the connection between the diversity tension noted and the organization's success factors?
3. *If* the tension is interfering with maximum realization of the key success factors, the following questions should be addressed:
   a. What response options have been used in the past around this particular diversity?
   b. What have been the strengths and weaknesses produced by the use of these options?
   c. Given the organization's mission and success factors, what is the desired state with respect to the diversity tension?
   d. Which of the options have the greatest potential to bring about the desired state?

In light of the importance of the organization's mission and key success factors as context for action, diagnosis is critical. Only through accurate and insightful diagnosis can the manager assess the potential for gain as a result of addressing a given diversity mixture and its related diversity tension.

Question 2: If we use the diversity framework with its multiple dimensions, will my preferred issue receive less attention? Under the diversity framework, it is possible that a diversity tension analysis will determine that an individual's pet issue offers a low potential for gain. If that happens, it is true that less attention will be given to this issue.

However, less attention under the diversity framework would not necessarily mean less progress for the issue involved. As attention is focused on the critical dimensions, progress will be made with understanding and using the diversity framework. A result would be spillover benefits for diversity issues that were not assessed as critical. Indeed, in the long run, for noncritical issues, I suspect that even mere spillover progress will be greater process than would occur otherwise.

This would be true because of the transferability of the Managing Diversity capability. Regardless of the dimension or diversity mixture, where the manager hones his Managing Diversity mind-set and skills, they will be available and applicable to other diversity arenas. The critical prescription is to learn about diversity and Managing Diversity, as opposed to becoming proficient with one diversity mixture. Our challenge with the dimensions of race and gender is that they have been so emotionally charged that they have been less than excellent learning arenas. Indeed, because of this reality, managers seriously and effectively could address "workforce diversity" and "racial and gender diversity" without ever getting in touch with "diversity" per se.

Question 3: What difference does it make? Despite all the noise about diversity, aren't we talking primarily about race and gender? If so, why not just say race and gender? This is a key set of questions. What do you gain by using the diversity framework? This diversity framework highlights the reality of the diversity forest that is greater than an individual's pet diversity tree. This realization, in and of itself, suggests the opportunity to gain economies of learning through the experiences others have had with different diversity issues.

In addition to economies of learning, the diversity framework offers an opportunity to rise above the fray and to gain perspective in search of greater understanding. A frequent comment by longtime managers has been the following: "In my corporation, we're doing what was done 15 and 20 years ago. We're simply recycling as if what we are doing is new." I am seeing a growing readiness for new perspectives and freshness, not as a way of denigrating past paradigms and accomplishments but as a way of building on them.

Another potential gain with the diversity framework is the possibility of progress with all dimensions, not just those involving the workforce. Now when the word *diversity* is used, an assumption is made that the topic is workforce diversity. This narrow focus excludes all the other arenas characterized by mixtures of differences and similarities. The diversity paradigm broadens the focus and greatly enhances the possibility of progress on many fronts.

* * *

My purpose in this brief chapter has been to contribute to the ongoing discussion and evolution regarding the nature of diversity. Before we decide what to do about diversity, I believe that we must spend more time attempting to understand the concept of diversity. Once we understand what diversity is, we can more easily evaluate affirmative action, understanding differences, managing diversity, and other action approaches.

Note

1. The following are examples of works that have explored diversity with respect to workforce issues.

Cox, T. (1994). *Cultural diversity in organizations: Theory, research, and practice.* San Francisco: Berrett-Koehler.
Cross, W. E., Foster, B. G., Hardiman, R., Jackson, B., & Jackson, G. (1988). *Workforce diversity and business.* (Available from the American Society for Training and Development, Customer Support Department, ASTD, 1640 King Street, P.O. Box 1443, Alexandria, VA 22313, 703-683-8100)

Fernandez, J. P. (1981). *Racism and sexism in corporate America.* Lexington, MA: Lexington.

Galagan, P. A. (1991, March). *Tapping the power of a diverse workforce.* (Available from the American Society for Training and Development, Customer Support Department, ASTD, 1640 King Street, P.O. Box 1443, Alexandria, VA 22313, 703-683-8100)

Jamieson, D., & O'Mara, J. (1991). *Managing workforce 2000.* San Francisco: Jossey-Bass.

Loden, M., & Rosener, J. B. (1991). *Workforce America: Managing employee diversity as a vital resource.* Homewood, IL: Business One Irwin.

Madden, T. R. (1987). *Women vs women: The uncivil business war.* New York: Amacom.

Thiedereman, S. (1991). *Bridging cultural barriers for corporate success: How to manage the multicultural work force.* Lexington, MA: Lexington.

Thomas, R. R., Jr. (1991). *Beyond race and gender: Unleashing the power of your total work force.* New York: Amacom.

References

Lawrence, P. R., & Lorsch, J. W. (1969). *Organization and environment.* Homewood, IL: Irwin.

Peters, T. J., & Waterman, R. H. (1982). *In search of excellence.* New York: Harper & Row.

William, B. J., & Packer, A. H. (1987). *Workforce 2000: Work and workers for the 21st century.* Indianapolis: Hudson Institute.

Author Index

Subject Index

About the Contributors

MARTIN M. CHEMERS is the Henry R. Kravis Professor of Leadership and Organizational Psychology and Director of the Kravis Leadership Institute at Claremont McKenna College. He is also Adjunct Professor of Psychology and Management at the Claremont Graduate School. He received his Ph.D. in social psychology from the University of Illinois, Urbana, in 1968. His primary research area is leadership and organizational effectiveness, particularly the effects of cultural differences on leadership processes. His books include *Leadership and Effective Management* and *Improving Leadership Effectiveness: The Leader Match Concept* (both with Fred Fiedler), *Culture and Environment* (with Irwin Altman), *Leadership Theory and Research: Perspectives and Directions* (with Roya Ayman), and the forthcoming *Function and Process in Leadership Effectiveness: A Theoretical Integration.* He is currently editor of *Basic and Applied Social Psychology.*

MARK A. COSTANZO is Associate Professor of Psychology at Claremont McKenna College and Claremont Graduate School. He received his Ph.D. in social psychology from the University of California at Santa Cruz in 1986. His research areas include human communication, social cognition, and social influence. He is especially interested in the application of basic theory and research in social psychology to the legal system, environmental issues, and education. He coedited (with Stuart Oskamp) and contributed to two previous volumes in this series: *Gender Issues in Contemporary Society* and *Violence and the Law.* Recently he coedited (with Lawrence White) and contributed to a special issue of the *Journal of Social Issues* devoted to the topic of the death penalty.

TAYLOR COX, Jr. is Associate Professor in the Department of Organization Behavior and Human Resource Management of the School of Business at the University of Michigan. He is also founder and president of Taylor Cox Associates, a human resources consulting firm specializing in the management of workforce diversity. He holds B.S. and M.B.A. degrees in management from Wayne State University and a Ph.D. in organization behavior and psychology from the University of Arizona. He is author or coauthor of more than 20 articles and cases on topics such as performance appraisal, promotion processes, manufacturing strategy, and cultural diversity. His research and consulting emphasis in recent years has centered on workforce diversity. His 1993 book, *Cultural Diversity in Organizations*, was a co-winner of the 1994 George R. Terry Award given by the National Academy of Management. He has been an active consultant and speaker on the topic of workforce diversity and other human resource issues.

TERRI D. EGAN earned her Ph.D. from the University of California, Irvine. She is currently Assistant Professor of Management and Organization in the School of Business Administration at the University of Southern California. Her current research interests include organizational justice, business ethics, and organizational demography.

BERNARDO M. FERDMAN (Ph.D., Yale University) is Associate Professor in the Organizational Psychology Program and Director of the Organizational Consulting Center at the California School of Professional Psychology in San Diego, where he specializes in diversity and multiculturalism in organizations, ethnic and cultural identity, and organizational development. He is also a consultant affiliate with The Kakel Jamison Consulting Group, Inc., a national firm specializing in strategic cultural change and management consulting. He previously taught at the State University of New York at Albany. He is editor of *A Resource Guide for Teaching and Research on Diversity* (1994) and coeditor of *Literacy Across Languages and Cultures* (1994). In 1991 he was awarded the Gordon Allport Intergroup Relations Prize by the Society for the Psychological Study of Social Issues for his paper, *The Dynamics of Ethnic Diversity in Organizations: Toward Integrative Models.*

JOYCELYN A. FINLEY is a doctoral candidate in the Organizational Behavior Human Resource Management Department at the University of Michigan. She received her Master of Business Education and Bachelor of Business

Administration from Eastern Michigan University. Her research interests include cultural diversity, communication, crisis management, and training and development. She is a coauthor of several journal articles nominated for Best Paper awards, including one with Taylor Cox, Jr., who serves as her dissertation chairperson. Her dissertation focuses on the dilemma of talk and silence about racioethnicity issues in organizations and the effects on anxiety in interracial work relationships.

SUSAN E. JACKSON is Professor of Psychology at New York University. In addition to workforce diversity, her research interests include strategic human resource management and decision-making processes in top management teams. Her work on the topic of workforce diversity emphasizes the consequences of diversity for teamwork in organizations and the importance of linking diversity issues to business imperatives. This perspective is reflected in her book, *Diversity in the Workplace: Human Resources Initiatives* (1992), which describes how several major companies have been attempting to improve their ability to effectively use a workforce that is diverse along many dimensions.

SUSAN E. MURPHY is Assistant Professor of Psychology and Associate Director of the Kravis Leadership Institute at Claremont McKenna College and Adjunct Professor of Psychology at the Claremont Graduate School. She received an M.B.A. and a Ph.D. in organizational psychology from the University of Washington. Her research interests include leadership and the relationship of self-efficacy to leader performance and subordinate perceptions of leaders. She has conducted studies in cross-cultural leadership and is currently examining diversity issues related to leader behavior and mentoring. Before joining Claremont McKenna College, she worked as a consultant in leadership and management.

STUART OSKAMP is Professor of Psychology at Claremont Graduate School. He received his Ph.D. from Stanford University and has had visiting appointments at the University of Michigan, University of Bristol, London School of Economics and Political Science, University of New South Wales, and University of Hawaii. His main research interests are in the areas of attitudes and attitude change, environmentally responsible behavior such as recycling and energy conservation, and social issues and public policy. His books include *Attitudes and Opinions* and *Applied Social Psychology*. He has served as president of the American Psychological Association Division of Population and Environmental Psychology and the Society for the Psychological Study of Social Issues (SPSSI) and as editor of the *Journal of Social Issues.*

BELLE ROSE RAGINS is Associate Professor of Management at Marquette University. Her research interests include gender and power, mentorship, and diversity in organizations. Her research has been published in *Psychological Bulletin, Academy of Management Journal, Journal of Management, Journal of Organizational Behavior, Journal of Vocational Behavior,* and other journals. She reviews for numerous academic journals and has received the Dorothy Harlow and Addison-Wesley Best Paper Awards from the Academy of Management.

VALERIE I. SESSA is a Research Associate at the Center for Creative Leadership. She received her Ph.D. in Industrial and Organizational Psychology from New York University. Her work on the topic of workforce diversity emphasizes the consequences of diversity on teamwork in organizations and the importance of fitting diversity programs into the existing organizational environment. She has published several articles and book chapters on these topics. In addition to workforce diversity, her research interests include executive selection and the impact of technology on leadership. She is a member of the Academy of Management, the Society for Industrial and Organizational Psychology, and the American Psychological Association.

DARYL G. SMITH is Professor of Education and Psychology at the Claremont Graduate School. She received her Ph.D. in psychology and higher education from the Claremont Graduate School. She previously served 23 years as a dean and vice president in areas spanning student affairs, planning, and institutional research. She is the author of numerous articles on diversity in higher education, the role of women's colleges, strategic planning and governance, and the impact of college. She is a frequent consultant and speaker on these topics.

R. ROOSEVELT THOMAS, Jr. is founder and President of the American Institute for Managing Diversity, a nonprofit research and education affiliate of Morehouse College. Among his publications are two books, *Beyond Race and Gender: Unleashing the Power of the Total Work Force by Managing*

Diversity and *Differences Do Make a Difference.* He is author of the *Harvard Business Review* article, "From Affirmative Action to Affirming Diversity." His previous experiences include serving as Dean of the Atlanta University Graduate School of Business Administration and Assistant Professor of the Harvard Graduate School of Business Administration. He and his colleagues at the institute have worked with numerous corporations and other organizations.

HARRY C. TRIANDIS obtained his Ph.D. (1958) from Cornell University and has been Professor (since 1966) at the University of Illinois in Urbana—Champaign. His books include *Attitudes and Attitude Change* (1971), *The Analysis of Subjective Culture* (1972), *Variations of Black and White Perceptions of the Social Environment* (1976), *Interpersonal Behavior* (1977), *Management of R. & D. Organizations: Managing the Unmanageable* (1989), *Culture and Social Behavior* (1994), and *Individualism and Collectivism* (1995). He was general editor of the six-volume *Handbook of Cross-Cultural Psychology* (1980-1981), editor (with Dunnette and Hough) of the fourth volume of the *Handbook of Industrial and Organizational Psychology* (1994), and coeditor with Uichol Kim and others of *Individualism and Collectivism* (1994). He has published more than 80 chapters in books and 100 articles and monographs in journals.

ANNE S. TSUI is Associate Professor of Organizational Behavior in the Graduate School of Management, University of California, Irvine. She received her Ph.D. from the University of California, Los Angeles. Her current research interests, in addition to organizational demography, include the study of managerial reputational effectiveness, effectiveness of the human resource management function in complex organizations, and employee-organization relationships.

KATHERINE R. XIN is Assistant Professor of Management and Organization at the University of Southern California. Her doctoral work has been at the University of California, Irvine. Her current research interests include the processes of supervisor-subordinate exchange relationship, organizational demography, and influence tactics.